3 –

## the IT Girl's™ Guide to

# Blogging

## with Moxie

# Blogging

## with Moxie

by Joelle Reeder
and
Katherine Scoleri

Wiley Publishing, Inc.

**The IT Girl's™ Guide to Blogging with Moxie**

Published by
**Wiley Publishing, Inc.**
111 River Street
Hoboken, NJ 07030-5774

www.wiley.com

# About the Authors

The Moxie Girls, Joelle Reeder and Katherine Scoleri, are like vodka and olives — tasty on their own, but even better together. As pioneers in the blog design market, Joelle and Kathy have been designing stylish blogs and websites as Moxie Design Studios since February 2003.

**Joelle Reeder** has been blogging since January 2003. As the author of personal blog Tenth-Muse.com, Joelle's descriptive and humorous writing style quickly earned her a loyal readership of both women and men, resulting in thousands of visitors a day. Designing websites since 1996, Joelle's unique and bold style caught the attention of many a blogger, so joining forces with Kathy to form Moxie Design Studios was only natural!

**Kathy Scoleri** started blogging in 2001 under the guise of PixelSphinx.com. Kathy now authors the blog PinkMartinis.com, where she discusses the comedy that is her life as a new mother and busy designer. Kathy has maintained her vast readership over the years and enjoys comments from a wide variety of readers — everyone from long-time blogging friends to people looking for the other half of The Moxie Girls. Kathy started teaching herself HTML back in 1998 and built a career as a website and blog designer. Her clean, slick style is the perfect complement to Joelle's fun, bold flare, making this team invincible.

Moxie Design Studios launched to a huge response, and they've been busy ever since! In a time when blog design consisted of boxy default templates and simple banners with pictures of celebrities, the Moxie Girls pushed the envelope with fresh, unique, and completely personalized concepts for blog design.

The success of their personal blogs, as well as their business, led to the launch of their extremely popular diet and fitness blog, PutDowntheDonut.com, featured in a national women's magazine by the Lifetime Network, in 2004. The Moxie Girls are part of several professional blogging and design networks, are select members of the EllisLab Advisory Board, and have been notably mentioned on national radio program Air America. They've also been interviewed by several websites and have been speakers at high-profile industry conferences such as South by Southwest Interactive (SXSWi) in Austin, Texas.

Joelle resides in San Diego, California. When she's not designing websites, you can find her singing jazz standards, soaking in a bubble bath, or mastering the art of the cocktail. Kathy splits her time between Atlanta, Georgia, and Palm Beach, Florida, where she enjoys picking her son's Cheerios out of her hair, getting a pedicure, or coming up with things to mix with champagne.

# Authors' Acknowledgments

## Joelle Would Like to Thank . . .

First and foremost, I'd like to thank my best friend, business partner, and co-author of this book, Kathy Scoleri. You make starting every day so much fun, and I couldn't possibly ask for a better friend. You're the cream in my sugar-free, non-fat, hazelnut coffee. It's been nothing short of an honor to be your other half.

The following people put a spring in my step, and if I didn't have their support, none of this would have been accomplished: To Heika Muller, thank you for your continued love and confidence in me and for putting up with my shenanigans all these years. To Michael Sampaga, thank you for being one of my dearest friends, for being the kind, giving man you are, and of course, for killing all the spiders. I have to give kudos to Peter Zielinski for knowing how to push *all* my buttons and still managing to remain the closest friend I've never met. And to Ross Lawson, thank you for being so wonderfully in tune, for listening, and for letting me be myself. Thank you Internet.

Finally, I'd like to thank my parents, Jamia and Jerry. I can only hope that I've made you as proud as I am of having had you as my mom and dad.

## Kathy Would Like to Thank . . .

At the risk of sounding like an actor making her acceptance speech at the Oscars . . . I would like to thank my co-author, business partner, and friend Joelle Reeder. Without her immaculate sense of grammar, her creativity, and her imagination, this book would not have been possible. I value our friendship, and it has been a great pleasure to write this book with you.

I would like to thank my family and friends for their endless support and unabashed pride in what I do. I'd like to thank my husband, Steven Scoleri, for his help, support, and love during the writing process and for being one of my biggest fans. Thank you to my son, Reilly Scoleri. Even though you are only a toddler, your love and smiles made the stressful days bearable and the goal worth it. Last and certainly not least, I would like to thank my mother, Carol McClenin, for being my biggest cheerleader during the writing of this book and in everything I do. It is you who have made me strive to do great things with my life no matter how big or small. Your confidence in my talents, your encouragement, and your love are some of my most cherished possessions. Oh, and thanks for babysitting.

## The Moxie Girls Would Like to Thank . . .

A huge thank you to Yvonne Valtierra for the joy she brings to the blogosphere and the laughter she brings to our friendships — and for being a great technical editor, too! To Melissa Connelly, an honorary Moxie Girl, we appreciate your professionalism, optimism, and friendship. Thanks for being you! We'd be remiss if we didn't thank Bob Roth for his endless patience with our code freakouts over the years. You've always been there when we need you! To the boys at EllisLab — Rick, Paul, Les, and the Dereks, as well as the rest of the EllisLab team — thanks so much for your continued support and friendship. ExpressionEngine forever!

### A Huge Moxie Thank You

And finally, a huge Moxie Girls thank you to all of our readers, clients, and every blogger in the blogosphere. Without you, we wouldn't have had this incredible experience. Keep on blogging, and remember, whatever you do, do it with moxie!

We'd like to thank Wiley Publishing and our editors — Katie, Kim, Heidi, and Melody. Thank you for this amazing opportunity and for your support throughout the creation of this book. We appreciate your listening to our ideas for making this book the *best* blogging book, not just for women, but ever! We're so tremendously proud of *Blogging with Moxie* and the principle behind the entire IT Girl's series. Here's to its success!

# Publisher's Acknowledgments

Some of the people who helped bring this book to market include the following:

### Acquisitions, Editorial, and Media Development

**Project Editor:** Kim Darosett

**Senior Acquisitions Editors:** Katie Feltman, Melody Layne

**Copy Editor:** Heidi Unger

**Technical Editor:** Yvonne Valtierra

**Editorial Manager:** Leah Cameron

**Editorial Assistant:** Amanda Foxworth

**Sr. Editorial Assistant:** Cherie Case

### Composition Services

**Project Coordinator:** Lynsey Osborn

**Layout and Graphics:** Carrie A. Foster, Jennifer Mayberry, Ronald Terry, Erin Zeltner

**Proofreaders:** Laura Albert, Cindy Ballew

**Indexer:** Broccoli Information Management

**Anniversary Logo Design:** Richard Pacifico

**Book Design:** Michael Trent, Erin Zeltner

### Publishing and Editorial for Technology Dummies

**Richard Swadley,** Vice President and Executive Group Publisher

**Andy Cummings,** Vice President and Publisher

**Mary Bednarek,** Executive Acquisitions Director

**Mary C. Corder,** Editorial Director

### Publishing for Consumer Dummies

**Diane Graves Steele,** Vice President and Publisher

**Joyce Pepple,** Acquisitions Director

### Composition Services

**Gerry Fahey,** Vice President of Production Services

**Debbie Stailey,** Director of Composition Services

# Table of Contents

eing the smart, savvy goddess that you are, you may be bored with all the ho-hum technical guides out there. You want to learn about blogging, but with your busy schedule, you don't have time to decipher nerd words.

You're looking for flavor, and we're dishing it out! So without further ado, let's dig in!

## Bye-Bye Blah!

The book you're holding in your French-tipped fingers is not just a book, but a fun, engaging approach to blogging with the best. In it, we empower the reader to take the Internet by storm, all while maintaining her usual sense of style.

Yes, it's a reference book, but it's written for women, by women. In a world where women are expected to bring home the bacon, fry it up in the pan, and then drive it to soccer practice, we appreciate the need for on-point information that doesn't leave you asleep at the wheel.

## How to Make the Most of This Book

For your convenience, this book is divided into three sections: Learn IT, Live IT, and Love IT!

- In Learn IT, we cover the blogging basics, such as what blogging is and how you can use a blog to connect with others, beef up your business, and find out what all the cool kids are blogging about.

- In Live IT, jump right in with quick-start blogging options or host your own blog, get advice about blog design, and much, much more.

- Love IT serves up insider tips on blogging superstardom, including hints about blog popularity, promotion, and advertising.

And the glossary comes in handy if you need a vocabulary refresher. Throughout the book, you'll also discover relevant suggestions and ideas for making the most of your blogging experience.

## Blogging with Moxie Puts the Chic in Geek

*Blogging with Moxie* is so much more than just a reference guide. It's a conversation between girlfriends. We're pretty sure that flavor you're looking for isn't vanilla, and *Blogging with Moxie* is anything but! We encourage you to be the kind of blogger *you* want to be, whether that's a famous blogging A-lister or a more private personal journaler. Either way, *Blogging with Moxie* is the way forward!

You'll find interviews with high-profile and respected female bloggers, as well as notable, sometimes hilarious quotes by well-known women. Coupled with our dishy, hip dialogue and rewards loaded with goodies such as cocktails and spa treatments, you'll find this book an easy read. You'll be ready for your blogging debut in no time!

## Ready, Set, Go!

If you're a total newbie and not familiar with blogging at all, we recommend starting with Chapter 1: Blogging Basics. Following the book chapter by chapter will guide you through the ins and outs of setting up a blog for the first time.

If you're already a seasoned blogger and looking for tips on blog design, promoting your blog, or just general hints on enhancing your existing blog, feel free to flip around and choose the chapters that suit your needs.

So, come on, IT Girl! What are you waiting for? Let's get started!

# ①  Learn IT

"Every woman has a story."

–Tyra Banks

## To Do List

- Find out what a blog is and how it works
- Get the dish on the benefits of blogging
- Figure out which type of blog platform is best for you
- Learn about blogging's potential
- Give yourself a hand!

# Blogging without Breaking a Nail

**Y**ou may have read about it in magazines or heard about it on TV. Perhaps your friend does it or your receptionist does it, or maybe even your mom or daughter does it. No, we're not talking about the latest trend in beauty, we're talking about blogging, the hottest thing to hit pop culture since Jennifer Aniston's *Friends* haircut.

In this chapter, we'll go over the basics of what blogging is and how you can benefit from it. If you're familiar with the Internet and blogging in general, feel free to skip ahead; but if you don't know a blog from your bum, read through this chapter to get a feel for the lingo and a grasp on the concept. And away we go!

# Blog Anatomy: The Essential Parts

You wouldn't start your first day at Starbucks without knowing what *Venti* means, would you? Nor would you claim to be a hairstylist, but not have a clue what a pair of shears are. The same is true for blogging. We've provided a very handy glossary in the back of this book for you to reference if you run across something you're not familiar with, but along with Figure 1-1 from soapbox.SUPERSTAR (thescanlons.net/weblog/), here are some of the common elements of a blog and their definitions:

- **Header:** This is sometimes called a banner, as well. In a traditional blog structure, this is usually found across the top of the blog, displaying the blog name or a graphic.

- **Blog name/blog title:** A blog name or blog title is whatever you've named your blog. This is often represented with text or a graphic treatment. (Learn more about blog names in Chapter 6.)

- **Content area:** The content area, sometimes called the body, is the most essential element to any blog. This is where your blog entries live. There are many variations for how one might display the content area of a blog, but traditionally, you find it on the left or right if you only have one sidebar (described next), or in the middle if your sidebars flank either side.

- **Sidebar:** The sidebar (or sidebars, if you've got more than one) is commonly the area where blog authors display links they enjoy, a short bio, perhaps their Flickr photo stream (more on that in Chapter 18), links to their most recent posts, or archives.

- **Footer:** Not all blogs have an obvious footer, per se, but this is the area at the very bottom of your blog where you might list design credits, additional navigational links, copyright information, links to privacy policies, or anything you like.

- **Navigation:** This is how people get around on your blog. Some blogs, as shown on Tenth-Muse.com in Figure 1-2, have a graphic navigation along the top in lieu of a traditional header. Some choose to create simple text navigations in their sidebar or footer. The choice is yours! Navigation most commonly includes a link back to the main page of your blog, a link to some kind of archives, a link to an about or bio page on the blog author, and sometimes a contact link. You're free to include whatever you like in your navigation, but we recommend keeping it simple.

Comments link

Blog name

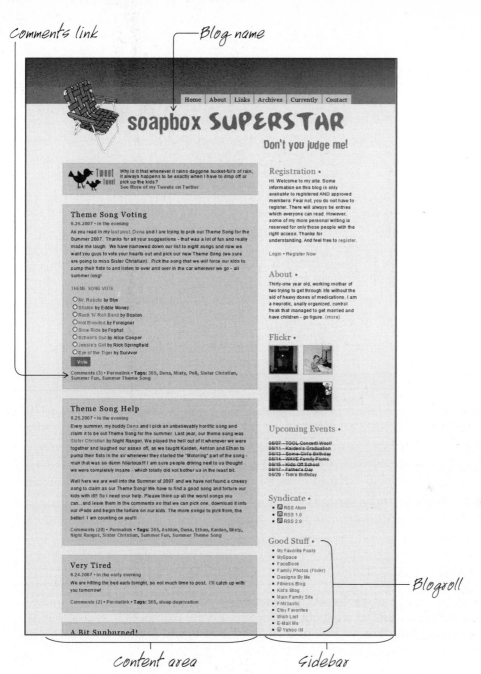

Content area

Sidebar

Blogroll

Figure 1-1

Header/banner     Graphic navigation

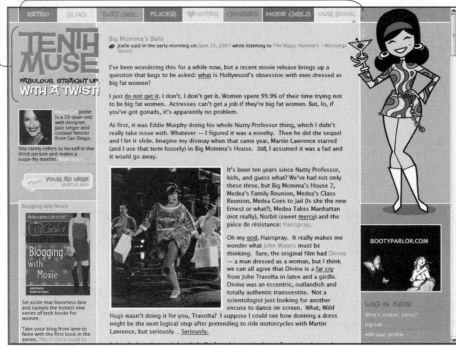

Figure 1-2

- **Blogroll:** A blogroll is a list of links to other blogs that often appears in the sidebar. Occasionally bloggers set up a separate page for their links, so you may find it there.

- **Comments and trackbacks:** We go over these in more detail in Chapter 9, but essentially, these are the areas where visitors to your blog comment and/or notify your blog that they have posted something relating to one of your entries.

# Blogging Doesn't Mean Blah

In the beginning, blogging was relegated primarily to techie types or ubergeeks. But, since new blogging tools and platforms have made it so easy for the technically challenged to share their thoughts, blogging is one of the biggest, fastest-growing trends around. We mean big. Bigger than Paris Hilton's sunglasses — and that's *big*.

Lots of cool people blog! You may not realize that everyone from news anchors like Meredith Vierra (meredithtoday.ivillage.com) to famous comedians like Margaret Cho (margaretcho.com/blog/) have blogs. Following its debut, blogging was primarily done by individuals sharing their personal thoughts and anecdotes. They included everything from statements like "I just had a cheese sandwich" to a complete, detailed, blow-by-blow account of the birth of one's child, including photos. Ah, good times! Personal blogging certainly has run the gamut.

Since blogging's burst into the mainstream, it continues to reach everyone from individual to community, from company to celebrity. Even politicians have made their way onto the blogging scene. In fact, political blogs, news blogs, and politicians are partially responsible for the exposure of blogging in traditional media.

Blogs have gained tremendous clout in the world on varying levels. If you have something to say, it just might be heard by the powers that be. You may be thinking, "Who cares if I blog?" Believe us when we say that blogs are now a force to be reckoned with and the power of numbers is on your side, especially when it comes to opinions on politics and current events. While your grass-roots blog campaign to decrease the price of shoes at Saks Fifth Avenue may not make the impact you're hoping for, if you feel strongly about current issues like the government or the state of affairs in the country, your voice can be heard. You just have to throw your opinion in the mix.

# Home Is Where the Blog Is

You may wonder where you get a blog and even if you had one, where would you keep it? There are two main methods for blogging: hosted blog services and stand-alone blog platforms. Your level of technical know-how really helps determine which of these choices is best for you.

A *hosted blog service* is usually owned by a company and offers blogging solutions on its own servers either for free or for a small fee. These services are great for new bloggers looking for instant gratification and are a way to try out blogging without making a financial commitment. Some of the best quick n' easy hosted blogging services are WordPress.com and Vox, primarily for their fast and simple set-up. With both, you could be blogging in under five minutes. Read more about hosted blogging services in Chapter 5.

A *stand-alone blog platform* requires that you install a downloaded blog software program and then install that program on your own server space, usually rented through a hosting provider. You will need an FTP (File Transfer Protocol) program and a bit of your inner geek in order to accomplish this, but it's not that challenging if you're patient and pay attention to the details. Some examples of outstanding stand-alone blog platforms are ExpressionEngine Core, Movable Type, and Word Press.org. Check out Chapter 6 for more information about stand-alone blog platforms.

## Women with Moxie

"In order to be irreplaceable, one must always be different."

–Coco Chanel

## The Doc Is In

It's important with either blogging method – hosted or stand-alone – that you read through the documentation and keep it handy. While initial set-up of most blog platforms is fairly simple, you never know when you might need to reference something. If you have a question, always consult your documentation first before seeking other alternate solutions.

# You've Got Potential

Blogs were born from personal journaling, but they've developed into something much bigger than "Here is my grocery list." The possibilities of blogging are pretty boundless as long as you have an imagination and some extra time.

There literally is a way for everyone to utilize a blog in some capacity that benefits her or his life or business. Here's a list of just some of the ways people are using blogs today:

- **Calling all moms!** Mothers and parents all over the world are embracing the beauty of blogs as a way to chronicle the lives of their children, from pregnancy to birth to teen. Remembering everything about your pregnancy, even down to the heartburn, may sound like a chore, but for most, it is an endearing way to keep track of your life during that time. You can wax nostalgic for years to come over the day you posted your first ultrasound photo or reread your birthing experience.

- **Getting hitched!** Everyone knows that Bridezilla wants to keep track of everything that went down in the planning of her wedding. Keep a wedding blog to post news about your upcoming nuptials. Post directions to the hotel, links to your online registry, and a list of local attractions for out-of-towners. Or update the family on time changes, transportation options, and hotel reservation tips. It's one thing to mass email your guest list and quite another to have a spot where your friends and family can all come to get the 411 about your big day.

- **Enhancing business!** Blogs have changed the way professionals handle their business websites. Not only have companies embraced blogging as a way to connect with customers and lure potential clientele, as shown in the Dog Blog! in Figure 1-3, but blogs have morphed into the hippest and easiest way to manage your site's content. Blogging isn't just a hobby anymore; it's a tool. It makes the Internet a more information-rich place that is constantly fresh. Even if its sole purpose is to showcase press releases, your business or company can only benefit from using a blog.

- **You're crafty!** We know those of you with creative flair can think of *something* for which a blog might be useful. Blogs are huge among crafty people. Start a knitting blog and chronicle your latest projects or write tutorials, post sewing

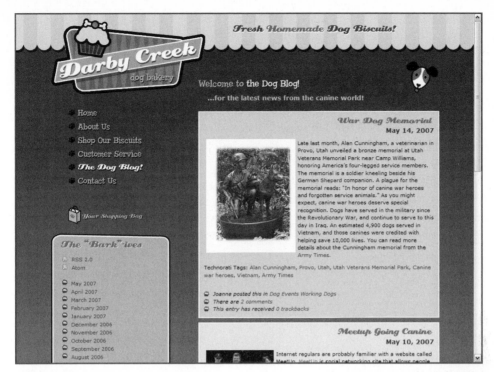

**Figure 1-3**

patterns, or share instructions on making a tea cozy. Whatever you like to create, using a blog to showcase it can be a lot of fun. By connecting with other people who enjoy creating as much as you do, you could eventually start a group blog with other like-minded crafties. (Learn more about group blogging in Chapter 3.)

- **Podcasting!** Podcasting has become yet another explosive trend that stemmed from blogging, and if you haven't heard of it yet, you most certainly will soon. *Podcasting* is, essentially, blogging with a microphone. It's like being on the radio — only, the coolest part is that *anyone* can do it. You don't have to be a radio deejay or even a professional speaker. You just need Chapter 13 and an idea.

- **Picture this!** Are you an amateur or professional photographer? Make blogging an art by showcasing your views of the world in a photoblog. You can make the Internet your art gallery by cleverly displaying your amazing photography skills or just show us pictures of stuff on your cat — whatever makes your flash bulb flicker!

This is just a short list of basic ideas and samples. You can do or blog just about anything. If you're the type who would prefer to blog for the sake of blogging, by all means, get yourself a domain name and start crackin'. The world needs to hear what you have to say, after all! What is crucial to remember is that blogs in any form are hot, hot, hot, so you better get your butt on the bandwagon or be left in the dust!

Finally, even with all these benefits aside, it's still just a whole lot of fun!

# Relax, Refresh, Reward

As we're here to hold your hand through the fast-moving, exciting new opportunities awaiting you in the blogosphere, we should warn you now: Blogging can be addicting. Once you get the hang of it, you may find yourself composing blog entries in your head while in line at the bank, tinkering incessantly with your layout, and manically checking your comments when your boss isn't looking. All that typing action can leave your cuticles looking worse for the wear.

## Give yourself a hand

To battle the dreaded dry hands, we keep an arsenal of hand creams, lotions, and potions on our desks at all times, in a variety of scents and textures. The small sizes work great as desktoppers and are usually reasonably priced. So, you don't have to spend a fortune to keep your digits diggable. Here are a few of our favorites for you to try and details on where to get them:

- **True Blue Spa Look Ma, New Hands! from Bath and Body Works:** This fresh-scented hand cream locks in moisture to make your hands feel as though they've been given a hot wax treatment — they're *that* soft. You can pick this up at most Bath & Body Works retail stores or online at bathandbodyworks.com. Prices vary from $5–$20, depending on the size you choose.

- **Hand Crème with Meadowfoam Seed Oil in Pink Champagne or Buttercream Frosting by Jaqua:** Of all the yummy flavors that Jaqua has to offer, these two are our absolute favorites. If the delectable scent wasn't enough, they make your hands softer than a baby's caboose and don't leave you feeling greasy. This heavenly treat runs about eight bucks, and you can get it at jaquagirls.com or bathandbodyworks.com.

- **High Intensity Hand Cream by Bliss:** *Silky* doesn't even begin to describe this decadent moisturizer. *Intense* does, though! This stuff deeply conditions your hands, leaving them super soft and not too slick! Like most Bliss products, High Intensity runs a bit more, at $18 for a full-size bottle at blissworld.com, but you can sometimes find travel sizes at places like Sephora retail stores.

## To Do List

Get the dish on popular blog topics

Consider what kind of impression you want to make

Peruse fabulous blogs of various genres

Enjoy a tasty treat while you do it!

# Become Part of the Buzz

**Y**ou've decided you want to blog, but do you really know what you want to blog *about?* You may choose a general topic blog just to wax poetic about your day, or you may have a more specific purpose in mind. Some bloggers choose to focus their energies on one particular topic. Doing so can create a sense of community with like-minded readers by allowing you to share your passions about everything from dessert to dolls to deep sea diving.

In this chapter, we cover some of the most popular topics in the blogosphere, especially among women. You may find yourself choosing something similar, or perhaps this chapter will inspire you to create something totally new. You trendsetter, you!

# Personal or General Topic Blogs

The most common blog on the Internet is a personal, or general topic, blog. These bloggers tend to write from a first-person perspective, usually providing insight into the blogger's day-to-day life. It's important with personal blogs to consider your privacy and security when sharing information such as where you live, where you work, any information about your children, and even your name. (See Chapter 14 for more information on privacy.)

There are so many blogs out there, but we would be remiss if we didn't share a couple favorites.

## Dooce.com

Heather B. Armstrong, a.k.a. Dooce, has been blogging since February 2001. Originally known as The First Blogger to Get Fired for Her Blog, she's since built a *massive* following and reputation as a hilarious writer with a penchant for bad television, bourbon, and bowel issues (see Figure 2-1). From that description, you might not think that's a good read, but trust us on this one, she's one funny broad. We should add that she not only takes beautiful daily photos of everything from her darling daughter to her kooky dog, Chuck, but her blog entries are well-written and engaging and make us laugh out loud. Heather has won several awards for her blog and been featured on assorted websites, TV shows, and even had a feature spread in *Glamour* magazine.

Figure 2-1

# On the Line with Mac of Pesky' Apostrophe

Mac, as she's known on her blog (pesky apostrophe.com), immediately came to mind when we thought "well-rounded personal blogger." In fact, not only is she well-rounded, she's prolific! You can always count on Mac for fresh content several times a day. Just about every post is as well thought out as the last, and she's refreshingly honest in her social commentary.

You can't hang a label on PeskyApostrophe .com, as its content is as eclectic as its author. Mac is quite possibly the busiest woman in Philly, as she grows her own vegetables, is an avid and talented photographer, knits like a fiend, and is more than a bit of a culinary dabbler. Lest we forget, she also has a full-time job, a husband, and of course, a blog. Talk about bringing home the bacon and frying it up in the pan!

Mac was kind enough to take the time to answer some questions for us.

**When did you start blogging and what was it that inspired you to start your blog?**

My foray into blogging began in April 2002, first at the now-defunct Diary-X and then later with a URL of my own. I've always kept a paper journal, so online journaling just naturally appealed to me. Reading other blogs is what put the idea of starting my own into my head, though.

**You've been blogging for a long time. Do you feel that blogging has changed for personal bloggers over that time?**

I do feel like things have changed. Things used to be much more independent back when I first started blogging — now you have more community blogs (like DailyKos or BlogHer) and more blogging for money (ad revenue). Not that there's anything inherently wrong about either of those things, but it contributes to the homogenization of the blogging world.

I also feel that there's a huge emphasis on blogging specifically to become popular — there are blogs that focus on what you can do to be a popular, A-list blogger. Luckily, there are still lots of bloggers who don't really care about all that and simply blog because they enjoy it.

**Do you feel there are more or less quality blogs in the blogosphere these days? Any favorites?**

Less. With the advent of places like MySpace and Facebook, it seems like there's been a proliferation of blogs full of text messages. I like some political and religion blogs (allspin zone.com/, possummomma.blogspot.com/, scienceblogs.com/pharyngula/), but my favorites are the people I consider my friends through blogging — Joelle and Kathy, Mikey (heyfreak.com), Statia (itssonotaboutyou. com), and John (thudfactor.com), among others.

**Do you ever feel blogger burnout?**

Every now and then I think about just quitting, but blogging is about venting and getting it out of your system. Without blogging, I would bore everyone to death about my political and religious viewpoints. No one wants that.

*(cont'd)*

**From your blog, you seem to be full of boundless energy. You grow your own vegetables, cook like a gourmet, take professional-grade photographs, are part of a rowing team, sew, spin your own yarn, knit, and still find time to blog four or more times a day. Admit it — you're superhuman.**

I'm an anal-compulsive Type A person who feels like a failure unless I'm multitasking. Plus, I don't have children. That's 99% of Why Mac Has Extra Time. Well, that, and I'm preparing for going off the grid or the apocalypse. One or the other.

**Okay, seriously. Any tips for new bloggers looking to keep their content fresh?**

Get a boring desk job and be hyper efficient. You'll have oodles of time to fill your head with mundane facts and learn more than you ever wanted about U.S. politics.

**Thanks, Mac!**

## JoyUnexpected.com

Y, as she's known on her blog, is one of those bloggers that you can't quite pigeonhole. Some call JoyUnexpected.com a mommy blog, but we feel she's more eclectic than that. Her posts are absolutely, side-splittingly hilarious at times, and in more intimate entries about her body image or depression, she reaches her audience in a wonderful way (see Figure 2-2). Her readers connect with her, whether she's talking about her reign as the self-proclaimed Queen of Aerobic Dance or sharing her latest adventures with her three beautiful children. And if you ask her nicely, she might even break dance for you.

## Mommy Blogs

Often, personal blogs by women tend to fall into the mommy blog category, but sometimes they get stuck there. We feel this is an unfair labeling, as often blogs by women get pegged as mommy blogs simply because the bloggers happen to be mothers. Even if a woman with children blogs about the stock market, someone somewhere will call it a mommy blog just because she has kids. There's absolutely nothing wrong with writing a mommy blog, but let the label fit the blog. In our opinion, a mommy blog is much more than a mention of your child or the fact that you happen to have one.

**Figure 2-2**

# Blog Valley High

Many people find creating personal blogs cathartic, a way for them to get things off their chests, like writing in a diary or journal. This is one of the great things about blogging! We encourage people to speak their minds, but remember that sharing your most intimate feelings or personal insights on the Internet can leave you vulnerable to attack by others with opinions that you may not care for.

Those that just pop in to leave nasty comments are usually called *trolls*. For some reason, it's usually men, but sometimes it's women. They are called *trolls*, too, but usually we just call them … well, it rhymes with *witches*. You get the idea! It's surprisingly juvenile, and it's not something that happens to everyone, but we want you to be prepared. The bottom line is, post what you're comfortable with, and if someone doesn't like it, shine them on, honey! It's only the Internet, and their opinions don't count. Unless it's your boss … then you might want to hide that entry where you admit to spiking the nog and photocopying your butt at the company Christmas party. (See more on privacy in Chapter 14.)

Mommy blogs tend to focus on the day-to-day life of a mom, with the majority of entries specifically about her children, parenting, and coping with being a mom in this crazy world we live in. Mommy blogs are ways for moms to connect with one another to get advice or read about other moms' experiences. Or, sometimes it's a way to spend time *not* discussing their children, as a way to have some adult interaction and support from those in the know.

Some mommy blogs aren't personal blogs per se, but more of a collective or community blog that shares personal anecdotes, parenting tips, and advice. (See more on community blogs in Chapter 3.) Moms are getting in on the video blogging and podcasting markets, as well, so there's room for you and room to grow if you're interested in starting a mommy blog. (You'll find more on podcasting and video blogging in Chapter 13.)

Of course, the flipside to the mommy blog is the daddy blog; although, you don't often see it called that. And people usually call a blog written by a mixed gender couple a *parenting blog.* Mommy blogs are big business right now, as women make up the majority of the advertising target audience. A blog that contains quality content and receives reasonable traffic can make money from advertising. (See more on how to drive traffic to your blog in Chapter 16.)

With mommy blogs appearing to grow faster than any other blog demographic, there are a myriad to choose from. Here are two of our favorites and hopefully, some new reads for you.

## TheMommyBlog.com

The name says it all, no? Melinda "Mindy" Roberts, author of *Mommy Confidential: Adventures from the Wonderbelly of Motherhood,* has one of the most popular and longest running mommy blogs in the blogosphere (see Figure 2-3). She's written about everything from her personal relationships to her jobs, but it all comes back to her three, cherub-faced kidlets. Mindy's writing is charming, self-deprecating, and funny. Definitely worth a look!

## CheekyLotus.com

Lena, a lovely Southern California mother of a little girl, blogs at Cheeky Lotus (see Figure 2-4), and you can also find her at the mom-community, ClubMom. Her writing is authentic, amusing, and has just the right amount of edge for a hip young mom. Check out our twist on her recipe for a Cosmolito at the end of this chapter. Yum!

### Women with Moxie

Latte

"You live but once, you might as well be amusing."

–Coco Chanel

Figure 2-3

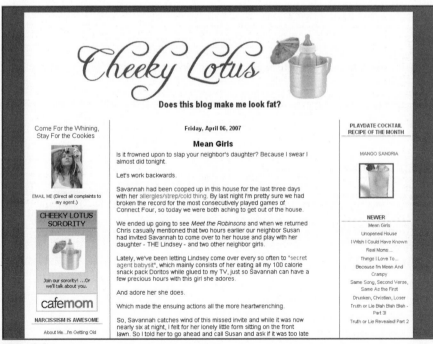

Figure 2-4

# Gossip Blogs

Girl, who doesn't love to sit around and gab about the latest celebrity scandals, fashions, and romances? We do! We do! Gossip blogs have to be rivaling mommy blogs for the fastest growing segment of the blog community, and it seems like every day a new one pops up.

Most gossip blogs tend to be a bit on the catty side, dishing up editorial commentary about celebs, in addition to the actual scoop. Often, the entries are accompanied by photos, sometimes with *watermarking* (captions to prevent theft or indicate where the image originated). Some gossip sites even include celebrity sightings in real time!

When it comes to gossip blogs, for us it's quality, not quantity. Some gossip blogs overwhelm you with too much information (or TMI, as the kids say). Some gossip blogs give us new content on every little detail about 4,000 times a day. Okay, maybe 20, but even that seems like a lot. However, if gossip is your bag and you absolutely, positively cannot go one more second without reading about Orlando Bloom's latest tan lines (or lack thereof . . . ahem!), maybe a gossip blog is just the ticket for you.

## PopSugar.com

Oh, PopSugar, how we love thee! PopSugar (shown in Figure 2-5) is the way, the truth, and the gossip-lovin' light! Okay, maybe we're getting carried away, but if you're looking for a feminine take on gossip and sick of sifting through scads of "nipple slips" just to get some juicy tidbits, this is the site for you. The whole site is chock-full of entertaining goodies, and since they're always pumping in the latest 411, you'll dazzle your friends with all the dirt you've got to share at the next happy hour.

## Celebrity-Babies.com

It's a gossip blog . . . about celebrity *babies.* Who knew? The mini-starlets are no exception in a world hungry for gossip! They have famous babies as far as the eye can read! From the Jolie-Pitts' latest adoption to the hottest stroller that celebs are sporting these days, Celebrity Baby Blog (shown in Figure 2-6) has the latest for those addicted to hip celebrity kids.

Figure 2-5

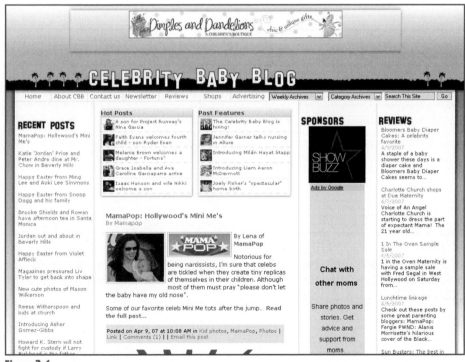

Figure 2-6

## Be Original

While gossip blogs are almost a dime a dozen, it's those that put in the extra effort that really keep the readers (and advertisers) rolling in. Often, gossip blogs simply repost a photo found on another gossip blog with a link back or create an entry compiled entirely of links to other gossip blogs. How is that creative?

If you decide to start a gossip blog, give it your own edge, your own flavor. Take pride in your content and quality of images and avoid churning out regurgitated links and entries. We don't need to see Britney's naked underbits mentioned at every turn. If you want to discuss it, do so and move on to the next big thing! Keep it fresh!

## Dieting and Fitness Blogs

The diet and fitness industry is a multibillion dollar business, and many people, especially American women, are *perpetually* trying to achieve their ideal weight or fitness goals. Enter diet and fitness blogs!

As many weight loss programs and diets there are in the world, you can find about an equal amount of websites dedicated to the subject. Some are commercial in nature, but many are blogs. While you can run across very disturbing blogs that are pro-anorexia (pro-ana) or pro-bulimia (pro-mia), these are *not* the sites to which we are referring. We're talking about healthy fitness and nutrition.

A diet and/or fitness blog is most often written from a first-person point of view, chronicling one (or more) person's journey to get fit. In this vein, you'll sometimes see bloggers logging their food intake or tracking their workouts. Other times, the diet or fitness blog is written more as a resource, providing recipes or workout tips.

If you're on a journey to get fit, consider starting a diet and fitness blog. While it can be scary to put yourself out there like that, it's a great way to garner support and encouragement, as well as keep you honest about your intake and exercise level. Sharing recipes and tips draws in new readers with like-minded goals enabling you to connect with others on your same path.

We don't see as *many* diet and fitness blogs as we used to, but the ones we do see tend to be very rich in content and information. Here are some of our favorites to get you started.

## FitSugar.com

Okay, so the name is a bit of an oxymoron, but the blog is the cat's pajamas! Hands down one of the most thorough and well-informed fitness blogs we've found on the net (see Figure 2-7). It's got a woman-centric perspective and a girlfriend's tone that make it feel like you're chatting with a workout buddy. The recipes are ever-flowing, and product reviews tip the scales in FitSugar's favor. Plus, with simple workout videos at your fingertips, there are no excuses, missy!

## Poundy.com

In November 2000, Wendy McClure began Pound (shown in Figure 2-8) to write about body image, weight issues, and diet culture. As author of one of the longest-running, personal-perspective diet blogs around, Wendy writes candidly with dry wit and a humorous take on what can otherwise be the discouraging topic of weight loss. Wendy also is the author of *I'm Not the New Me* (Riverhead Trade), a "poignant, comic memoir," and the gut-busting and truly bizarre collection of vintage weight loss recipe cards aptly titled, *The Amazing Mackerel Pudding Plan!* (Riverhead Trade).

**Figure 2-7**

Figure 2-8

# Knitting Blogs

Knitting is the new black. Since knitting exploded into the pop culture in the early 2000s, everyone from your grandma to Julia Roberts seems to enjoy the many benefits of knitting. Many people find it meditative, others appreciate always having a gift on hand for that last-minute baby shower invite, and junk food addicts like that it keeps your hands busy when you're tempted to plow through a bag of sour cream 'n' cheddar chips during *Grey's Anatomy*. There are a zillion knitting blogs and communities with all the information you could possibly need to become a needle-wielding diva. Give a few a read, share your insights by commenting, and watch as you spin your way into the knitting blog circle.

# Knitty.com

Knitty (shown in Figure 2-9) is a online knitting magazine that's updated four times a year. The magazine provides free knitting patterns contributed by readers from all over the world. The site has over a million readers a month, a discussion forum where you can chat with fellow yarn junkies, and the blog features personal tips and anecdotes from the editor herself, Amy Singer (knitty.com/blog).

# Keep your cool, Kitten!

Are all these options freaking you out? You don't have to pick one right this second! It's easy to get overwhelmed, but consider what you want to achieve with your blog, decide who you're writing *for* (yourself or your audience — see more on this in Chapter 8), choose your topic, and then make it happen!

The Internet is littered with old, worn-out, raggedy blogs that contain a dozen entries and then fizzle out into crickets and tumbleweeds. Don't be one of those blogs that starts out with a bang and can't go the distance. Give yourself some time to let it sink in and visit assorted sites to get a feel for what kind of blog interests you. Find something you feel passionate about. Decide what the best fit is for you and then pace yourself. The Internet isn't going anywhere.

Figure 2-9

# KnitSisters.com

The Knit Sisters (shown in Figure 2-10) is a shared knitting blog authored by real-life sisters Ellen and Sarah Bales. Blogging since June 2006, the Knit Sisters have shared their trials and triumphs of the needle, as well as their daily lives. We found some tasty recipes, too! Sarah and Ellen's casual and familiar writing style engages the reader and leaves us wanting to learn to knit.

Figure 2-10

# Relax, Refresh, Reward

We've discussed so many wonderful blogs in this chapter, you must be parched! Why not have a cocktail created by one of our featured mommy bloggers, Lena of Cheeky Lotus. With a few tiny twists from us, this delectable treat is pink like a Cosmo, but packs the south of the border punch of tequila. Olé!

## Cosmolito

*1 ½ oz. 1800 Silver tequila*

*¾ oz. Grand Marnier*

*2 oz. cranberry juice*

*¾ oz. fresh Key lime juice*

*Cocktail sugar*

*Cocktail or margarita salt*

Rim the glass with an equal mixture of the cocktail sugar and salt (available at bevmo.com or most quality liquor stores). Combine ingredients in a cocktail shaker filled with clean ice. Shake well and strain into a chilled martini glass. Garnish with a fresh Key lime slice.

# 3 Group/Community Blogging:

## To Do List

Get the dish on blogging groups and communities

Decide who's in charge

Think about how to communicate and manage effectively

Get the girls together for a slumber party

# Playing Well with Others

In this chapter, we discuss all the cool things that you can achieve when you've got each other. Cheesy? Absolutely, but creating a little blog posse to share their thoughts can take your blog from boring to bodacious and cut your work in half!

# Hey There, Lonely Girl

Blogging solo can be a daunting prospect for many people. The pressure to find something interesting to say and keep people reading is a challenge sometimes. Safety in numbers and the support and enthusiasm of others can inspire you to write more, and it gives your blog fresh content on a more regular basis.

Some people use the terms *group blog* and *community blog* interchangeably, but we feel there's a slight distinction. Keep reading to get our take on that.

## Women with Moxie

"If I don't have friends, then I ain't got nothing."

–Billie Holiday

## The group scoop

A *group blog* tends to be on a bit smaller scale than a community blog. Usually, two or three friends get together and share one blog, each writing entries in their own unique voice. The topics of group blogs are varied, just like a solo blog, and can run the gamut from personal blog to gossip to fashion. (See more on hot topics in Chapter 3.)

Working with a couple of people can be a good way to start out, as it can be more exciting than blogging alone and easier to manage than dozens of authors. It still gives each blogger a feeling of empowerment without it spiraling into something bigger than you can handle. When you get too many cooks in the kitchen, sometimes the tone of a blog can change, and you or your readers can become disinterested. So it's important to choose bloggers that mesh with your groove to write with.

One of our favorite group blogs is the hilarious duo, Heather and Jessica, at GoFugYourself.com (shown in Figure 3-1). These ladies pull absolutely no punches when it comes to celebrity slamming, and it reigns among one of the most popular gossip editorial blogs. If it's fugly, the Fuggers, as they call themselves, will be the first to let you know.

## The good of the community

While writing with bloggers that are similar to you is great in the small scale, a larger blog with more authors, a *community blog,* can bring diversity to your audience. Having an eclectic group of authors allows your readers to connect with the blogger that's most like them — it offers a little something for everyone. Variety is the spice of life, and while some people may like things as hot 'n' spicy as your homemade guacamole, others may not.

**Figure 3-1**

Community blogs are a growing trend, as they build . . . well, community! A community blog can provide a haven for people with similar interests or attitudes to commune and chit-chat with not only the blog authors, but also with each other. Some community blogs offer additional features, such as forums or message boards, so that readers can connect, set up profiles, and create even more content than you might otherwise be able to achieve with a solo blog.

ParentDish.com (shown in Figure 3-2) is a great example of one community blog shared by many, many authors. The website features 15 authors, each posting multiple times a day. Their topics range from adoption to child development, from choosing the best schools to the latest in gossip and style.

## Columns: The Russian nesting dolls of blogging

Some websites are collections of solo blogs tucked inside another, bigger blog community. These solo blogs, in this setting, are sometimes called *columns,* like in a magazine. They tend to showcase the writing of a single blog author in her own style

**Figure 3-2**

and often give her a dedicated section of the community site. Usually, there is a cohesive design brand overall, but sometimes the columns display each author's own decorative point of view. Great examples of these kinds of blog communities are Alphamom.com (shown in Figure 3-3) and ClubMom.com.

Occasionally, an independently-produced solo blog indicates that it's part of a larger blog network, such as Glam.com, by displaying a button or banner on its site. This indicates that it's part of an overall community, but neither a column nor, necessarily, a group or traditional community blog.

## Managing Group Dynamics

They say that all we need to know in life we learned in kindergarten. Put that to the test by sharing your blog with more than one person. It can be an exhilarating, bonding experience, or it can totally suck your will to live. You choose! We're here to share some ideas for managing multiples.

**Figure 3-3**

# Learn to share

We're talking to you control freaks out there. Yes, you. You know who you are. Sometimes it's hard to let go, but if you have any hope of sharing your blog with other authors, you need to leave the drama at the door. Here are some tips for getting the most out of the multi-author experience:

**Women with Moxie**

"Creativity comes from a conflict of ideas."

–Donatella Versace

## *Follow the advice of the Dog Whisperer*

Exercise, discipline, affection! Cesar Millan (cesarmillaninc.com/blog) rocks those methods with pampered pooches, and strangely, the same applies to group and community blogging:

- **Establish dominance.** It's wise to decide who's in charge. You can't *all* be in charge. Someone has the take the lead. Usually, it's the person who came up with the site concept or pays for the server space — or otherwise takes the first initiative to make the blog happen. Make sure your authors are clear and agree with whomever you decide to give the lead. That way, you can avoid power plays or hurt feelings.

- **Exercise.** Don't rule with a short leash. Let your authors stretch their legs a little. You'll have happier authors who feel more willing to contribute if they feel as though their voices are heard and they're permitted to speak their minds.

- **Discipline.** Sometimes, confrontation is just unavoidable. But you can express yourself without being accusatory or aggressive. Be calm, kind, and tactful, but direct. If your authors aren't projecting the image that you want to convey, it's not unreasonable to address it.

- **Affection.** Value your authors. You've chosen them for a reason, and if they're quality writers, nice people, and good friends, reward them either with small tokens or praise, publicly or privately. Let them know they're welcomed on your blog and in the community and that you value their contributions. You'll have happier writers and happier readers.

### The phone lines are now open

Talk to your authors. Make sure they know that the lines of communication are open and you're willing to listen, should they have a grievance with another author, a reader, or even with you. Be willing to listen with an open mind, even if you ultimately disagree. If you feel defensive, take a minute before responding to their email — or if you're on the phone or chat, let them know that you've heard them and that you need some time to digest everything before responding. It's better to respond with a cool head, especially if this is an author you value. Burning bridges is rarely wise.

# Multiple personality disorder

When you get a slew of bloggers going all at once, such as with a larger community blog, it can get a little nuts. While you want to encourage your authors to post and you want fresh content, sometimes it's hard to keep up as a reader when there are several posts an hour. Here a few tips for helping your authors and your vision play nice.

### Who's on first?

Before you start taking on this grandiose project of 20 blog authors, message boards, advertisers, and start booking your spot on *Oprah,* consider delegating certain topics or site responsibilities to specific authors. Like a group blog, someone needs to be in charge. When you get a *lot* of authors, you can end up with multiple entries about the same thing, an overwhelming amount of entries in general, or just a disconnect between the site's overall purpose and an author's agenda.

For example, let's say your community blog is called TheNeedtoFeed.com. Perhaps it's about food and cooking and you have six authors. Consider assigning the authors their own specialty, such as baking, cocktails, entrees, appetizers, salads, or soups. . . . Or you might choose to assign each author a specific cuisine, such as Mexican food, Chinese food, or Italian. Match the topic to the author and, of course, make sure they're comfortable writing about their assigned subjects.

### What's on second?

Create a team atmosphere! Your blog authors should be as committed to your blog as you are. If they feel as though they're part of something big, part of something exciting, and that they're appreciated, they'll be more apt to post creative entries and contribute to the growth of the site.

If your fictional TheNeedtoFeed.com has six authors, perhaps you would give them a cute nickname, such as Chic Chefs. Maybe you'll allow the authors to choose their own icon or *avatar* that signifies them as a Chic Chef to the readers at large. (Flip ahead to Chapter 9 for more on avatars.) It might be fun to have a monthly meeting, either in person, if possible, or online via chat just to regroup and connect in a nonblog atmosphere. Or initiate a team-building project or exercise, such as a contest or a sweepstakes that encourages authors to drive in more traffic or create a unique recipe. A little public praise and a free t-shirt can go a long way — you'd be surprised.

### I don't know who's on third!

No one's perfect, and once in a while you'll get an author that might be one sandwich short of a picnic when it comes to your blog. The fictional TheNeedtoFeed.com is about cooking, so why does Chic Chef Nancy keep posting entries about Justin Timberlake? Some blog administrators don't mind if their authors occasionally post something off-topic. It applies in various instances, but if it's a regular occurrence and you don't approve of it, this is one of those times you'll have to practice tactful discipline. We realize she might be trying to bring sexy back, but she can bring it back on her *own* blog.

## Single-Subject Straightjacket

Keeping your authors organized is great, but if you do assign them only one topic to discuss, make sure it's something they can be prolific with. If they're experts in the preparation of chocolate-dipped grasshoppers, but nothing else, you might not want them to cover the entire dessert category. However, if they're really well-versed in several cuisines, you might consider assigning them more than one subject to discuss.

The key is to keep your authors engaged, as well as engaging. Blog authors in a community setting generally appreciate leadership and guidance, but don't stifle their creativity. You want your authors psyched, not psycho!

# Patience, Grasshopper

We are Idea Queens. We have a fabulous new idea every 30 seconds, so when we get excited about something *big,* it's easy for it to take on a life of its own. Many bloggers have this problem when they first decide to create a community blog. Don't get ahead of yourself! Remember, when you open your blog's virtual doors, unless you've done one hell of a public relations job, you won't be flooded with readers. We hate to break it to you, but you just won't. It takes some time, quality content, a pleasing design, good energy, great communication, and a little optimism.

While your community blog might be the next big thing — and we don't doubt that it will — don't feel as though you have to hire 20 bloggers, purchase advertising during the Superbowl, and sink every last dime into the project right off the bat. Time and again, we've seen blogs with great ideas pull out all the stops, only to fizzle out in a few months. Usually, it's because the blog author didn't have realistic expectations, became discouraged, and eventually lost interest. Start small, build a following, write strong content, and your traffic will increase. With traffic comes advertisers, and with advertisers comes publicity. *Then* start shopping for the perfect outfit to wear on *Oprah*.

# Relax, Refresh, Reward

We've covered a lot of ground about building friendships and community in this chapter, so what better way to get some face with your girlfriends than a good, old-fashioned slumber party?

Slumber parties aren't just for kids anymore! Bust out the fuzzy slippers and the chick flicks, grab some snacks, and call your best gal pals for a Friday night pajama jam session. There's nothing like a little gossip, tasty goodies, and a clarifying masque to put you right again. Put a grown-up twist on a slumber party favorite . . . punch! After your girlfriends have a few of these, good luck keeping your bra out of the freezer.

## Packs-a-Punch Champagne Punch

*1 3 oz package of cherry Jello*

*1 cup boiling water*

*3 cups cold water*

*1 6 oz can of frozen lemonade*

*1 6 oz can of frozen pineapple juice*

*1 quart cranberry juice*

*1 pint champagne (or ginger ale)*

Thaw frozen lemonade and pineapple juice until soft. Combine boiling water and cherry Jello until dissolved. In a large punch bowl mix dissolved jello, lemonade, pineapple juice, cranberry juice and cold water. Add ice and top with cold ginger ale or champagne.

Optional: Float frozen sorbet on top or mint sprigs or both.

# Business and Blogging:

## To Do List

- Promote your business and talents with a blog
- Combine your blog and your business
- Bust business stress with a simple salad

# Putting Your Talents to Use

**W**e can't tell you how many times we've been asked what the best method is for business owners to drum up new leads, or better promote their company, or sell more products. Time and time again, we drill "Start a blog" into the heads of our clients. It can be much more time consuming than it seems. As you've learned so far, a lot goes into putting a blog together and giving it a chance at success. However you define what success is in your mind.

No smart businesswoman ever got ahead by sitting back on her Jimmy Choos waiting for things to happen. You have to get in there and work, get dirty, and be involved to see results. Just like with any type of project, you need to play an active role. For some, a blog can be the key to finding that avenue of participation that can lead to better business tactics.

# Promoting Your Business

Starting a blog for the purposes of business may sound silly, but in essence, you're extending your business in a direction that is accessible to anyone with an Internet connection. It's not a tough sell. Committing to a business blog can be a little overwhelming, but the benefits, if you really give it a fighting chance, can be rewarding not only to you personally, but also to your potential sales, leads, and business connections.

You might be asking yourself, "Why?" Blogging and business really can go hand in hand in many situations. For starters, in order to get potential customers to your business site, you need to market to them and generate traffic by direct marketing or search engine ranking or both. By introducing a blog into the mix, you're catering to a built-in customer base. Search engines love blogs. And what better way to get your blog and business discovered by new customers than by providing them with relevant information. It gets you off on the right foot from the beginning.

Marrying a blog to a business website can really give your company some desirable results, if you execute it correctly. There are a few things to be mindful of when taking this step forward. Consider the following:

## Mind Your Ps and Qs

Naturally, you can blog however you want. But in the case of using a blog for business purposes, you might want to keep your potty mouth in check. We know you're a classy gal, but we all have our moments. Just keep your moments off your business blog, okay?

- **Relevance:** Anyone can stick a blog up and start writing, as we've learned. But with business, you need to be careful what you explore content-wise. If you run an online doggie boutique and your sales are floundering, start a small blog discussing how to sew your own dog clothes, bake your own dog treats, or talk about the latest trends in doggie couture. Sell corresponding gift packs in your store that correlate with your discussions. Maybe sell a bake-your-own treats kit and blog about how to enhance your recipes. The key is to make the blog enhance what you're trying to sell. Whether it is goods or services, keeping in the same vein will draw people in. If you start a blog and talk about cats, chances are the readers aren't interested in your latest supply of dog booties. Keep it relevant.

- **Content:** A blog about your business can run drier than last night's martini. Not many people, except your own mother, perhaps, want to hear you go on and on about what's new at your store or business. Sure, it's okay to mingle those types of entries into the content, but the key is to keep it interesting. Variety is the spice of life and all that jazz.

- **Participation:** We feel like a broken record on this one, but it's imperative that you stay involved in your industry if you want to spike interest in your blog. Comment, read, and subscribe your little heart out to industry colleagues, and the promotion will begin to handle itself.

- **Strategic design:** If your business is going to benefit from having a blog, you may consider hiring a professional to help you determine your best course of action. How to present your material and how to best cross-promote your company with your blog may be things a professional can help you with. You'll want to be careful with link placement. Brandishing your company logo all over the place is not necessarily the way to go. Subtlety is key.

- **Brand development:** You can blog all day long on a free, hosted solution with a free domain name that the hosted blog service hands out to you, but as Coca-Cola will tell you, branding is everything. If you are serious about building your blog for business purposes, a design that goes with your company branding can be a good tactic.

## Back to Basics

Remember, it's still a blog in its simplest form, so keep blogging basics in mind. Participate, contribute, and be involved in the community. Those three things should be stamped on your forehead.

# Promoting Your Talents

Whether you're a photographer, artist, crafter, writer, or musician, blogging is an open forum that is limited to no one. It's the best way to obtain objective feedback and criticism. Finding a way to merge your creative talents with a business plan can come together in a blog.

Using a blog to display your talents is a good business strategy. You are the business, so you might as well sell yourself. Blogs open endless possibilities when it comes to what you can create. If you're a photographer, you can build a photoblog, and when you're confident enough, sell some prints. Make gorgeous, hand-knitted tea cozies? Blog about knitting and showcase some of your work. People respond well to creativity, and if you plan on making your talents into a money maker someday, using the blog format to promote yourself is a great place to begin.

Thinking in terms of starting from scratch, it doesn't have to go in any particular order. If you already have a creative job and want to promote the work you've already done, a blog can be a way to do that. You can journal how you did your work, how you hoped it would turn out, and what you accomplished with it. With some pretty easy-to-use tools, you can build a nice portfolio for further business development like on MyPaperCrane.com, shown in Figure 4-1.

Figure 4-1

## Think Outside of the Box

If your talent is shoe collecting rather than something creative, don't let that deter you. A lot of women adore shoes (and some fetish enthusiasts too, ha!). You might be surprised to find that your shoe collection sparks a big following, and you're rolling in free shoe samples, posting shoe reviews, and doing designer critiques. The point is, don't limit yourself! You never know when creativity may strike, and if it's in the form of those fetching Cavalli wedges you scored last weekend, so be it.

Whether you choose to do sock monkeys or landscape watercolors, remember that with any creative outlet, blogs aren't bound to definite limits, and you can take things in any direction you wish.

## Turning Your Blog into a Business

Blogging with money on the brain isn't always the best tactic, but in some cases, your ideas just strike a chord and take off. Blogging with the intent to turn your blog into a business, however, if done the right way, can help you rid yourself of that cube farm desk job and springboard you right into working from home or launching a huge online business! Imagine that!

# Chew on this: Business blogging considerations

Things to think about when turning your blog into a money maker mover and shaker include:

- **Keeping your options open:** Be careful not to corner yourself into one particular topic. Think expansion. If you drill too specifically into one particular topic, you leave no room for inspiration and growth. Make sure you leave yourself some options with regard to business direction.

- **Accepting advertising:** Determine whether a driving force of your revenue will eventually be advertising. If so, you'll need to design your site accordingly to accommodate it without it being totally overwhelming. Too many ads can be a deterrent, and poor ad locations can stifle advertisers — or worse, you may have trouble finding some.

- **Staying true to your content:** Don't get derailed too quickly. If you run a blog about cooking and your biggest traffic bait is low-fat recipes, be sure to keep those readers swimming in them. Keep it real.

- **Cross-promoting:** If you notice a spike in popularity in a certain area of your blog that could potentially take off in a big way, consider splitting your blog into different areas to draw your readers into different parts of your site. For example, if your cooking blog is getting heavy traffic in your Low-Fat Recipe category, maybe make it into a separate blog that can cross-promote with another section of your site. Divide things up but keep your readers drilling into other areas. Maybe your cooking blog now turns into a low-fat cooking blog, and then you open a second connected blog for low-sugar baking. Tie recipes together; get the readership moving between the two blogs. You double your target audience and potentially double your advertising opportunities.

## Burn, Baby, Burn

We've all done it. We've flopped face down onto the couch and just wanted to curl up and sleep rather than think of something to write about. Don't let the burnout get you down! Take a quick break, find your inspirational center, and blog on. If you have to get some help to take the pressure off, call on a guest blogger to pick up the slack while you recharge your batteries.

- **Getting help:** We know you can do it all — and do it all in style, for that matter — but every woman should know her limit. Recognize that people are out there with similar interests that can potentially make wonderful contributions to your endeavor. Bring on guest bloggers, rope industry professionals into your discussions, or have a cross-blog promotion. When you can afford to expand, do so. Finally, invest in some professional design if you can't do it yourself the way you think it should be done.

- **Picking up some literature.** There are lots of books about marketing and books about blogs available online or at you local bookseller. You might want to check out Susannah Gardner's *Buzz Marketing with Blogs For Dummies* (Wiley) to help you get started.

## Marketing: Put the Avon lady to shame

All that work and no one knows about it? Start spreading the news, honey! We know you've been commenting your little heart out, but if you want to get the ball rolling on your blog business, you can take a few extra steps to help give your site that extra boost. Go the distance by trying some of these techniques:

- **Buy some ad space on other popular blogs.** There are some great programs, most notably Blogads.com, that allow you to purchase prominent ad space on blogs that cater to your target market. It could be a wise investment if the traffic pours in.

- **Offer a newsletter.** Enticing readers who've visited your site to come back — as a gentle reminder that "Hey! There are new tips over here! Come back and check it out!" — could get those old site stalkers back in the palm of your hand.

- **Send email blasts.** Although unsolicited email is not the group favorite, some people have much success using this tactic. If you collect a list of business contacts, it might behoove you to email them when you launch a new product or service.

- **Distribute press releases.** If you get to a point with your blog business where you warrant a press release, by all means do so. Any way you can get the word out is worth doing.

- **Show off your links.** You never know where you can get a potential reader or customer. Put your blog URL in the signature of your emails, put it on your business cards, heck, have it written on your car's rear windshield. (Is that legal?) Get your URL out there where people can see it.

## URL Reminder

Now that you're out there promoting your blog, you have yet another reason to make sure your domain name and URL are short, easy to remember, and make some sense. Choose something that will be easy for people to recall if they see it in a random place.

# Relax, Refresh, Reward

So you're ready to start a blog business. We can't wait to visit your site! But all that work surely leaves you pining for something at lunch time, and you just don't want to go through the motions of making something healthy. We get it! It happens to us all the time. This salad is one of our tried-and-true, all-time, tested-and-approved salads that is a quick dish to whip up during the day.

The nice part about it is you can adapt it to fit your tastes rather easily. Like gorgonzola rather than feta? No problem! Out of pears, but have an apple? Walnuts instead of almonds? Swap them out! Hate spinach? Try romaine or green leaf lettuce instead. We've changed this recipe from its original a dozen times. Here's the basic recipe. Have this stuff on hand and ready to toss together for a fast and healthy lunch that will keep you going until dinner.

## Stress-Free Spinach Salad

*2–3 cups baby spinach (rinse and pat dry)*

*3 tablespoons of feta cheese, crumbled (low-fat or fat-free works, too)*

*Handful of dried cranberries or dried cherries*

*2 tablespoons sliced almonds*

*1 ripe pear, thinly sliced*

*2–3 tablespoons of your favorite vinaigrette dressing*

In a bowl, toss baby spinach, feta cheese, dried cranberries, and almonds with dressing and dump onto a chilled plate or bowl. Top with sliced pear and a few sprinkles of feta and dressing. To turn this yum-fest into a dinner, add grilled chicken or shrimp.

# II Live IT

"I always say, 'Don't make plans, make options.'"

–Jennifer Aniston

# 5

## Blogging Tools:

### To Do List

Shop the hottest hosted blog services

Find the right fit

Dress up your blog

Accessorize!

Celebrate your blog shopping success

# Bargain Blogging Out of the Box

**A**ntsy to get started, but don't want to give up your precious pedicures to pay for hosting? Don't you fret. A hosted blogging service is the solution for you. A generous handful of quality hosted blogging services are out there – most of them free! And who doesn't like free?

This chapter shares some of our favorite "quick-start" blogging services for you new blog starlets out there, as well as provides an overview of some of the other hosted options available to you. We won't sugar-coat it for you – they're all basically the same. Hosted blogging services provide a simple web-based interface from which you can post and manage your own blog with minimal drama and cost. Of course, each service does have its own unique features, and we're here to give you the skinny so you can make the best choice for you. If you need a refresher on some of the basics of blogging, we recommend you jump back to Chapter 1 or cruise the glossary to get the lingo down.

So, grab yourself a latte (or beverage of choice), fire up the ol' web browser, and let's get this party started, shall we? You'll be blogging by the end of the chapter!

# WordPress.com

With the runaway success of the blogging software WordPress.org, in 2006 the developers expanded to a hosted blogging service, WordPress.com, to bring the wonder of WordPress to a larger audience. Confused? Just to be clear, *WordPress.org* is a type of blogging software. *WordPress.com* is the hosted blogging service that *runs* the WordPress.org software.

WordPress.com allows users to start their own blog in *seconds* without having to know squat about technical stuff like FTP, databases, hosting accounts, and the like. This is great for a newbie with basic Internet savvy who is trying to get a feel for blogging without any real commitment. WordPress.com wanted to make it easy and fast to sign up and get started — and we have to agree, they certainly did.

While the service is free, for a few bucks (anywhere from $15–$90), you can upgrade your blog with enhanced functionality. Extra goodies include more server space to hold photos of your precious shoe collection and customizable CSS (or Cascading Style Sheets, which is one of the methods used to give your site its design) for those who are a little more advanced. Check out the WordPress.com website to get a full list of their features (wordpress.com/features/).

## Got 5 minutes?: Setting up your WordPress.com blog

Ready to get started? In a matter of minutes, you will complete the super-easy setup. Before you know it, you'll be blogging with WordPress!

Follow these steps to get your very own WordPress account:

1. **Visit WordPress.com (**wordpress.com**). Look for a link such as Sign Up Now and click it.**

2. **Fill out the signup form to set up your WordPress.com account.** Because you can create multiple blogs at WordPress.com, you need to set up an account first.

   - *Choose a username.* This will be your login, so choose something meaningful to you.

   - *Enter a valid email address.* With all the spam we get these days, the temptation is great to enter a faux email address. However, WordPress.com registration emails are sent to this address, so use a real one!

- *Choose Gimme a Blog!* You have the option to create just a WordPress.com account, but for now, choose Gimme a Blog to set up a blog as well.

- *Select the I Have Read and Agree to the Fascinating Terms of Service check box.* Make sure you read and agree to the terms and conditions before continuing.

3. **On the next page, complete the signup process.** Almost finished! Just take care of these last few simple steps, and you're on your way:

   - *Choose your blog domain.* This will be your actual URL, so be sure to choose wisely. By default, WordPress.com populates the field with your username, but you're free to choose whatever blog domain you prefer (such as avidknitter.wordpress.com or ilikecheese.wordpress.com, and so on).

   - *Choose your blog title.* Again, you're free to title your blog whatever you like, although commonly, people choose a title similar to or the same as their blog domain.

   - *Choose your language.* This is fairly self-explanatory. Feel free to choose the language most appropriate for your needs.

   - *Choose your level of privacy.* We go into more detail about blog privacy in Chapter 14, but for now, you can decide to list or not list your blog publicly. Consider whether you want your blog known or if you'd prefer to stay off the radar. You can always change this setting later if you want.

4. **Click Sign-Up.** At this point, you're directed to a confirmation page requesting that you check your email account.

5. **Locate your activation email from Word Press.com and click the included activation link.** *Voilà!* You're blogging!

## Motivate to Activate

Don't forget to check your email account for the WordPress.com activation email and click the link to activate your blog. The link expires two days from the date of registration, so be sure to click it!

After you've clicked the link in your activation email, it directs you to a page with a preassigned password. You are free to keep this password, but we recommend changing it to something more memorable and meaningful to you. Visit your profile on WordPress.com to change your password.

## Adding options: Making love out of nothing at all

So, you've got your blog. Now what? Well, nothing says "blah" like a boring, default blog design! You need to give it some love! WordPress.com offers a few different options for customizing your blog and making it a little more personal.

As with any free hosted blogging service, there are limitations to how much customization you can do. But with just a few clicks, you can definitely jazz it up!

## Your WordPress.com Dashboard

WordPress.com has a handy-dandy dashboard control panel, shown in Figure 5-1, that allows you to manage your blog layout and entries from one simple location. It also offers a library of almost 60 predesigned templates, or themes, for you to choose from! Whatever look you're going for, you should find something to get you started. Follow these steps to choose a template:

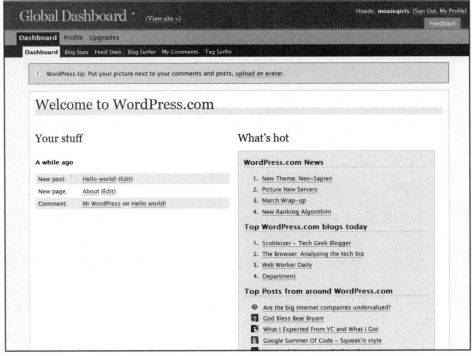

**Figure 5-1**

1. **Visit WordPress.com** (wordpress.com). **Look for the My Dashboard icon or link and click it to enter your blog control panel.** Or you can enter your control panel via a link similar to this: *yourblogname*.wordpress.com/wp-admin/, which should be in your activation email.

2. **Click the Presentation tab.** You're offered a collection of themes from which to choose.

3. **Click the theme you'd like.** Ta-da! Your blog is dressed and ready for its unveiling!

### Additional customization

More, huh? Well, WordPress.com, at the time of printing, doesn't offer a *whole* lot in the way of additional customization — at least not for free. But, never fear! You can do a few things to add a little more bling to your blog for next to nothin'.

Depending on the theme you've chosen, you may have the option to customize your header image further. This is a free option. Follow these steps to upload your own header image:

1. **Choose Presentation→Custom Image Header.**

2. **Click the Browse button, navigate to the image on your hard drive, and click Open.**

3. **Click the Upload button.**

4. **Drag the image selection up or down to choose the part of the image to use as your header. Then click the Crop Header button.**

WordPress.com also offers a way for you to play with and preview custom stylesheets. However, if you wish to actually save and *use* those stylesheets on your WordPress.com blog, you have to pay an upgrade fee ($15.00). To edit CSS (or the Cascading Style Sheets, the code that alters the look of your blog), follow these steps:

1. **Choose Presentation→Edit CSS.**

2. **Edit directly in the CSS editor and preview your changes as often as you like for free.**

3. **To save and use your custom CSS, click the Custom CSS Upgrade link and follow the instructions to purchase this feature for your WordPress.com account.**

# Blogger

Blogger is a very popular free blogging platform available to anyone with a Google account. Upstart web developers started Blogger back in 1999 as a pet project and later sold it to the Internet superstar Google (google.com). Eventually, Blogger developed into the vastly popular service we know today.

Using Blogger is *beyond* easy and requires almost no technical knowledge to get your blog running. While it's not all that feature-rich, with a decent amount of pre-made templates to choose from, all you need is a Google account and something to say. The best part? It's free, so it's great for bloggers on a budget or inexperienced bloggers looking for a way to get their feet wet without jumping head-first into the deep end.

# Easy peasy: Setting up a blog using Blogger

Setting up a new blog using Blogger is, in a word, simple. The only caveat is that you must have a Google account.

Visit the Blogger website (blogger.com) and follow these steps to set up your own blog on Blogger:

1. **Set up your Blogger account.** The nice part about Blogger being associated with Google is that signing up is a breeze. If you already have a Google account, your information may already be plugged in on the Sign Up page. If it's not and you have a Google account that you wish to associate with this blog, go ahead and fill in your email address and password to login and then skip to Step 2.

   If you do not have a Google account at all or do not want to associate your existing Google account with this blog for privacy's sake, click the link that says Create Your Blog Now. This will take you to a page where you can set up a Google account and your blog at the same time! In the interest of this example, we'll assume you do not have a Google account.

   - Enter an existing email address (not a Gmail address — if you have one of those you wish to use, try logging in on the main page first and skip to Step 2.)

   - Choose a secure password. Blogger will tell you how safe your password is as you enter it. You have the option of changing it at any time in your Blogger Dashboard settings.

   - Re-enter your chosen password for confirmation.

   - Enter the word that's displayed in the box for verification that you're a real human being.

   - Accept the terms of agreement and click Continue.

**thisdomainnameishardtoread.blogspot.com**

When choosing your URL, avoid using run-on sentences or overly complicated words that are hard to spell. It's also a good idea to choose one that matches or closely matches the title of your blog. Clarity is important. We cover name selection in more depth in Chapter 6.

2. **On the next page, fill in the rest of the info:**

   - *Choose a title for your blog.* Again, some of these details can be changed later, but it is wise to choose carefully from the start.

- *Choose a blog address (URL).* As with any free blogging service, you are bound to their limitations, and in this case, your blog's URL will look something like this: *yourblogname*.blogspot.com. All Blogger blogs have the blog spot.com domain name required unless you pay for the upgraded service.

- *Click Continue.* Blogger will offer you the option of selecting advanced features in order to host the blog on your own website. For the purposes of this example, please skip this step.

3. **Choose your template.** Blogger provides about a dozen different looks to choose from. Just choose one and off you go!

Now you're ready to start blogging!

# Adding options: Expand your Blogger wardrobe

As we've mentioned, with any free blogging service there are limitations. But now that blogging is becoming so widely used, the free services are beginning to offer more features — not to mention making customization a snap. Blogger tends to be one of the most minimal hosted services in terms of bells and whistles, but they do have a few features you can take advantage of.

### Your Blogger Dashboard

Once you're set up, you can start making this blog yours. Own it! From the dashboard, shown in Figure 5-2, you can manage your lovely blog and its contents. You may add sections to the sidebar of your blog so your readers can learn more about you and navigate through the rest of your blog. On your dashboard, look for the Layout option to customize these areas:

- **Page Elements:** This provides you with a list of existing Page Elements and the ability to add extra items, such as photos, RSS feeds, and ads. Neat!

- **Fonts and Colors:** Right next to Page Elements, you find the Fonts and Colors options. Blogger has a nice little color selection palette that lets you choose and preview your font colors. Easy!

### Additional customization

Now that you've found your way around, you want more, right? We know you're hooked! You should be feeling confident in your technical skills and maybe you want to muck around in the CSS and design your own Blogger blog. Great! From the Layout link on the dashboard, here are a few more options worth checking out:

- **Edit HTML:** If you're a little more adventurous, you can choose the Edit HTML tab and

**Call a Do Over!**

Blogger provides links to all the original HTML and CSS code, so you don't have to fret if you forget.

directly edit the code guts of the template. Be very careful when doing this — or at the very least, back up a copy of the original before you start rearranging HTML. You can revert to your original if you make a mistake.

**Figure 5-2**

## HTML, CSS, and Other Acronyms

HTML? CSS? You may be wondering what all these kooky letters mean that we keep throwing around. HTML is short for HyperText Markup Language, and it's the foundation language used to structure web pages. CSS is an abbreviation for Cascading Style Sheets, which is the language used to apply the design elements to a web page. Think of it like one of those gingerbread houses you put together at Christmas. The HTML is the gingerbread house itself, and the CSS applies all the frosting, glitter, and treats. Don't try to eat it, though. You'll never get the code out of your teeth. We cover more design-type stuff in Chapter 7.

Blogger uses its very own code syntax, or language, to output your posts and comments from the database. These bits of code will need to stay intact, so be sure not to accidentally delete them while you're getting down and dirty. If this all sounds like a foreign language, just stick with the basic default settings until you're more comfortable.

- **Pick New Template:** If you're over it or the look you chose initially just doesn't fit your personality and you want to trash it, never fear! You can select Pick New Template from the Layout area of your Blogger Dashboard and change your duds in a click. (You never wear the first thing you put on before you go out, right?)

- **Customize your domain name:** Blogger grants members the perk of using a custom domain name, which allows you to register a personalized domain name and point it to your Blogger account. Click the link that says Customize Your Domain from the Settings area of your Blogger Dashboard. This lets you control your blog a little more and allows you to operate from a real domain name rather than a blogspot.com domain.

## Bad Business

If you're considering using your blog for business, we recommend steering clear of communities and social networks like MySpace. While many businesses do find an *added* benefit to having a MySpace profile, it's not recommended as your primary professional web presence.

# Vox

Vox! Oh, how we *love* playing around with this service. Like Blogger, Vox (vox.com) is probably the easiest and most fun, free blog service out there. It was created by the good folks at Six Apart who, not coincidentally, are the people responsible for Movable Type (discussed more in Chapter 6) and TypePad (covered later on in the chapter). Vox is totally fun and casual, and it makes adding content simple and easy. You can add video, audio, photos, and Amazon.com merchandise in one or two EASY steps without ever touching one single bit of code. Integrate YouTube.com videos or photos from your Flickr account seamlessly and effortlessly. (See Chapter 12 for more on Flickr.) The whole thing is totally automated and super slick. It's also completely free.

Vox is great for any type of blogger, experienced or not, but it's really ideal for people who are more interested in a point-and-click type setting — very user-friendly. This can be said for all of the services featured in this chapter, but it's especially easy with Vox. Those who may be interested in a more exclusive, private setting for their blog or those who enjoy a community vibe might enjoy Vox, as well.

One of Vox's fabulous key features is its supreme privacy controls. These controls are far more robust than those of WordPress.com or Blogger, and they offer more flexibility. While privacy isn't the sole reason to join, Vox was born in an effort to allow people to share video and photos without exposing them to the entire Internet. Since then, it's grown into a much larger blogging tool with many benefits. Take a moment to check out the Vox tour of features on the Six Apart website (sixapart.com/vox/tour/).

# Rock Vox: Setting up your Vox blog

While there are a few more steps to setting up your Vox (vox.com) blog than there are for WordPress.com or Blogger, it's not too much trouble, and once you're finished, you're ready to start blogging!

Just click the Join Now icon and then follow these simple steps to get your new Vox blog up and running:

1. **Fill in the information on the setup page to create your account.** Don't you just *love* filling out forms? Oh, it's not that bad! Start by filling in your email address and choosing a password (preferably something you'll remember fairly easily). Then provide the rest of the following information:

   - *Choose a member name.* This is public, so choose wisely if it matters. If you prefer to be a little more anonymous and don't want Aunt Millie knowing you had too many cocktails Friday night, choose something anonymous or something silly that won't directly identify you. Otherwise, you can use your regular name.

   - *Enter your gender.* Everyone likes to know who they're dealing with, but you can decline to state it.

   - *Enter your birthday.* It's a requirement for legal reasons, so be truthful.

   - *Prove you're human.* Standard anti-spam measures . . . just type the characters in to let the site know you aren't a bot.

   - *Agree to the terms of service.* Read the terms of service and select the check box.

2. **Click Sign Up!**

3. **Confirm your email address.** Vox will send you a confirmation email with a link that verifies your address. Those pesky spam bots make this extra step necessary. While you're waiting for your confirmation email, move on to Step 4, but don't forget to check your email because you'll need that confirmation code for Step 7.

4. **Enter other identifying information.** Enter your first and last name, gender, birthday, country, and postal code. This all remains private unless you opt to reveal it to certain member groups, such as friends, family, or neighbors.

5. **Choose a personal icon.** Don't worry, you can always go back and select something different later or upload one of your own.

## Blogging within a community or social network

Some people choose to use communities or social networks like MySpace (myspace. com), LiveJournal (livejournal.com), and Yahoo! 360° (360.yahoo.com) to make their foray into blogging. This is often because they are not comfortable venturing beyond their community niche, since that's where all their friends are. Or sometimes it's because they figure there's no need to — their community has a blog built right in! And MySpace often *is* the Internet to many of its users. Using the built-in blogs in these social communities is definitely an option, but in many blogging circles, it is not regarded the same as "having a blog."

In some communities or social networks, like MySpace for instance, they may use slightly different terminology than in the rest of the blogosphere. For example, MySpacers usually refer to each blog entry as a *blog*, as in "Hey everybody! I just posted three new *blogs* about my new job!" To some, this is misleading because bloggers out in the wilds of the free-range Internet refer to their blog as one single entity and that entity is comprised of many blog *entries*. This would be referenced like so, "Hey everybody! I just posted three new blog entries about my new job!" This is the traditional use. Calling each blog entry "a blog" in and of itself drives *some* people absolutely crazy. Not that we would know who those people are or anything ... ahem.

Social networks and communities also tend to be somewhat self-contained and often require you to have an account in order to read the associated blogs.

While this kind of community or network definitely has its appeal and its benefits, especially for musicians and artists, it might not be what you're looking for if you're trying to make your mark in the blogging community at large. Arguably, your blog may garner more street cred (and traffic!) if it's not within a social community.

6. **Select your Vox address**. Your blog address will look something like this: *yourblogname*.vox.com. Choose something that's easy to remember and spell.

7. **Enter your confirmation code.** At the top of the page, enter the confirmation code you should have received by now in your email into the field and click Confirm Account.

8. **Name your poison.** At this point, you're offered options. You can choose to fill out your profile, set up your Vox, or write your first post.

## Dressing up your Vox

Thus far, setting up a Vox blog is less painful than a brow wax, no? And customizing it is just as pain free; we promise. With this platform, you can add some fun

## Know When to Zip It

Vox offers various privacy settings. Want to dish about the latest drama? No problem with a Vox blog. Simply set the privacy settings in your Share This Post section and you're good to go.

multimedia with the flick of your perfumed wrist. It does have some limitations, as any free blogging service does, but the pros outweigh the cons in this area.

### Your Vox home page

After you've verified your email and are all set up, the fun really begins. You'll already be logged in and ready to make this blog shine. From the page that appears after activating your account, click the Set Up Your Vox link to customize your new blog. Or from your My Vox home page, shown in Figure 5-3, choose My Vox➔Design. Here are your options:

- **Select a Layout.** You can choose from four different layouts and customize your sidebars as you see fit. Before you realize it, you'll have a fully organized and designed blog that's just begging for content.

- **Select a Theme.** You can choose from over 250 predesigned themes. There are some really stunning and cute designs to choose from.

Figure 5-3

There are clear, concise step-by-step instructions right in the blog you just created. Vox is very forthcoming with the help, and you can find what you need in mere seconds.

### Additional customization

So, you have your Vox blog up and running and you want to really make it yours. We get it. So do the folks at Vox. You can create your own personalized banner graphic (within the specified size limits, of course), and upload and install it right on your Vox blog. Here's how:

1. **Click the Personalized theme category to upload your homemade banner graphic.**

2. **Click the Select Image button and navigate to the image you want to use for the banner.**

3. **Choose your palette.** You can choose from over 60 coordinating color palettes to complement your dazzling creation.

Blogging comes easy here. Not only can you just start typing with the click of your cute little wireless mouse, but if you're feeling a little stumped, or have blogging performance anxiety, Vox also provides a community atmosphere armed with daily questions and topics you can answer and discuss with other Vox members right from your blog.

Making a Vox blog your own is simple, quick, and really very painless. We wish we could say that about the last bikini wax we received, but we can't have everything.

# TypePad

TypePad (typepad.com) is a popular hosted blogging service launched in 2003 by the folks at Six Apart, the makers of other blogging tools such as Vox and Movable Type. (We'll go into more on Movable Type in Chapter 6.) While it is marketed as "the premier blog service for

professionals," TypePad works for the non-professional, too. TypePad is a fine platform — especially for those who are looking to start a business blog. But, it's not our favorite hosted service for first-time bloggers or bloggers who aren't sure if they want to get their hair wet — for a couple reasons we discuss in a minute.

Once upon a time, TypePad's basic service was free, but now requires a small fee (as low as $4.95 per month, at time of publication). Programmers and developers are skilled professionals who deserve a salary, so we can appreciate the fact that Six Apart is charging for this service. And it *does* offer a 30-day free trial after registering your credit card information. But, if you're just dipping your toe in, it may benefit you to go with a free service, like WordPress.

On the upside, the Six Apart developers provide an accessible control panel interface that allows comfortable users to smoothly add and delete features to their weblogs with a handy click 'n' publish structure.

TypePad offers various features (sixapart.com/type pad/features), as well as upgrades to TypePad Plus and TypePad Pro ($8.95 per month and $14.95 per

### Caveat Emptor!

TypePad is not free, and getting the full benefits of the service can become costly. This can be confusing for a lot of bloggers who think they'll be able to get the whole enchilada with just the basic package. Make sure to read the fine print before submitting your credit card information!

## More Bang for Your Buck

If you decide that TypePad is the service for you, consider paying in lump sums. TypePad offers a discount when you purchase a year in advance. It's like getting two months free!

month, respectively) that allow you to customize your blog further and get more goodies for just a little more cash.

The downside is that TypePad can be complicated to customize if you want to do something beyond what the library of templates has to offer. To *fully* customize your TypePad blog, you need to pay for their highest level of service, and you need to be relatively proficient in HTML (or know someone who is!).

For the extreme novice, we feel there are other services, such as Vox, that are a bit more intuitive. However, if you're feeling daring, toss aside your water wings and jump on in! TypePad is definitely a solid choice if you're comfortable with basic lingo, have a working knowledge of blogs, and/or want a blog for your business.

## Cute Overload!

Think your blog can't gain popularity on a hosted service? Not the case! There are a number of insanely popular blogs out there garnering acclaim and adoration by millions. A perfect example is the squishy, feel-good blog run by Meg Frost, called Cute Overload (cuteoverload.com).

CuteOverload.com is hosted on TypePad by Six Apart. With a readership of primarily "fine, fine women," this blog reaches 55,000 visitors a day. It's been featured on or in numerous highly regarded news outlets and publications such as CNN, *The Washington Post, New York Magazine,* and *Entertainment Weekly,* among others.

With a darling design, an engaging hostess, and content cute enough to kill (or at least maim), Meg Frost has made an adorable dent in the blogosphere.

# Relax, Refresh, Reward

In this chapter, you find out about effectively starting your own blog on a hosted service. Hooray! As easy as it was, we think it's still a feat worth celebrating.

And what better way to celebrate than with a little bubbly? Don't go drinking out of the bottle just yet! You've dressed up your blog, so why not dress up your drink?

While celebrating the launch of a project, we created a champagne cocktail with a sexy little twist. One glass became another, and it soon became one of our favorites. It's fabulous for brunch, too!

## Blogging Betty

*6 oz chilled pink champagne*

*Half a shot of peach nectar*

*Drizzle of raspberry liqueur*

*Fresh raspberries*

In a chilled champagne flute, pour half a shot of peach nectar (Kern's works well). Add a drizzle of raspberry liqueur (Chambord is easy to find), but not too much! Just a few drops. Fill the rest of the flute with pink champagne. Plop in fresh raspberries to sweeten the deal and drink. Cheers!

# 6 Hosting Your Own Website:

## To Do List

- Choose your domain name, registrar, and web host
- Find the right blogging software
- Set up your domain and install your software
- Make your space inspirational

# You Say Who, When, and How Much!

**Y**ou're feeling confident enough to get down and dirty with your own blog on your own terms, rather than rely on a free, hosted service (as described in Chapter 5). Rock on, sister! But hold up – there are a few things you need to know in order to get started. Before you give up and head for yoga class instead, setting up your own blog really is a lot less complicated than it sounds.

In a nutshell, here are the general steps for setting up your own blogging site:

1. *Choose a domain name.*

2. *Register your domain name.*

3. *Select a web hosting provider.*

4. *Pick a blogging platform.*

5. *Install blogging software.*

This chapter gives you the lowdown on completing all these steps to get you on your way to blogging independence!

# Choosing a Domain Name

Choosing a domain name (*yourdomainname*.com), a simple but memorable name used as an address, is a rather simple task. However, choosing the *right* domain name is an entirely different animal. And you want to get it right the first time because domain names — while they aren't permanent like that butterfly tattoo on your tailbone — can be a hassle to change. Here are a few questions you should ask yourself when choosing a domain name:

- **Is it readable?** It's okay to choose a domain name that represents you, but if the letter arrangement when squashed together looks like something else entirely, it might not be the best choice.

- **Does it make sense?** So you want to register iamaflyingpotatoheadmonster.com, but your blog is about vintage clothing stores in Manhattan. It's not that you won't get hits, mind you, but matching your domain name to your content is a perfect way to establish branding (if that's important to you). Of course, if the point is for it to be total nonsense, then go to town. But it's something to consider before spending your rainy day money on a domain name.

- **Does it fit you?** This domain name should represent who you are — or at the very least, have some significance to you. You'll be with a domain name for at least a year or more, so make it count.

- **Is it catchy or memorable?** You want to increase your traffic. If people can remember your domain name easily, chances are they will come back again and again, even if they have forgotten to bookmark or subscribe to your blog.

Finally, choosing a domain name that matches the "title" of your site (or that you use in your logo, if you have one) is good blogging business. Of course, if the domain name is for personal use and you don't care so much, full steam ahead. But consider matching your domain name with your title or logo. Remember that thing we said about making it memorable? It applies here. If they remember, they will come, just like they did in *Field of Dreams*.

## For Rent

While you can register and use domain names, they're never really yours to keep. You're more or less renting them. But as long as you renew each year, you have the full rights to the domain name for as long as you pay for it.

# Registering Your Dream Domain Name

You've settled on a domain name! Pat yourself on the back. But before you get too excited, remember that you don't own it yet; you must register the domain name in order to use it for your blog. To do so, you need to buy the domain from a *registrar* (a company that sells and administers domain names). There are hundreds of web hosts and websites that perform registrar duties as well, so if you are more of a one-stop-shop kind of girl, you can sometimes handle this with your web host. But if you need more control over your domain registration, you can purchase it from any registrar. Table 6-1 lists a few popular registrars that offer quick, easy, and cheap domain name registration.

## Checking availability

Before you can buy a domain name, you're required to check it to ensure it isn't already registered by someone else. If you've come up with something unique, you have a good shot at getting the domain name — or something close to it. But if your desired domain name is along the lines of something commonly used, you might have a bit of a challenge on your hands. Typical registrars (like GoDaddy.com) offer a multitude of suggested alternatives if your precious domain name is taken.

## Considering .org, .com, and .biz — .huh?

One additional decision you'll need to make concerning your domain name is what *suffix* to go with. People tend to gravitate toward domain names ending with .com because it's the most recognized suffix around. Most people hear "dot com" and know what it means and where to go. Other suffixes available, such as .org (which is typically used for nonprofit organizations), .gov (for government websites), and .net (for network organizations), aren't quite as widely recognized. (Originally, .com was reserved for commercial businesses, but it's become more a way of life than anything.)

### Thrifty Chic

Make sure to prowl around Google (google.com) for discount codes and coupons on domain registrations. On sites such as GoDaddy.com, we've found 10-percent-off discounts on bulk registrations – or similar discounts for first-time buyers. Even if you come up empty handed, it's worth checking out!

## Table 6-1     Popular Registrars

| Name | Address |
| --- | --- |
| Go Daddy | godaddy.com |
| Dotster | dotster.com |
| Network Solutions | networksolutions.com |
| Register.com | register.com |

Not sure what to choose? You should choose your domain name's suffix based on what suits your tastes and budget. Some registration companies promote .biz or other domains with alternate endings as a way to offer the domain you want, at a cheaper price. Reason being, .biz or .info domains aren't as common and are therefore less desirable.

## Selecting a registrar

So how do you know which registrar to use? You'll find quite a few on the Internet (see Table 6-1 for a few suggestions) to choose from, so keep your budget considerations and hosting needs in mind when choosing a registrar:

- **Price:** Pricing can vary widely. A domain name can cost as low as $4 a year to upwards of $35 a year or more. Make sure you shop around. Some companies offer a highly discounted price on domain names, but there are sometimes strings attached, such as requiring you to sign up for a specific length of contract or purchase other services from that vendor.

- **Flexibility:** Do a bit of comparison shopping to make sure the company you use meets your needs. Both registrar companies and web hosts offer a variety of services that can add on to your bill. If all you want is a domain name, then working with a registrar might be for you. But if you want the whole enchilada and need everything from a domain name to hosting and email, then getting your domain name through a hosting company might be smarter and more economical. Just be sure the company you pick fits the plan you have for your site.

When you find a domain name that suits you, is available, and makes sense, you should secure it for the minimum of one year. Some companies offer a discount for prepaying for more than one year of service. If you plan on keeping the domain name for a while, you might as well go for the savings.

## You Can Take It with You

Make sure when registering your domain that *you* are the listed contact and owner of the domain name, not the registrar or the hosting company. Some hosts or registrars register the domain name for you, but under their company name, thus making it owned by them and not you. If you change hosts or switch registrars, you can't take the domain name with you if you don't own it. So, be sure to read the fine print.

## Protecting your privacy

A few domain registrars offer some privacy services as well. Right now, most domain name registration information is *public* — meaning anyone with an Internet connection and a nosy tendency can look up your email address, mailing address, and name. (Anyone with an Internet connection can use a WHOIS database to find the name server, registrar, and full contact information for a particular domain name and its registrar. All registrars are required to maintain a WHOIS database with contact information for the domains they host.)

If you prefer the extra privacy of keeping your contact information hidden, you can sometimes pay for a *masked registration*. This keeps your information hidden from public snoops, but the catch is the additional fee. GoDaddy.com, one of our preferred registration companies, provides Private Registration as an added service for approximately $7 a year.

To register a domain name with GoDaddy.com, follow these steps:

1. **Visit GoDaddy.com, and in the search form at the top of the page (see Figure 6-1), enter your desired domain name and select your desired suffix from the drop-down list. Then click Go!**

Figure 6-1

2. **If the name you want is taken, repeat Step 2 until you find one that is available.**

3. **Select the check box under the domain names/suffixes you want to purchase.** See Figure 6-2. GoDaddy will give you more available domain name options, which you can purchase at this time as well.

Figure 6-2

4. **After you have selected all the desired domain names, scroll to the bottom of the page and click Continue.**

## Getting only the bells and whistles you need

Tons of domain registration companies out there mean competition and harsh marketing strategies. During the signup process, they'll try to lure you into spending all your hard-earned bucks on every service they provide. While it may be tempting to sign up for everything, read the terms and conditions and choose only those services you need.

If you get roped into buying additional services, make sure you read the fine print. Just when you think you're getting a deal, you actually might be purchasing three years of hosting (for instance) that you might not be able to use.

5. GoDaddy gives you the opportunity to purchase hosting and other add-on services, but you can skip these and click on Continue to Checkout to get to the buying part.

6. On the page shown in Figure 6-3, fill out your personal information and credit card information and finish your purchase!

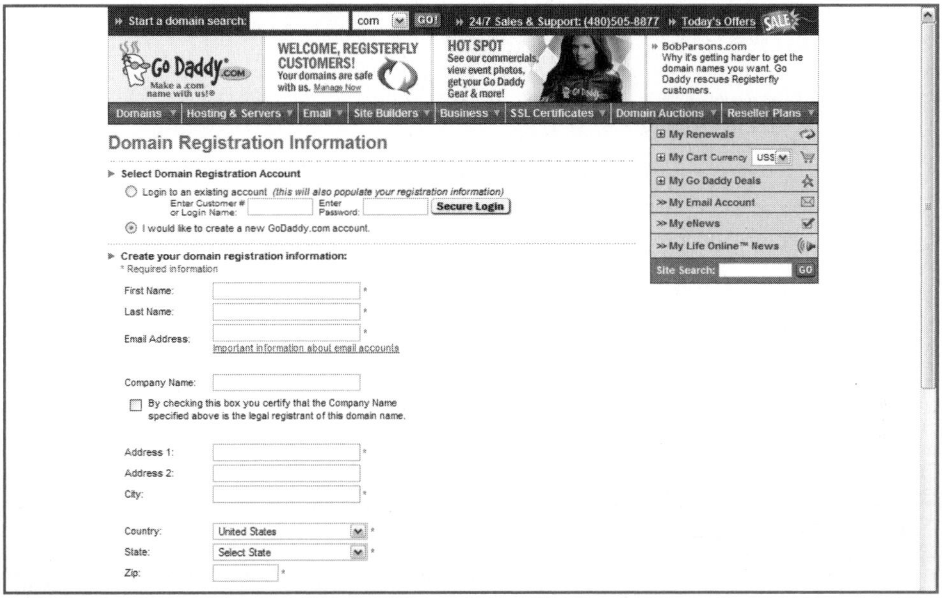

Figure 6-3

# Choosing a Web Hosting Provider

If you have successfully registered your domain name, let's press on. You've got a hot date with a blog! Your domain name is like your personal mailing address, and the Internet needs to know where to go to find your house. Now, you just need to rent a house for the masses to visit.

Think of your new website as a person or a friend who needs a place to live. Web hosting is like a virtual apartment building where your domain name can rent a place to stay and keep all its stuff. You have to choose the size of the apartment and length of the lease, and you need to make sure it has the proper amenities to run a blog. In technical speak, you lease space on the web hosting provider's *server,* which is a computer that stores all the files associated with your blog.

Zillions (okay, maybe not zillions, but maybe thousands) of web hosting providers are available for hire. The question is which one to use. You can do a search for *web hosts* and compare the ones you find that have the criteria you require at your price range.

Or you can ask around. Usually, other people with blogs that aren't on free, hosted services use a hosting provider, and they can give you recommendations. If you don't know anyone with a blog, just find one you admire and ask. Bloggers are generally eager to offer up the information (especially if they get a referral bonus out of the deal). People are nice, so ask away! Table 6-2 is a quick reference of web hosting providers you can investigate.

Typically, the smallest package (or the package a step up from that) is suitable for running a blog. If you aren't sure, check the documentation on your chosen blogging software for guidelines on what you need to run an installation.

If you anticipate thousands upon hundreds of hits a day and massive quantities of blog entries and multimedia, then you may think about going for something with a bit more disk space. If this is the case, you will want to talk to the web hosting company before you buy. Ask to speak with a sales contact who can direct you to the right hosting package for you.

## Deciding on a studio apartment or three-bedroom condo

Deciding how much space you need and how much to buy is a daunting thought. Before you purchase the biggest hosting package the provider offers, check out the minimal packages first and work up from there.

## Lease options: One year or infinite?

Most web hosts require that you sign up for a one-year hosting agreement, while some let you pay in three-or six-month chunks. Purchasing your hosting in one-year chunks is usually more cost effective, but don't buy more than one year at a time. If for some reason you encounter a problem with the host you've chosen and decide to move, you won't be throwing away money by abandoning the extra years you paid for.

Table 6-2     Popular Web Hosting Providers

| Name | Address |
| --- | --- |
| Hosting Matters | hostingmatters.com |
| Wired Hub | wiredhub.net |
| Living Dot | livingdot.com |
| Engine Hosting | enginehosting.com |

# Making sure you have the right amenities

Most blog programs require a few things in order to run properly and at their full potential:

- **MySQL:** Almost *every* platform requires you to run one *database,* which is a system that enables you to store data in an organized manner that can be accessed by a program, in this case a blogging tool. Most blogging software packages run well using MySQL, a type of database management software, and your web host should provide the ability to add a MySQL database to your account. The larger the package you purchase, usually the more databases the web host lets you add. If you'll be running multiple instances of software requiring more databases, you'll need a more upscale package to accommodate it. However, for running a blog, you usually just need one single database.

    Installing a MySQL database can typically be done through your web host's *control panel,* an area of your hosting account where you administer items like setting up email addresses. Most web hosts provide an easy step-by-step section for creating and setting up a database. Setting one up is as far into databases as you will need to get to set up and run your own blog. Once you have it created, the hard part is done.

- **Perl and PHP:** Many blogging software programs use *Perl* and *PHP* for their basic functions, so your web host will need these programming language packages installed on their servers. Most web hosts do; just make sure that the package you obtain includes them. Don't fret, you aren't required to know how to use Perl and PHP; you just need to ensure your web host has and supports them in order to run most blogging software tools.

- **Some type of image-resizing module such as ImageMagick:** A lot of blog platforms can automatically resize photos that you use in your blog entries — thumbnails included. This depends on whether your blog platform has an image-resizing module installed. In addition to ImageMagick, other popular image-resizing modules are Gif Draw and Graphics Draw. Whether your web host has and supports this feature is something to investigate before you buy any web hosting packages, but if the host you chose does not have it, it isn't the end of the world. It's just a nice perk that will make your blogging software run at its fullest potential.

- **A control panel user interface such as cPanel:** Inquire with web hosts about whether they have cPanel or some other type of control panel user interface. This interface enables you to manage your site, email, and databases yourself, rather than rely on someone in tech support to do it for you. Figure 6-4 show you an example of what a host using cPanel looks like and the options it provides you.

Figure 6-4

# Choosing a Blogging Platform or CMS (Content Management System)

Choosing a blogging platform, also referred to as *blogging software,* is an important step, so consider it carefully. You have quite a few platforms to select from, and each has its own set of benefits that can influence your choice, given what you want to accomplish. If you plan on building a straight-up simple blog, most any platform will suffice. Some platforms have more bells and whistles than others and provide ample opportunities for expansion down the line.

Now that blogging is somewhat mainstream, a handful of blogging platforms double as a method of managing other content, otherwise referred to as a CMS (content management system). Consider choosing a CMS for its ability to help you produce a full-blown website, complete with blog. A CMS is a software package that allows you to edit and manage website content easily, such as basic site text and images, without fiddling with HTML code. If you plan on having more than just a blog and need to display extra pages of content or news, you might investigate using a CMS to manage your whole website.

There are many blogging platforms out there, and a quick comparison of features can help you decide what platform will benefit you. There are a few pinch hitters and a slew of others that are worthy of a gander. In the sections that follow, we show you the benefits and options of a few platforms that are widely used and let you decide which one best suits your needs.

## Movable Type

Movable Type (movabletype.org) was created by the company Six Apart, the makers of TypePad and Vox. Movable Type has garnered widespread use and praise for its contributions to the growth of blogging, as a tool and resource to the blogging community. What started out as a simple blogging tool has grown into a rich and dynamic content management product. Yet, it still manages to keep the blogging simplicity intact.

Movable Type has a very what-you-see-is-what-you-get, point-and-click approach to its setup. Depending on what licensing option you choose, you can run multiple blogs off the same installation. You can customize your blog with a templating system that is very accessible, right in the control panel of the program, which is shown in Figure 6-5.

### Hire It Done

Movable Type offers installation and upgrade services for a small fee. Check out their website for information, details, and pricing.

Movable Type (also known as MT) has a handful of basic features that give you the chance to dive into blogging head first. Here's a quick rundown:

- **Comments and trackbacks:** We give you the details on comments and trackbacks in Chapter 9, but basically, MT provides the functionality for people to leave comments on your blog, in addition to sending and receiving trackbacks.

- **Search feature:** Lets your readers search through your previous entries.

- **Archiving system:** MT automatically files your blog posts by month, by week, and by category. You can display links to these sections for easy reference by your readers, and you.

- **RSS:** RSS is described in detail in Chapter 11.

- **Email notification and subscribers:** Allows you to send a notification email to users who have subscribed to your site, alerting them of site updates.

- **A bevy of widgets and plugins:** Customize to your heart's content with added features, downloadable from the MT website (sixapart.com/pronet/plugins/).

*Click to access templating system*

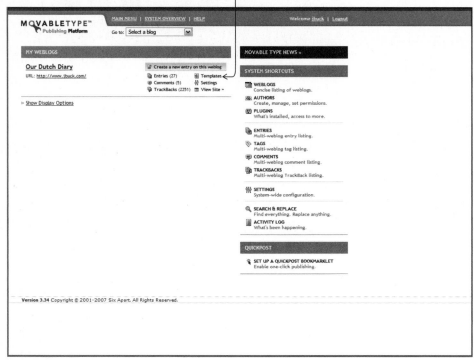

Figure 6-5

# Plugins out the Widget

In case you're wondering, *widgets* and *plugins* are small scripts that you can install or add to blog software to enhance it in some way. A good example of a plugin is a script that allows you to display your latest Netflix rentals, or the last few books you read, complete with links to the books on Amazon. Widgets are more drag and drop in nature, and are usually associated with hosted blog services, but they allow you to pull information from other websites in order to enhance the content of your site.

Movable Type has several licensing options for download and purchase directly from their website. You can get a free personal license that limits you to one user but no support. You also have the option of purchasing a personal one-user license for about $49.95, which includes one year of support services. Although you can find your way without the company's support, purchasing the support license gives you peace of mind. You know that the company is available to answer questions or resolve installation or performance kinks that their handy Knowledge Base (list of commonly asked questions) might not answer. Movable

Type also offers a couple of multiuser licenses, educational and nonprofit licensing, and the Movable Type Enterprise edition, which caters to larger commercial needs.

With Movable Type, you can easily add nonblog pages (or *static content*) to your site, although you'll need to know a bit of HTML to get the full potential of those features. However, as soon as the program is installed and running, you can begin blogging right away.

## ExpressionEngine

ExpressionEngine (expressionengine.com) sprouted out of a blogging tool, called pMachine, conceived in 2001 by Rick Ellis. In 2004, the company EllisLab released their "next generation publishing system" ExpressionEngine, which is an extremely flexible and powerfully slick content management tool and blogging platform. EllisLab refers to their product as a publishing system for the simple reason that it's much more than just a blog tool. Its flexibility makes it useful in just about every website situation or project, and it packs a powerful punch as a blogging platform, too.

In 2005, EllisLab created a slimmed down version of ExpressionEngine, called ExpressionEngine Core, which is more of a basic blogging tool. ExpressionEngine Core is a free version for personal use, albeit without any technical support. It gives you the basic functions of the software, which include these main components:

- **The weblog module** — the basic functionality that allows you to publish blog entries
- **Commenting and trackbacks**
- **Search and archiving**
- **Spam control**
- **RSS**

You can spring for the complete version of ExpressionEngine (for about $99.95 at the time this book was written). The full version includes unlimited tech support and gives you some highly useful goodies on top of the core program, including

- **Membership capabilities:** Give your readers the opportunity to register for an account on your site. You can save their profile information, give them insider access to private blog posts, and give them the chance to skip over the comment form on return site visits. See more about comment forms in Chapter 9.
- **A photo gallery.**
- **A wiki module:** A *wiki* is an application that lets multiple users post and update information to keep it current, like a reference that is always being updated.

- **A mailing list:** You can notify site members or subscribers of new content or make special announcements.
- **A really cool Simple Commerce module:** This allows you to integrate shopping with your site if you need it.

You will have to judge whether your blog needs ExpressionEngine or ExpressionEngine Core. Either choice gives you a fully functional blog, ready to use after you install it. Figure 6-6 shows the basic blog post publishing screen.

**Figure 6-6**

One of the many things we love about ExpressionEngine (lovingly referred to as EE by its dedicated users and followers) is just how flexible it is. You can literally rearrange almost every field to suit your needs. Don't want an Entry Body field? Make a new one and call it Grocery List — or anything you want!

Unlike Movable Type, there is no need to rebuild anything. MT requires you to sit through a rebuilding step when publishing or when making changes to template content. EE is an instant-gratification type of software. We like that. Who wouldn't?

# WordPress

WordPress (wordpress.org) is another pioneer in the blogging world. Born in 2001 as a bit of code, WordPress quickly gained popularity and was installed on hundreds of thousands of sites in the blink of an eye. WordPress is an *open source project,* which means it's freely available for you or anyone who can write code to use and modify. Due to its open source nature, it's always being improved by programmers everywhere, and a handful of web hosts provide installation of WordPress right on your site with the click of a button. Ask your web host or dig around in your hosting control panel for something like Fantastico, which is a program that installs software automatically on your hosting space without making you jump through all the hoops.

Even though it's a free open source project, WordPress is a pretty powerful little tool for blogging and managing content. It's customizable, lightweight, and speedy. One of the coolest features in WordPress is the availability of multiple themes that you can change at the click of a button. The Themes Available number dips into the thousands, so you can easily find a look that fits you. Figure 6-7 shows the WordPress Dashboard area, which functions as the command and control center for running your blog.

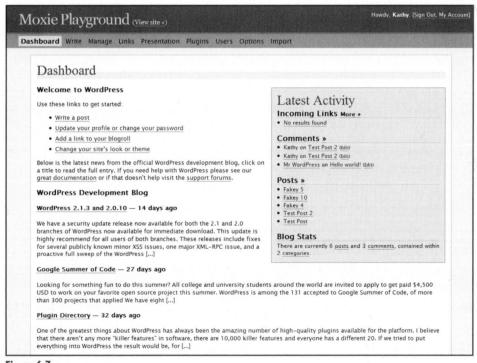

**Figure 6-7**

## Mambo, Drupal, and Textpattern

Life is about choices. Right? Well, just like there are many domain names and many web hosts, there are also many other blogging platforms and content management systems. Aside from the tools we outline earlier in the chapter, here are a pile of other systems you may want to investigate:

- **Mambo** (mamboserver.com), a robust program gaining ground, is more of a content management system than a blogging tool, although it does provide a blogging module for use with its system. But it has its publishing benefits, such as its sleek template system. You can use one of Mambo's completely free templates to style your site in minutes.

- **Drupal** (drupal.org/) is a software platform that helps users easily publish and manage website content. The nice thing about Drupal is its web installer, which takes the headache out of installing software. Just a few clicks, and it's ready to go immediately. Drupal provides content management and blogging capabilities, while providing a bunch of add-on modules to beef up the original installation. Like WordPress, Drupal is free and open source!

- **Textpattern** (textpattern.com) is another program in the free category. Textpattern classifies itself as a content management system, but it does handle weblogs, too. One of the most attractive features of Textpattern is Textile, a tool that allows a user to type in a what-you-see-is-what-you-get style, much like typing in Microsoft Word or similar, where you can see how it'll appear before you publish it. Textile converts your post to the appropriate HTML and eliminates your need to fiddle with any kind of HTML or markup. Neat!

In truth, almost any blogging tool will do in a pinch, but if you have specific needs, one or another might suit you best. Compare, price, and pick the one that fulfills your blogging agenda. For quick convenience, we've whipped up a comparison chart for the top blogging software players. There are dozens out there on the Internet, but Table 6-3 provides a quick rundown of the default features supported by Movable Type, ExpressionEngine, and WordPress.

# Pointing Your Domain to Your Web Host

You have all the elements in place to get your blog up and running, just not sure what to do next? Never fear; your work is almost complete. As we said earlier in this chapter, a web host provides server space for your website to live. It's a cozy place for your blog and its files and database to hang their collective hats. In order for someone to find where your website lives, they need the address, and you need to associate your address with its new dwelling — or in technical terms, point your domain name to your web host.

# Table 6-3   Blog Software Feature Comparison Chart

| | Movable Type | ExpressionEngine (and EECore) | WordPress |
|---|---|---|---|
| Comments and trackbacks | Yes | Yes | Yes |
| Archiving and site search | Yes | Yes | Yes |
| Blogroll/lists | No | No | Yes |
| # of blogs available off one installation | Depends on license | Unlimited | 1 |
| Moblogging | No | Yes | No |
| Photo gallery | No | Yes | No |
| RSS/atom feeds | Yes | Yes | Yes |
| Site membership/registration | No | Yes | Yes |
| Basic content management | Yes | Yes | Yes |
| # of authors | Depends on license | Unlimited | Up to 10 |
| Spam control | Yes | Yes | Yes |
| Price | $0-$800 | $0-$249 | $0 |

Every registrar is different, but most let you edit the *DNS* (domain name system), which is a service that translates your domain name into an *IP address* (a number that identifies a particular location on the Internet). When you register a domain name with GoDaddy.com, for example, GoDaddy.com holds your domain name in place for you until you tell it which IP address it should point to. IP addresses are held by servers (called *DNS servers*), and the web host you choose has its own set to identify its location. To point your domain name from your registrar to your web host, you have to change the DNS for your domain name to the DNS specified by your web host. Phew!

When you sign up for hosting, your web host should provide you with information on what you need to do to point your domain name to their services. If not, they likely have it in the help section of their website. Your web host's name server information should look something like this:

NS1.*SOMEWEBHOST*.COM

NS2.*SOMEWEBHOST*.COM

## Women with Moxie

"I succeeded by saying what everyone else is thinking."

–Joan Rivers

You'll want to log in to your account with your registrar and take the following steps to change the name server information so that it points to your new web host. In this example, we show you how to complete the steps with GoDaddy.com:

1. **In your GoDaddy.com account, click My Domains in the top-left side of the screen, and from the small list of links that pops down, choose Manage Domains.** Your Domain Control Center appears.

2. **From your list of domain names, click the domain name you want to edit.** If you have just one domain name, click on that one! This will take you to the domain detail page where you can edit the information associated with your domain name, including DNS.

3. **Click the Nameservers icon, shown in Figure 6-8, to go to the Nameserver editing area.** The Nameserver 1 and Nameserver 2 fields, shown in Figure 6-9, indicate where GoDaddy.com has their DNS servers set. GoDaddy.com is currently holding your domain name until you tell them otherwise.

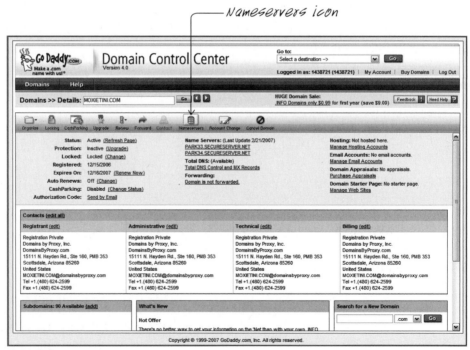

Figure 6-8

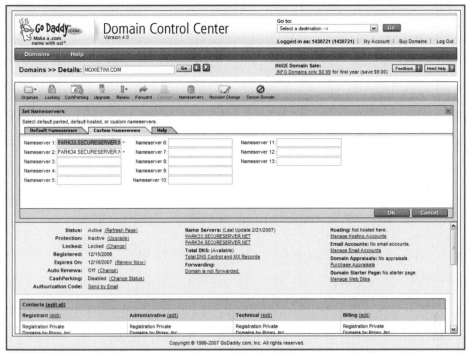

Figure 6-9

4. **Replace the old nameservers with the nameserver information your web host gave you.**

5. **Click OK.**

Your name server information should be processed rather quickly. After you change it, it'll take the Internet a little while to catch up — just like when you move to a new home, it takes a brief period for your mail to start coming to your new address. The rule of thumb is that it takes approximately 24–48 hours — but usually less.

# Installing Blog Software

Now that your domain name points to your new web host, you need to install your chosen blog software. The steps for installing blogging software vary depending on which software you chose.

Before you try to install anything, find out if your host has a Fantastico feature, sometimes referred to as "one-click installs." Some hosts provide software installation as an automated service, and you can sometimes install programs like

WordPress with one or two clicks instead of going through all the steps of installing it yourself. Or if you're the type who wants to get your hands dirty, keep reading.

Most blogging tools, such as Movable Type, ExpressionEngine, and WordPress, require a MySQL database to run correctly. The database holds all your data, such as your blog entries, in an organized manner that is quickly accessible by the blog software. Setting up a MySQL database is easier than it sounds. Hopefully, you chose a host that has cPanel, which makes creating a database a snap.

## Setting up a database

Here's a general idea of what steps you need to take to set up a basic MySQL database through your web host:

1. **In your web host's control panel, find the place where you can manage your MySQL databases.**

2. **Create a database, create a user, and then add the user to the database.** Make sure to jot down the database name, username, and password; you'll need this information when installing your blogging software.

3. **Go forth and install your chosen software.** Each blogging platform comes with explicit step-by-step installation instructions and troubleshooting tips, both with the downloaded software and online.

   As we mentioned, the exact steps you take to install the software depend on which software you're installing. If you've chosen to go with a paid license, don't hesitate to ask for help. The fine folks at the company will be more than thrilled to give you a hand.

Here is a list of the online documentation for installing a few blogging software tools:

- **ExpressionEngine:** expressionengine.com/docs/
- **WordPress:** codex.wordpress.org/Main_Page
- **Movable Type:** sixapart.com/movabletype/docs/
- **Drupal:** drupal.org/handbooks
- **Textpattern:** textbook.textpattern.net/wiki/index.php?title=Detailed_Installation_Instructions
- **Mambo:** help.mamboserver.com/

# Uploading files with FTP

*FTP (File Transfer Protocol)* is a method used to move material from one computer to another over the Internet. In order to install any blogging software, you need to use FTP to upload your software files to your web host in order to complete the install.

Lucky for you, there are many programs available that are made specifically for FTP. Most FTP programs offer a 3-day trial period to test them out so you don't have to commit to a purchase until you find one you like.

Here are a few you can download for free to try:

- **CuteFTP:** cuteftp.com/cuteftp/
- **SmartFTP:** smartftp.com/
- **FlashFXP:** flashfxp.com
- **WS_FTP:** ipswitch.com/

# ASCII and binary file formats

A few terms may pop up during a blog software installation that might puzzle the mind. There are two formats to upload files in FTP:

- **ASCII** (American Standard Code for Information Interchange) is a character encoding based on the English alphabet and is used to represent text in computers. Most files are moved in this format to ensure they are preserved in an FTP transfer.

- **Binary** is a file that typically contains bits of data that are meant to represent something other than textual data. In FTP terms, this usually means images and photos.

Be attentive to your blog software's installation instructions, as they will usually tell you which files need to be moved via FTP in what format, whether it is ASCII or binary.

# File permissions

Once you've got your software files all moved to your web host, your blog software may have you check the permissions on certain files and folders. Changing file permissions isn't too tricky. It just requires that you use your FTP program to edit the file permissions. Every file needs a Read, Write, and Execute permission combination, which you can edit right from your FTP program. See Figure 6-10 for an example.

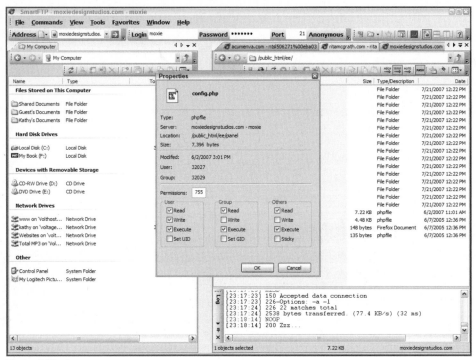

Figure 6-10

# Relax, Refresh, Reward

In this chapter, you register a domain name, choose a web host, and select and install a blogging platform. When you mash the three together, you have a fully functioning blog and website. Now all you have to do is make riveting content that will keep the masses drooling for your next update. Content may come easy to you, or you may find yourself staring at a blank Publish screen for an hour while your top coat dries. Here's an idea from our bag of tricks that may keep you inspired.

## Master of her domain

Surround yourself with ideas at home or work to keep your ideas fresh. To keep ourselves inspired and otherwise interested, we have both created inspiration boards that hang above our desks. There we each pin items, photos, and cards that evoke a smile or have a nice color palette.

To make a quick inspiration board, get a cheap bulletin board from your local superstore or nearby hardware or craft store. Or get squares of cork from a nearby office supply joint and pin them up in random places. Decorate the board with strips of your favorite fabric or paper, photos of friends or family, pins, bits of yarn, a card from a dear friend, a new cocktail recipe you want to try . . . whatever will help you be creative or inspire new material for your blog.

Hang your board where you'll see it when you're typing — next to the big chair where you sit with your laptop, near your office desk, in the kitchen, wherever you think the mood will strike!

# 7 Dressing Up Your New Blog:

## To Do List

- Find out what look highlights your best features
- Scope out the freebies and specials
- Consider something couture
- Tap into the designer in you
- Pamper yourself before your big reveal

# Feel Pretty, Oh So Pretty!

**Y**ou've chosen your domain name, set up your hosting, and installed your blog software. Aren't *you* a rock star? But, you're left with whatever boring design the blog software offers out of the box. As a new blog starlet, you'll want to set yourself apart. Before you walk the blogosphere's red carpet, you need something unique, something eye-catching, something that suits your domain name, content, and personal style.

This chapter covers what to consider when choosing your new look and where to find easy-to-change designs for those on a budget. Or you may be interested in investing in a couture blog design from a professional designer. If you're the adventurous type, you can always give designing your own blog a go. The options are many, and the choices are yours! Now, let's shop for something that fits.

# Blog Design: Choosing the Perfect Outfit

Before you email your new domain name to all of your friends, you might want to make sure your site's dressed appropriately for the big unveiling. The first thing you need to get rid of is that tired default blog design! While a default design serves its purpose, your blog is about *you,* so it should reflect your personality.

## It's all in the name, dah-ling

One of the first things you should consider when deciding on a new look for your blog is the name. You chose your domain name for a reason, and unless it's something extremely straightforward (like your name), we are willing to bet you already have a creative way to illustrate it in mind.

### Domain name

Let's say your domain name is StellaLikesCosmos.com. That suggests that, hey, you're Stella, and you like Cosmopolitans. It also says that maybe your site could be about cocktails, about women and the *Sex and the City*–esque lifestyle, or simply about you, Stella. A good rule of thumb is to consider what your domain name implies and then decide if that's the look you want your blog to have: sexy (not lewd, sexy!), modern, cosmopolitan, or feminine. Rockstar Mommy of RockstarMommy.com is a shining example. Check her out in Figure 7-1 sporting the rocker boots and Elmo — her design perfectly illustrates her domain name.

### Blog title

For starters, it's best to keep your blog title and domain name the same (if not similar), just to avoid confusion. You don't have to add the suffix if you don't want to, but keeping the blog title and domain name close makes the most sense. Titling your blog something that coincides with the domain name can also help influence your blog design concept.

Occasionally, the domain name is just a shorter variation of the title. For example, using the blog title *Stella Jones Likes Cosmopolitans* with the domain name StellaLikesCosmos.com and designing it with a vintage cocktail theme is a good correlation between domain name, blog title, and blog design.

## Women with Moxie

*"I wanted so badly to study ballet, but it was really all about wearing the tutu."*

–Elle MacPherson

Figure 7-1

On the other hand, if your domain name is StellaLikesCosmos.com, but you title your blog *Dancing with Cats,* and design the site with nothing but cats doing the Lambada, you can see how that might be a little confusing to someone looking for a blog about cocktails. Instead, Stella might want to stick with *Stella Jones Likes Cosmopolitans* and use an image of a cocktail or urban nightlife setting in her design to enforce her domain name. Or, if hot-stepping cats are really her thing, she might consider changing her domain name altogether to something dancing cat–related.

Sometimes you can't avoid a disconnect between the domain name and the blog title, but keep it in mind. Some bloggers opt to do this sort of disconnection, either because they happen to own a domain name already or they like to change their look periodically or from season to season. For the utmost blog recognition, keeping things consistent is recommended, but ultimately, it's a matter of personal preference.

## *Taglines*

Accessorizing with taglines can showcase a blog owner's sense of humor. Some taglines are clever nods to pop culture or self-deprecating one-liners. Others are more direct, simply telling you exactly what the blog is about. The Bloggie Awards (bloggies.com), one of the most popular blog awards out there, until recently offered a Best Tagline category. So it's clear that taglines, if chosen carefully, can be a sparkling accessory.

Some examples of clever taglines include:

**Pesky' Apostrophe** (peskyapostrophe.com; see Figure 7-2): *Always Better than an Unexpected Period*

**The Mommy Blog** (themommyblog.com): *Adventures from the Wonder-belly of Motherhood*

**Words for Snow** (wordsforsnow.org): *Tastes Like Lime Jell-O — Feels Like Love*

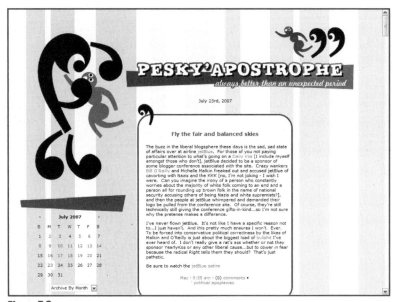

**Figure 7-2**

# Show 'em what you're workin' with

You've thought about your domain name and taken titles and taglines into consideration, but you're still not sure what kind of look you should choose — or even where to start. More than anything, you want your blog to be a reflection of you. For instance, if StellaLikesCosmos.com is a blog about you and you want it to have a sophisticated, metropolitan look, you probably don't want a design that's fluorescent green and black à la *The Matrix*. If StellaLikesCosmos.com is about cosmopolitan cocktails but you detest pink, you might want to consider other colors that might convey the concept without using pink (or using pink just as an accent). Read on for some other things to mull over when coming up with a blog design concept.

### Match your design with your own personal style

Are you one of those lovely, hippie, earth-goddess types? If that's the case, you probably don't want a flashy site full of pink feather boas and stilettos. If you're conservative, a muted, subdued palette might be your preference. While you're reaching an audience, this is really about what *you* like best. You're the one who'll be looking at it the most, so show your attitude!

### Let the design flatter the content

If your blog is called knitandtuck.com, you might want to choose a design or palette that highlights the content. Maybe choose a palette from your favorite yarn or use imagery that features knitting or knitting needles. Obviously, you don't want to choose a theme that revolves around puppies or square dancing when your blog is about knitting. Unless, of course, you knit costumes for square-dancing puppies.

These are some guidelines to help you choose a look, but no law says that you can't do whatever your heart desires — even if that means covering a cooking blog with pictures of bagpipes or putting an orange cat on a blog called Maison Pants, as shown in Figure 7-3 (or House of Pants, for the French-impaired). Expressing yourself is really what blogging is all about, so if bagpipes and cooking are your things . . . blow on, girl.

# Templates: The Slipdresses of Blogs

A very cool thing about templates is their simplicity to change. The fact that they're ready to go and often free makes them ideal for swapping them out on a whim. And a very cool thing about the blog community is its willingness to share. Many wonderful novice designers out there (and even some professionals) offer free or reasonably priced templates for download. A template generally includes all the HTML pages, images, and style sheets required to easily dress up your blog and change its outfit as often as you like.

## Need Help with Your Zipper?

Some designers will help you implement your new design if you don't feel comfortable doing it yourself. When choosing your templates, look for words like *installation* and *implementation* on the designer's website. Designers sometimes charge a small fee for this service, or if you purchased your template, include that fee in the price of the template. Be sure to ask, as each designer's policies may vary.

Figure 7-3

# In This Season: Free Design Templates

Searching for the best free blog templates can be like weeding through the clearance bin trying to find a Gucci handbag. You'll find a lot of "so-so," but if you know where to look, you'll find a whole lot of "whoa!" Here are a few of our favorite sites featuring beautiful, free blog templates:

- Smashing Magazine's 83 Beautiful WordPress Themes You (Probably) Haven't Seen smashingmagazine.com/2007/02/09/83-beautiful-wordpress-themes-you-probably-havent-seen

- Pink Design's Free Diary/Blog Templates pinkfreak.niftykeen.net/design/archives/templates/index.html

- Beccary's WordPress Themes beccary.com/goodies/wordpress-themes

- Gecko & Fly's Blogger Templates geckoandfly.com/blogspot-templates

- EllisLab's Free ExpressionEngine Templates expressionengine.com/templates/themes/category/site_themes/

- Movable Style movablestyle.com

# Bargain hunting for blog style

The key to finding the perfect blog template is to wade through all of the slightly-irregulars and get to the real, quality pieces. Here are a few ways to find bargain blog fashion:

- **Ask around.** One of the best ways to find quality designs is to *ask*. Do you read a blog that has a design you admire? Ask the blogger who did the design work. You can also look for links to templates or designers that may appear on the site credits, usually in the sidebar or the footer.

- **Google it!** As with every question in the universe, consulting the Oracle of Google — or another search engine of your choice — delivers a bounty of resources. Simply visit google.com, type **blog templates,** or **free blog templates,** or **free *Movable Type* templates** (replace *Movable Type* with the name of any blog software), or any variation thereof into the search engine, and let her rip!

- **Check with your blog software website.** Most blog software websites include links to resources for blog templates — or even offer some themselves. You might also check discussion forums for your chosen blog software for links and recommendations.

## What to expect from off the rack

Each template site or designer has their own set of terms and conditions. Look for verbiage such as *terms and conditions, policies,* or *usage rights* and be sure to read them thoroughly. These designers worked hard to create these pieces for you to download, so it's only fair that you comply with their rules, especially if you're getting the templates for free.

While some designers do offer limited support for paid templates, most free templates come with little to no support, so be prepared to know what you're doing when it comes to HTML — or know someone who does. Need a crash course in HTML?

## Can I Get Fries with That?

Keep in mind that whatever blog software you use – whether a hosted service or a stand-alone blog software you installed yourself – there may be some limitations. Check what blog platforms designers are able to work with, and remember that if you are utilizing a hosted blog service such as Vox or TypePad, you might be limited in what you can have installed. Vox allows you to customize the top banner only, while TypePad can have custom designs installed if you upgrade to a Pro account. Be sure to investigate what your service allows before purchasing a design. Of course, if you have stand-alone blog software running on your own hosting space, you are limited to only what the designer you choose offers.

## No one likes Miss Sticky Fingers

It's a common misconception that if it's on the Internet, it's free for the taking. But not everyone's blog designs are free. You wouldn't go into a stranger's closet and steal her best dress, would you? It's essentially the same thing. We can't count the times our clients have come to us frustrated because the couture designs they paid for were downloaded and used on someone else's blog without permission. It's violating, especially when someone has painstakingly designed her *own* blog only to have someone else blatantly rip it off — or worse, claim it as her own design.

Don't be one of those people, even by accident. You've read this, so you know better. Stick to downloading from template sites that are specifically marked *free*, *freeware*, *linkware*, or otherwise indicate that they're free for the public to enjoy. Or, if you're so inclined, learn to make your own designs. And no, downloading someone else's design, free template or otherwise, and changing a few colors here and there doesn't make it yours. It's a small Internet, and while you think no one will notice, design theft has a surprising way of being taken to the court of public opinion — in this case . . . blogs. Not the best impression to make, so be honest.

---

Pick up a copy of *HTML 4 For Dummies* by Ed Tittel and Mary Burmeister to start wrapping your brain around it.

In most cases, the downloadable template set should be complete and include all the images used to create the template (usually files with .jpg or .gif suffixes), the HTML files required (.html or .php are more commonly used file extensions), and the CSS style sheets (it will have the file extension .css). On occasion, the style sheet is embedded in the HTML files and not a separate file. If you don't see a file with .css in the template folder that you downloaded, we recommend that you email the designer and ask, to be sure.

# Springing for Couture Blog Design

So you don't want to settle for something off the rack? That $39.99 slipdress just didn't flatter your figure, and you need something superstylish and perfectly tailored to your shape? Just as there is haute couture in the fashion world, there is an equivalent in the design arena. Your blog must have the best of the best, something that is unique to you and you only. Your designer prayers are answered in the form of professional blog designers.

## Designers for every taste

Some people adore Yves Saint Laurent, some prefer the sleek, feminine characteristics of Chanel, and some women can't get enough of Dolce & Gabbana. Whatever your tastes are, some blog designers out there produce the type of design work you are interested in. It's only a matter of finding them.

There are designers that cater to different types of design — such as slick and professional, if that's your

## Hot designers

Here are just a few of the many designers that we think do gorgeous, high-quality blog couture for reasonable rates. Tell 'em the Moxie Girls sent you!

- **Emtwo Webstudios** (emtwowebstudios.com): Melissa Connelly does lovely, clean design that's easy to look at, whimsical, and reflective of the blog owner's personality. We've worked with Mel for years, and she's really a joy to work with. Mel specializes in ExpressionEngine and she's very talented with other platforms as well.

- **E.Webscapes** (ewebscapes.com): Lisa Sabin-Wilson, author of *WordPress For Dummies* (Wiley Publishing), is an established designer with a potpourri portfolio of design ranging from fun and nutty to slick and professional. She specializes in WordPress design and has experience in lots of other blog software. She also offers hosting!

- **Moxie Design Studios** (moxiedesignstudios.com): Hey, that's us! Moxie Design Studios offers full-service couture blog design! We Moxie Girls specialize in ExpressionEngine, but work with many other blog platforms, as well. With over 400 very assorted design projects under our stylish belts, Moxie Design Studios is sure to create just the look you're seeking.

- **Endeavor Creative** (endeavorcreative.com): Taughnee Stone at Endeavor Creative does really lovely, detailed work. Her designs are beautiful and precise, and she is knowledgable in many aspects of her field.

bag, or colorful and retro, for the not so faint of heart. Try some web searches for **blog design** and see what you come up with. To determine a designer's style of design, first evaluate their own website. Is it fun and flirty? Is it serious and classical? Whimsical and trendy? However, don't judge the boutique based solely on what's in the window. Dig around in the designer's portfolio to see what kind of stretch his or her designs have. You may be surprised at what you find!

## Have it your way

Don't be afraid to speak up. Designers want nothing more than to give you the design of your dreams. It can be frustrating to have you say, "Oh, just do whatever you think. You're the designer." While creative freedom and carte blanche to do whatever we like is glorious, it can also lead to a lot of extra work and miscommunication. Don't be passive-aggressive, sugar! Speak up!

Remember, this is *your* blog, and if you want it purple and green, then by golly, you shall have purple and green. Your designer may guide you in choosing a visually pleasing and easy-on-the-eyes palette using your chosen colors, but there's no reason you can't have what you want, within reason. If a designer tells you that he or she is struggling with your ideas, which can sometimes happen, it's good to have a backup plan in mind — such as another palette or concept. In any case, if you have a professional designer, you should be able to come to a workable solution. Speaking up tactfully ensures that you get what you want without any hurt feelings or buyer's remorse.

Once, our company had a client who requested, quite specifically, a design that involved a female, red-headed pirate drinking coffee. Yes, you did read that correctly. That's what the client wanted. If that's not a specific request, we don't know what is. What to do? We gave her a red-headed, female pirate drinking coffee, of course! And she was thrilled with the result. It just goes to show that if you think it can't be done, sometimes it *can*. You just have to ask.

Of course, not everything is possible. There are times when your designer might suggest a less eye-searing shade of yellow — or simply is unable to find stock imagery of a leggy blonde flying over New York with a Fendi handbag. These things happen, and it's your designer's job to provide options when they do.

# What to expect from hot designers

Sold! You have found the designer for you. She (or he!) has a brilliant portfolio and an amazing website. You want in — but not so fast! Just like anything else in demand, others are trying to get in line for the same thing. Depending on the size of the shop and how popular the firm is, you might do a bit of waiting before you can wiggle in line. Be sure to allow plenty of lead time if you're seeking a truly custom design, especially if you want more than a simple blog. (Elements that are beyond simple include an additional photo gallery, contact forms, or other bells and whistles.)

Designers should make you feel at ease and welcomed. They should instill confidence, and you should feel as though you're in capable hands. Designers should be talented, yes, but they should also fit you, as well as your design. Are they friendly? Does their personality match your style? Do they make you feel like you're valued? The answer should be yes to all of these things. While your desired designer might be in high demand, it doesn't mean you should be ignored.

Most designers do like to work via email and usually respond in a timely manner, but your designer should be willing to chat with you over the phone — or if you're local, meet in person before any contracts are signed or work commences. A common practice among designers is to offer a design questionnaire, either via download or online form. This form usually includes questions about what kind of a style you're seeking, what sorts of functionality you wish for your blog or website to have, how quickly you want the design, and how much money you have to spend. This allows you to fill out the form at your pace and expound as much as you like while allowing the busy designer to review your request in a straightforward format. The designer can then research your needs, put together a thorough estimate, send it on to you, and await a response. If the designer is unable to take on your project, you'll usually receive a response indicating so and thanking you for your interest. If you receive no response, you didn't want them anyway! La di da!

Assuming the designer responds and you accept the bid, you and she (or he!) can communicate directly about the next steps. Each designer has different methods, and these next phases might vary from designer to designer:

1. **Start the project with a phone discussion.**

   Most likely, a designer who's accepted your bid will contact you by phone — or try to set up an in-person meeting, if possible, although those are very rare. This is your opportunity to hear your designer's voice and get a sense of her character and personality. Is she professional? Does she sound knowledgeable? Do you click? This is also an opportunity for the designer to clear up any questions she may have about your project, go over additional ideas or ways the site can be improved, offer recommendations and expertise, and make sure that she understands the entire scope of work before preparing the final contract.

2. **Go over the contract.**

   The designer will most often outline any changes in the estimate that occur after the phone conversation in the contract and/or as an addendum to her original proposal. The designer will then send you the contract and any other paperwork via email or postal service for your review and signature. Be sure to read the contract thoroughly and know that anything beyond the scope of said contract is subject to additional charge. A deposit of 25–50 percent of the estimated project cost is commonly required along with your signed contract. This may or may not be refundable, so again, read the contract thoroughly. Your signature and your designer's signature commences the project. Woo! Time to get started!

3. **Look at the mock-up.**

   After a series of conversations, via phone or via email, the designer will usually provide you with a flat picture of their concept for your website. This is called a *mock-up* or a *comp* and isn't functional.

## Wrap It Up!

We understand that you want to get it just right. The desire to change a little of this and add a little of that is almost too much to bear, especially for you perfectionists and control freaks out there. Have faith in your designer. You hired that person for a reason. To keep the revisions phase from going on *ad infinitum,* additional revisions outside the bounds of the contract are sometimes subject to hourly rates, so be mindful of that when you're tempted to nitpick.

This is meant as a way for you to view the designer's ideas for your new site. Reviewing the comp and giving feedback to the designer enable the designer to fine-tune the design to your specifications. Most designers offer one to three unique concepts per project, and a couple rounds of revisions per mock-up, but make sure to ask if you don't see it in the contract.

4. **Step aside for the development stage.**

Ah, you've happily settled on the design concept, and now it's time for your designer to get started on the development phase of your project. This is the time when the designer takes the image or mock-up they created for you and transforms it into a functioning website. During this time, your designer may or may not provide updates along the way. Some designers prefer to work through until the site is ready for the owner to walk through the finished project; others prefer to give a blow-by-blow. This is something you need to discuss with your chosen designer directly.

5. **Check out your new site.**

The walk-through is generally when the designer will finally let you slip into your new outfit and have a strut around to get the feel of it. Do the links work? Do the pages load as they should in your browser? This is an opportunity for you to point out any last-minute minor changes before the designer signs off on the project, so be sure to speak up. At this point, some designers require an additional installment payment or sometimes the remaining balance due. Review your contract again or ask your designer, if you're unsure.

6. **Launch your hot new design.**

Your project is finished! At launch time, your designer may provide you a CD or a zip file with all of your site templates so you have a backup copy. The designer will also submit a closing invoice with any balance owed, including additional hours you may have accumulated along the way. (If any. Your designer should alert you to additional charges before accruing them.) And that's that! Designers will generally post your completed site in their portfolio and list their credit link somewhere on your site, usually in the footer.

## Worth the Wait

Your designer should give you periodic updates about your project, so don't be hesitant to send an email if you don't hear from her for a while. However, on that note, emailing every other day, daily, or even multiple times a day (it happens!) is the web design equivalent of kids asking, "Are we there yet?" You know how everyone loves that!

# Finding Your Inner Betsey Johnson: Fashionable Resources

If you're crafty, handy, technically savvy, or otherwise a chick with chutzpa, you might give designing your own blog a go. It may seem intimidating, but it can really be fun. To let you in on a little secret, it's exactly how we got started. That's right! We started designing blogs by starting with our very own. We had to learn the ins and outs of blog platforms and style sheets, just like you. It really can be done! Slap on a pore minimizing masque, turn on some tunes, and check out some of the resources that follow to learn more about doing it yourself.

A quick trip to Google tells you that there are a million and one resources for learning to customize your blog. The best advice we can offer is to learn from someone else. Wait . . . didn't we just tell you not to use anyone else's work? Yes, yes, we did. But we're not talking about stealing. We're talking about *learning*.

## Learning from free templates

The designs may be someone else's, but you can learn a lot from looking at the HTML templates and CSS files that are included in free templates. Review them and apply their techniques to your own fresh new files, starting from scratch. Change different things in the code to see what effects it has. This gives you hands-on experience and an opportunity to play around with something already established. Again, this doesn't mean change a few link colors, slap it on your website, and call it your

## Get Stuck? Look It Up!

A plethora of books on the market can teach you HTML, CSS, and blog/website design. A trip to Amazon.com or a jaunt to your local bookseller should provide many options for you to choose from. You'll also find some handy and information-rich websites can help you in a pinch. Here are a few to get you started:

**Webmonkey** webmonkey.com

**A List Apart** alistapart.com

**Mandarin Design** mandarindesign.com

own. But there's nothing wrong with modifying a free or paid-for theme or template, as long as you make it clear to your site visitors and give credit to the original designer somewhere on your site in a visible spot. Putting a small credit link in the footer or sidebar of your site should cover it.

## Resources from your blog software's website

Most blog software platforms apply a default template to your site on installation. They may also have other templates available on their website for you to download, play with, and learn from. The same principles apply here as they do to free templates. Please don't try to pass it off as your own if it's not entirely yours. It's bad juju.

# Relax, Refresh, Reward

In this chapter, we've covered a lot of material! You've learned how to make your blog go from geek to chic in just a few simple steps. Whether your budget is big or small, you can still dress your blog to the nines.

Your blog has a new look, but does your closet? It gets so expensive to constantly update your wardrobe with the latest trends in fashion. Fortunately, many savvy women have come up with a fabulous way to get a fresh look without using their last dollar.

## Shopping by swapping

Essentially, you get your best girlfriends, family members, local online friends, or maybe a mix of everyone together in your living room or at a local gathering place, like a restaurant or coffeehouse that caters to small groups. Everyone is instructed to bring pieces from their wardrobe that they're ready to part with. You make three piles: inexpensive, midpriced, and high end, and guests place their items in whatever pile they feel appropriate. Then, everyone shops! There are no hard and fast rules about a clothing swap, so set up swapping rules that fit your group size. Limiting trades to the number of pieces you brought can be a fair rule. If it's just a couple friends, then swap to your hearts content!

Often, refreshments like cocktails or coffee are served along with snacks, gossip is shared, clothes are swapped, and everyone goes home happier. You can read more about shopping by swapping by visiting SwapStyle.com (swapstyle.com).

# 8

## Your Online Identity:

### To Do List

- Decide what audience you hope to attract
- Let readers know how to get in touch with you
- Think about copyrights and trademarks
- Plan to keep content fresh
- Treat your lips to something special

# Like Finding Your Signature Red Lipstick

It's now time to make decisions about why you're blogging and what you hope to achieve with it. That's not to say you can't change your mind. We all know a gal can do that sometimes without warning. But before you start ranting and raving, take a moment to consider how much time you want to invest in your blog, what you want out of the experience, and who you want to connect with.

Blogging, in essence, is a form of self expression, much like your favorite shade of red that you save for evenings out. It took you weeks to find it, and it suits you to a tee. You want your blog to compliment you as much as that perfect red lipstick, if not more.

# Targeting an Audience

As you already know, there are literally millions of blogs on the Internet today, and that number is continuing to grow. They cover just about every topic known to woman (good and bad), and a vast number of them are dedicated to personal journaling. When deciding what you'll blog about, you need to ask yourself, "Who is this for?" and decide who your target is. Here is a short list of possibilities for the type of blog you might want that have a specific target audience:

- A blog about the country's current administration and aimed at provoking other politically minded readers to participate in the topics you propose
- A group blog for knitters that you want to expand into a full-blown community some day
- A blog where you type your thoughts and feelings, intended as an outlet for you to express your emotions, and audience be damned
- A fashion blog that you hope will gain mass popularity and make you a bundle of extra cash

The audience you're aiming to please, whether it's yourself, your family and friends, the general public, or all of the above, is what should drive your content, as well as your blog format. Cater to your audience.

# Defining your blog type

We mentioned that there are copious blogs out there swimming around on the Internet — one, possibly, for every topic you can think of. That doesn't make deciding what your blog should be any simpler. If you've already decided what your blog will focus on, move on, but if you know you want a blog and just aren't quite sure what direction to take it in, we are here to help. In Chapter 2, we covered what the *hot blog topics* are these days, but just to give you a refresher, here are a few broad suggestions based on types of blogs we visit on a regular basis:

- **Personal:** Personal blogs are the bread and butter of the blogosphere. They're what the phenomenon of blogging grew from — and coincidentally, are responsible for your authors (that's us!) meeting each other. *Personal blogs* are basically just online diaries that are open to comments from readers. They express the personal thoughts, feelings, and experiences of everyday people. Entries can range anywhere from personal updates to anecdotes from people's daily lives.
- **Group:** Sometimes, people who share a certain interest come together and share a blog, called a *group blog*. A handful of people post to the same blog and welcome commentary from their readers. A good example is MamaPop (mamapop.com). This group of mommy bloggers runs a group entertainment gossip blog, as shown in Figure 8-1.

**Figure 8-1**

- **Topic-oriented:** Some people blog for the sole reason of exploring, reporting, and discussing a particular topic or realm of subjects. Politics, design, news, fashion, or gossip . . . the blogger posts entries that keep within a specific subject. The Bag Snob (bagsnob.com/) is a fun example.

- **Photo:** Bloggers commonly post photos or use their blog as a sort of portfolio. Robyn Pollman of Shutterblog.com uses her blog as a way to not only blog about her personal life, but also to display her photography as a focal point.

Of course, your blog doesn't have to fit in any one particular category. If you want to build a group political photo blog, you go right ahead! No one ever said blogs had boundaries! Just be certain that what you create will satisfy your objective.

## Playing to your fans

Determining your audience is key. Of course, you might not care who reads what you have to say and just want a place to vent, express yourself, or keep a running record of specific events in your life. In this case, it's not so important what goes where and how you set things up. It's a place for you, so get buck wild.

But if your objective is to gain popularity and maybe at some point make some extra dough, you should keep the following tips in mind:

- **Consider placement of your different blog materials.** Keep content in an easy to find area. Your posts should be a prominent feature, and readers should be able to easily find archives and other related information.

- **Write carefully and frequently.** Take time to check spelling and grammar before you hit the publish button. If you're interested in building considerable traffic, post as often as possible. Fresh content is key, but keep it meaningful. Aim to post at least three to five times a week or more if the topic warrants it. Gossip blogs are chock full of news about celebs, and they have new material to post multiple times a day, while a blog about gardening might not have as many updates, but longer, more info-packed entries.

- **Leave room for expansion, either with content or advertising.** Don't limit yourself to your chosen topic. Keep your options open and consider leveraging your blog to build new blogs about related topics that your audience will be interested in. Whether you create your blog yourself or use a hosted service, think ahead about what you want to achieve. If your goal is to include advertising or sponsor logos as a means of income, be sure to allow space to accommodate banner ads and sponsor graphics.

## Loose Lips

Make sure you know who's reading. You might not want your boss to know about the embarrassing, drunken table dance you performed at your best friend's bachelorette party last weekend. We don't encourage censorship, but be careful what you say if you don't want the wrong information to fall into the wrong hands. You might even consider blogging under a pen name.

# Tell 'Em Who You Are

Who you are as a person should shine through on your blog, not only for your own personal satisfaction, but because your online identity is what sets you apart from the Joneses. Like they say, "You get out what you put in," so make it count.

## Your bio and why it matters

If blog readers are going to continue to visit your blog or subscribe to your posts, they need a reason to connect with you in some way — even if they lurk and never make themselves known. Having something in common with your readers is what gives them something to identify with. The fact that you are a writer, a mother, an author, or a tightrope walker . . . someone, somewhere, has similar tastes.

Including a bio or an *About Me* section with your blog can deliver this information of who you are as a blogger to your readers. Write a paragraph or two about yourself, your interests, or perhaps why you chose to start your blog. A little bit of background information can go a long way in connecting with your readers.

If you just aren't comfortable divulging much personal information, then don't share it. You can still give people a feel for who you are and what you are about without providing identifying details about your personal life. Figure 8-2 shows the About Me page for Mamapop.com.

## Short, But Sweet

If you think you don't have enough to say to warrant a separate page, try starting with a short About Me blurb somewhere in your sidebar so people can easily get the gist of who you are and what your site is about. Even if all you're writing about is your Chihuahua, people want to know!

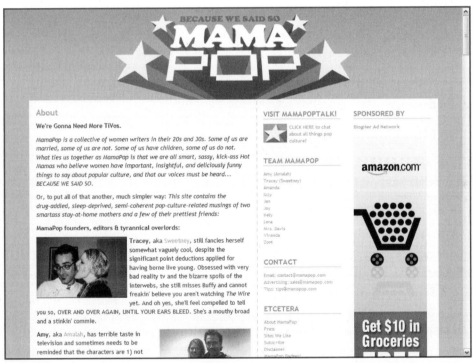

Figure 8-2

## Sharing your contact information

Most bloggers opt to provide readers a method to contact them, outside of leaving comments on their site for everyone to see. Say, for example, a reader wants to email you privately to ask a question, or someone wants to email a coupon to you for 10 percent off your next purchase at Bath & Body Works. Bottom line is, sometimes people just want to say hi and not make a federal case out of it.

You can provide your email address in your About Me information with a simple link. Of course, this leaves it open for anyone and anything to come your way. It's okay, as long as you don't anticipate a huge following. Some bloggers opt to create a contact form so that anyone sending you email has to provide a valid name and email address to contact you. Either way, keep in touch!

### Ew, Spam

Don't want to put your email on the Internet? We don't blame you. Sign up for a free account through Yahoo! or Gmail.com for use primarily with your blog. That way, your work address isn't up for public viewing – or worse yet, for harvesting by spam bots.

# What You Should Know about Copyrights

Copyrights and the Internet have a long and troublesome relationship. Unfortunately, it isn't unheard of for someone to copy your content and paste and publish it somewhere else. There isn't much to stop people from doing it, even though it's illegal to do so.

## Respect yourself, protect yourself

In a sense, you're protected by intellectual property copyright laws. But unless someone's stolen copy from your blog and used it to make a profit, there isn't a whole lot you can do. The good news is that your blog is copyrighted, by default, the minute you post it. It's okay to post on your site somewhere — usually in the footer — a copyright notice stating that you reserve all your rights to the work you publish. You can copyright your words, but you can't copyright ideas.

This doesn't mean, however, that you need to fret. Sure, there's the possibility that it'll happen, but in most cases, a nice cease-and-desist letter clears up any misconception that your blog posts are for the taking. Unless, of course, what you post *is* for the public to take — such as instructions or sewing patterns.

Creative property, such as a photograph, has varying levels of copyright protection. There is something called *Creative Commons* that allows people to use or copy your work for varying levels of uses, provided they give credit to the creator of the work.

## Creative Commons

Visit creativecommons.org for a more complete list of licensing options. Their License Your Work section provides a nifty little form you can fill out that lets you choose the conditions of your license. It also provides you with the proper license and some cute little buttons for your site.

## When to consider a trademark

A *trademark* is the legal registration of a service mark or a mark that otherwise identifies you or a business. Through a lawyer or trademark service, you can obtain a mark (as long as it isn't already in use by another individual) to protect your name, logo, tagline, or other identifying images, in legal form.

When you have a trademark, it prevents people from using your mark in any way, and you then have a legal leg to stand on with regard to your brand. However, this isn't really a solution to the protection of your blog entries and material. This, more or less, protects you if your blog's popularity warrants your becoming a business, or your branding is something you want to protect.

## Copy Cat

Place a © symbol and the date (usually just the year is sufficient) somewhere on your site to let others know you intend for your words to stay on your blog and nowhere else.

## Keeping Content Fresh

The main draw of a blog is the content. People want to come back for your next post to see what hilarious predicament you got yourself into that day at work. They want to come back every day and read about how you got stuck in line at the DMV behind Carrot Top and he smelled like Fritos. This is entertaining stuff, people! But how much is enough, how much is too much, and what if you draw a blank?

## How often should you blog?

How often you blog really depends on the type of person you are. If you're naturally chatty, of course you'll think up something to write about every few hours! And that's perfectly okay! If you tend to be a more laid-back and subdued personality, you might find that the "quality not quantity" approach works better for you. It's rather important to maintain some consistency in the frequency of your postings, unless your blog is completely non-audience oriented — in which case, you can do whatever you darn well feel like doing. But most bloggers think it's nice to have people coming back to check in on their latest adventures.

## Be yourself

The addiction to blogs is fed by people's desire to see what other people's lives are like — or in some cases, to connect with people with commonalities. If you're putting up a front that isn't reflecting your personality or your true self — or worse yet, putting up something deceitful — people will pick up on it. That's not to say that you won't have readers. However, the real you is someone with something to say, and people want to hear it. Your foray into cross-breeding fruit flies with sea monkeys is interesting to someone!

## Blogging burnout and taking a break

It happens to the best of us: blogging burnout. You just run out of inspiration and have nothing to say. That's okay! Sometimes we need to step back, gain some perspective, and recharge our interests. We all change our minds — or just plain need a break. This isn't a competition (usually), and there should be no guilt associated with taking a rest. In most cases, you can come back refreshed when you're ready, and people will still be there. Just jump right back in where you left off and let people know you're back in action. It'll snowball again, faster than you can click Publish.

# Relax, Refresh, Reward

In this chapter, you have the chance to ponder the meaning of life as a blogger and why being yourself is really the most important factor in enjoying your blogging success. Now that you know who you are and what you want the world to see, you need that perfect red lipstick we keep talking about.

## They should name a lipstick after you

For lip gloss addicts: Prescriptives cosmetics provides a custom service that allows you to create your own lip gloss. You choose the shade, which ranges from deep berries to light browns, the finish (which includes glitter! Who doesn't like glitter?), and even a flavor. Choose from latte, cocoa, and our favorite, Bellini. You can order them online from prescriptives.com or find a Prescriptives counter near you and place your order there! How fun!

For lip balm gals: Wouldn't you know it, there's a whole blog dedicated to lip balm and all things lip balm-related, called Chaptastic (chaptastic.blogspot.com). Chaptastic provides funny and honest reviews about the latest and greatest in lip balms, critiquing flavor, glide, lasting power, and appearance. See, there really is a blog about everything!

# Comments and Trackbacks:

## To Do List

Share your thoughts

Dodge the spam

Tell people you're talking about them

Meet your new online friends

# Like Champagne, Conversation Is Best Kept Flowing

Connecting with the Internet and its various communities (nevermind *staying* connected) is one of the most crucial things to consider when starting and running a blog. The real reason blogs have become so widely used and popular is that you can interact with people you never thought you would meet. It's like one big social event. So put on your favorite pair of heels and join the party!

Sure you can throw a blog up on the Internet in any ol' place, but you won't enjoy the benefits if you don't provide a way for people to talk to you. And don't forget to hand out the comments to your fellow bloggin' buddies. So get out there and participate in the world's biggest coffee klatch! Let's face it, you weren't a shy wallflower at the school dance, right? You were out there whoopin' it up. Why should this be any different? Get out there and socialize, and the benefits will trickle in.

# Comments: Give a Little, Get a Little

Let's say you start up a blog and click Publish on your very first post. Look at that! You put something out on the Internet! It's compelling and witty. People will laugh hysterically! You sit and wait for people to swarm and tell you how hilarious the story you just wrote is. Only there's one problem: No one knows your blog exists.

Comments, first and foremost, are the best place to start getting the word out about you and your blog. Surely, you've *read* someone else's blog. (We know, we know. Don't call you Shirley.) Maybe you've read a hundred blogs. That's great, but no one knows you read them unless you post a comment. Reading and not commenting is often referred to as *lurking*. Lurking is fine, as long as you don't expect to get anything in return. You get back what you put in. That said, commenting for the sheer benefit of just having something to say is great, too. People love comments!

## Save Me

When you submit a comment, most blogs offer you the option of saving your identifying information with a cookie the site harmlessly embeds in your browser. Then you don't have to fill your info out every single time. Look for a Remember Me check box or words along those lines so that next time you visit, you can just fill in your comment and go!

More and more blogs these days offer memberships features, like extra password-protected content for those who log in. Or, some just offer the login to make use of fun features their blog software may offer, like customized avatars. It's the choice of the blog owner what requirements they enforce regarding comments.

## Ego Check

Don't be offended if every blog you visit doesn't reply to your comments. They're reading them and may or may not email you back or respond directly on their site. That's okay! They still get your contribution and probably appreciate it all the same.

In order for others to find your blog, they need to know where it is. You wouldn't host a lingerie party and not tell the guests where to show up, right? Participating on someone's blog indicates to the blog author that you've read his or her post and have something to add to the conversation. Bloggers typically provide a link that directs you to a page with a small comment form where you can enter your comment. They generally ask for some kind of name or handle, an email address, and your website address (or URL).

When your comment publishes to the site, most blogs display your name and URL along with your charming contribution, as shown in Figure 9-1.

Other people reading that same blog may see your comment and follow the link back to your site. There they'll discover *your* latest anecdote and may even comment on your blog and come back the next time you post. It's not recommended to comment just for the sake of getting your link published, though. This would be the same as spamming someone and won't earn you any friends. You can read more about blog etiquette in Chapter 15.

The more you comment, the more places a link to your blog can be found. This betters your chances that people will come to your site to see what's new. You still have to post regularly to keep them interested, but getting them there is half the battle. Commenting doesn't mean instant traffic to your site, and it'll take some time to develop a readership. But it is a great place to start.

*Link to commenter's website*

**Figure 9-1**

## Nobody likes a bully

Sometimes when you get on a roll, it's hard to remember that real people are behind these websites. Real people with real feelings. You may not always agree with what people post, but most of the time, bloggers welcome a variation of opinion.

The most important thing is to be respectful. You can disagree respectfully and without confrontation. Blogs are built to encourage interaction with others on the web. Comment if you feel you have something to contribute, but remember there are human beings behind the Publish buttons. They have family and friends and a life outside of the Internet. What they portray on their blog is only 30 percent of who they really are.

If you really find yourself getting in a tizzy over something, take a step back and decide if it's worth getting jumpy over. Like our mothers say, "If you have nothing nice to say, say nothing at all."

# Comments: Open, Closed, or Moderated

There are three main status settings for blog comments:

- **Open comments** are just that — open and available for anyone to comment at will.

- **Closed comments** are also fairly straightforward — comments on a blog entry that are no longer open or available for commenting. There may already be comments on the entry, as the author may have had comments open in the past, but later decided not to offer new comments.

- **Moderated comments** appear on blog entries where the author has set the comments to go through an approval phase by her or him before the comment appears publicly to the blog. The comment has been received; it just will not post until the author makes it public.

A blog's popularity can garner tons of comment traffic, which may or may not include trolls. *Trolls* are people who, by false names or anonymously, comment with not so nice things on a person's weblog in a harassing way. It happens, so occasionally people need to put a choke hold on how comments are posted to their site. Instead of allowing anyone to post immediately to the site, bloggers can choose to set moderation on their comments and approve them before they're fully viewable to the public. This reduces the nasties and can help weed out any various spam comments that might leak in. Some people view it as a last resort, but if controlling the words used on your site is important, this is a definite option.

With the increasing popularity of blogs, there is an increase in businesses trying to hammer in advertising, which means spam. *Spammers,* the people responsible for the massive amounts of junk mail filling up our inboxes, have found a way to spam blog comments in order to get people to click through to various websites. They are a sneaky bunch! Spammers created *spam bots* that crawl around in the belly of the blogosphere and attack blogs where they can, such as in comments and trackbacks (described later in the chapter), by submitting fake ones to your site.

When spammers find your site, you can do little to keep them out. But you can cut them off where they feed. Moderating comments helps keep the spam at bay, but you can try other measures, such as closing comments after a set amount of days. Some blog software, such as Movable Type, ExpressionEngine, and WordPress allow you to automatically close comments to an individual entry or all blog entries after a set period of time. This prevents spammers from attacking older entries and clogging up the works.

## Troll Patrol

Trolls can be a bothersome annoyance for any blogger. You can ban their IP addresses or try blocking them on the server level through your host, but chances are they will always find their way back in. The best course of action? Ignore them. Trolls do what they do to get you to react, to get angry, and to lash out and give them a little show. Don't give in and give them what they're after. The less entertainment they get, the less interested they'll be in harassing you and your readers.

Using WordPress.com as an example, here's how to set your comments to moderated and closed by default (though you may override them individually per blog post):

1. **Log in to your WordPress.com account.**

2. **Choose My Dashboard from the top navigation.**

3. **Choose Options from the light blue navigation bar along the top.** Next, you will see further options in a dark blue navigation bar.

4. **Choose Discussion.** The Discussion Options page appears, as shown in Figure 9-2.

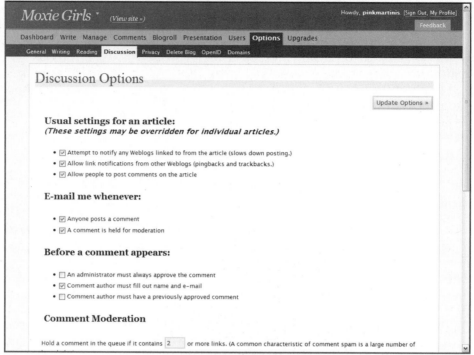

**Figure 9-2**

5. **About halfway down the page, you will see Before a Comment Appears with a list of three choices. Select the appropriate check boxes to change your default comment settings.** Here are your options:

- *An Administrator Must Always Approve the Comment:* Select this option if you wish to set your comments to closed and moderated by default.

- *Comment Author Must Fill Out Name and E-Mail:* This option is checked by default, and we recommend leaving it that way. Otherwise, it's like leaving your front door open for spammers and baking them cookies while they trash your house.

- *Comment Author Must Have a Previously Approved Comment:* If you wish to let previously approved commenters continue to comment unfettered by author moderation, also check this last option.

## Ew, Spam

Spam comments can spiral out of control. Check with your software documentation or support forums for spam control tips. Sometimes, something as simple as blocking an IP address in your control panel can eliminate a big pest. See more on IP blocking in Chapter 14.

If you truly want to let any visitors comment, without entering their name or their email address, completely free to leave anonymous links or hideous comments, by all means leave all the boxes unchecked. But again, we *really* don't recommend it.

Some software has antispam measures built in, but you'll need to do a little housekeeping to keep things tidy. Once in a while, a legitimate comment may sneak its way into your spam blocker, so it's important to do at least a quick scan of your moderated comments, should you have those turned on, before deleting the spam. If users complain that they can't get a comment through on your site, nine times out of ten it's because their comment has a word — in their text, URL, or screen name — that doesn't sit well with the spam filters.

Likewise, a spam comment will occasionally present itself as legitimate, for whatever reason, and make its way past your antispam filter. These filters are not 100% foolproof, but they are definitely better than the alternative.

# Spam Control

Spam is a growing and troublesome trend, and there probably isn't an end to it in sight. You can take steps to prevent and control it so that the volume doesn't get in the way of your fabulous content. Closing comments and moderating comments (as

**Housekeeping!**

Make sure to periodically update your blacklists and upgrade your blog software and any spam control plugins. With the rate of increasing spam, there are continuous efforts to combat those nasty buggers. Keeping your stuff up-to-date will keep your site on top of the spam war.

described in the previous section) are a start if you encounter a spam infestation. But if it gets to a point where you need to take more action, you can do a few more things.

# Controlling spam with blacklists and whitelists

As spam increases, so do the ever increasing lists of spammers, spam-related websites, and IP addresses of those spammers. Most blog software these days comes equipped with some sort of spam control settings, which should include an updatable list of known offenders. A *blacklist* is a list of those offenders, and you can usually download the latest list, as well as add to it yourself if you have a certain spammer causing havoc. You can also keep a whitelist of sites to always accept comments from. These lists are usually quite simple to update with just a few clicks.

# Letting Captcha filter good guys from bad

Captcha (which is said to stand for *completely automated public Turing test to tell computers and humans apart*) is like a small pop quiz that can determine whether the person behind a comment is a real human being. Comment spam is usually done with programs that crawl around the Internet looking for unsuspecting blogs to attack. The Captcha test is a step in the commenting form process that requires the user to type in a graphic word or series of distorted characters in order to validate that the user is in fact a person and not a program. (See Figure 9-3 for an example.) Captcha comes standard in some blog software such as ExpressionEngine.

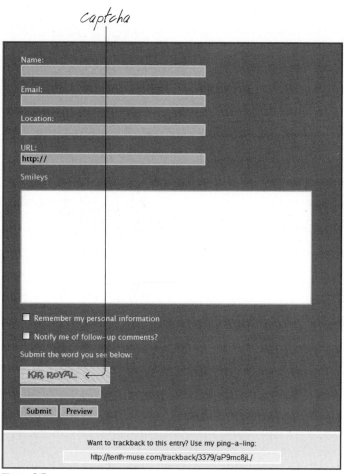

Figure 9-3

# Put Your Face on with Avatars and Gravatars

*Avatars* are little digital pieces of you. Awww! A lot of blogs and forum-esque sites allow you to represent yourself with a small picture or symbol. Whatever you choose, it typically appears next to *every* comment you make on that particular site. Avatars are usually square and range in size (see Figure 9-4). Blogs sometimes provide a preset list of avatars you can pick from, or you can upload one you made yourself. Choose it wisely, but don't fret if you get bored with it. You can always change it.

Avatar

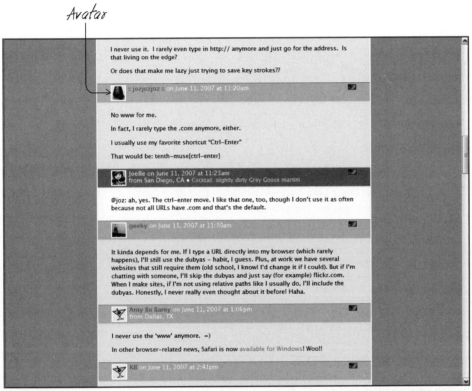

Figure 9-4

*Gravatars,* or *globally recognized avatars,* are in use on some blogs and forums. A gravatar is a small, square image that pops up when you comment on blogs enabled for gravatars. This means you sign up for an account on the gravatar website

(site.gravatar.com), enter your email address, and then upload an avatar you'd like to associate with that email address. Once you've done that, when you comment using that email address on *any* site that is gravatar-enabled (as set up at the blog author's discretion), your gravatar will appear next to your comment. You can even assign a different avatar to different email addresses in your gravatar account, if you like. It's a completely free service and much less of a hassle than changing your avatar on each and every site you visit. It's tempting to upload a big-old mug shot of yourself to represent you, but keep in mind it's seen wherever you comment (that has gravatars enabled), so it may not apply in every scenario. If you're big on privacy, you can choose to use something other than a photo to represent who you are. (See more about privacy in Chapter 14.)

Despite what seems like many steps, it takes only a few minutes to set up an account on Gravatar.com:

1. **Using your web browser, go to** site.gravatar.com.

2. **Choose Signup from the navigation on the top right of the screen.** The Signup page appears, as shown in Figure 9-5.

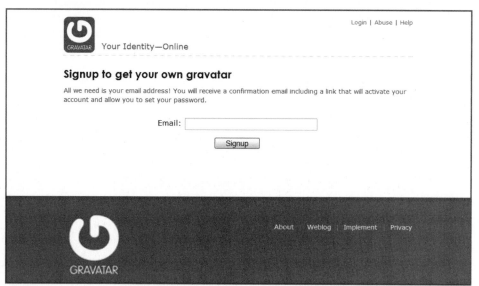

**Figure 9-5**

3. **Enter the email address you wish to use in the field and click Signup.** You're taken to a confirmation page instructing you to check your email account for an email containing a link to activate your registration. This is to confirm you are truly interested in signing up.

4. **Click the link as instructed in the email.** You're redirected through your web browser to an account activation confirmation page.

5. **Enter your chosen password twice and click Set Password.** Next, you're taken to a page offering you an opportunity to opt-in to the email newsletter.

6. **If you wish to opt-in to the newsletter, click that option and follow the instructions.** For the purposes of this example, we will choose No Thanks.

   You are now redirected to a page displaying your email address and an icon that states No Gravatar.

7. **To add a gravatar to this email address, click the blue Add a New One link.** You are then taken to a page that offers the option to upload your image from your computer's hard drive or to use an image located online. For this example, choose the image from your computer's hard drive.

8. **Click the Browse button, and then from the File Upload dialog box (shown in Figure 9-6), choose the image from your hard drive you would like to use as your gravatar.** You will have the opportunity to crop this image once you've uploaded it.

Figure 9-6

9. **Click Next.** You're taken to a page that gives you a little tool with which to crop your image, if you desire, as shown in Figure 9-7.

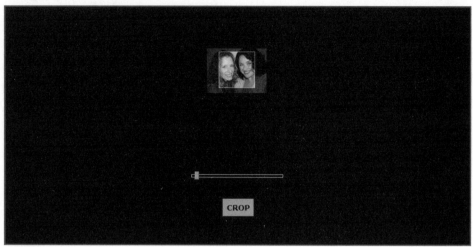

Figure 9-7

10. **Use the slide tool to position your gravatar image without the square to your liking. Then click Crop.** You're then redirected to a page for you to set your gravatar rating.

11. **Gravatar-enabled sites have the option of setting the rating level of gravatars they want displayed on their site. If your gravatar is family-friendly, choose rated G. If not, choose the rating level you feel is appropriate.** Next, you're finally taken to a page congratulating you for creating a gravatar.

## Gravatar Gravitas!

Like the idea of making your blog gravatar-enabled? You're in luck because the gravatar website provides a list of resources on how to set up your blog with gravatars (site. gravatar.com/site/implement).

12. **Click the Back to My Gravatars link to see your email, just like in Step 7, but this time your uploaded gravatar appears beneath it. Click the gravatar to associate it with your email address.** A pop-up window asks you to confirm this association before redirecting you back to your gravatars page. (See the final product in Figure 9-8.)

13. **You're finished!** At this point you can move on with your life or add more email addresses or upload more gravatars. You can host several email address and avatars on one gravatar account.

Figure 9-8

# Pinging: Pass It On!

A *ping* is, more or less, your blog's way of signaling other blogs or websites that you have written a blog entry directly referencing or relevant to one of their entries. Your blog can send out a ping to the other blog to notify it that you wrote a pertinent entry, and provided the blog you pinged has trackbacks enabled, your ping will display itself in the form of a trackback on the correlating blog entry. (Read more about trackbacks in the next section.)

Some sites collect pings as a way for people to see what has been updated in the blogosphere. You can visit sites like Technorati.com, Weblogs.com, or NewsGator.com for extensive lists of fresh content from blogs everywhere. You can ping one or all of them when you update your blog.

You can ping a site like this in one of two ways:

- Your blog software or hosted service may have a place to enter a list of sites you want to ping every time you update. This varies with each type of blog solution, but most have the option. For example, in ExpressionEngine, you can set your default ping servers, as shown in Figure 9-9.

- You can ping each site manually or take advantage of a pinging service, such as Ping-O-Matic

(pingomatic.com), and do it all in one shot. Pinging services save you time to put on that fresh top coat before you head out.

To use Ping-O-Matic, shown in Figure 9-10, enter your blog name and blog URL, and then select the check boxes for directories and services you want to ping. There are no hard-and-fast rules regarding which choices to select on Ping-O-Matic. The most popular options are usually preselected for you, but we recommend making sure that Technorati, Blogrolling, and Weblogs are all selected, at the very least. The form does offer some specialized selections, but unless you're producing a podcast or participating in one of the websites listed, there is really no reason to select those.

**Figure 9-9**

**Figure 9-10**

# Trackbacks: Know Who's Talking About You

The term *trackback* has been a source of confusion for years. It refers to a relatively simple process, but wrapping your head around it, initially, leaves some people saying "huh?" more than once. A trackback itself is an acknowledgement, a way for blog authors to be alerted when another blog is discussing and/or linking to a particular entry. Trackbacks originated with Movable Type as a way for bloggers to acknowledge one another through *pinging,* which, as mentioned in the previous section, is the term used to describe the act of sending a trackback alert.

## How trackbacks work

Let's say Sue writes a compelling tutorial on building a model of the Empire State Building out of bricks of cream cheese. Gail stops by and reads Sue's tutorial and thinks it's just the greatest! Gail jumps on her blog and writes an entry talking about Sue's tutorial. In order for Gail to alert Sue that she blogged about her tutorial, she obtains Sue's trackback link, typically provided with the original entry itself in the form of a URL. Sue plugs this trackback link into her blog entry in a specified field. This can vary by blog platform, but Figure 9-11 shows the field in WordPress.

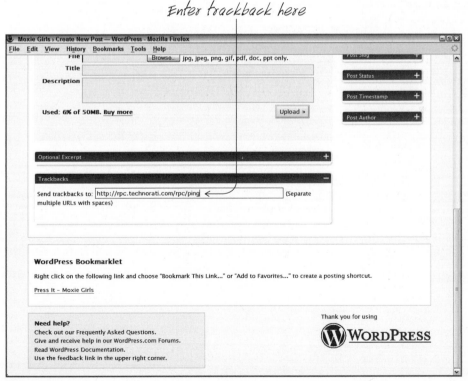

**Figure 9-11**

When Gail publishes her entry, her blog platform automatically alerts Sue via a network signal, or *ping,* letting her know someone has blogged about her tutorial and how to find Gail's blog to read about it. Some blog platforms allow you to be notified by email when someone tracks back to your entries.

In turn, Sue's tutorial entry shows that she has been pinged one time by displaying a link to Gail's blog entry. Readers on Sue's blog can then view Gail's

## Ew, Spam!

Your trackback URLs collect spam, too. Be sure to clean spam trackbacks out of your entries when they show up and don't forget to add offenders to your blacklist.

trackback link, along with any other trackbacks Sue may have received right in the entry about cream cheese architecture.

In order for this to work, of course, both sites need to have the trackback features enabled.

## Why they're helpful

You might wonder why bothering to track back to someone's entry is useful. Bloggers like to know when someone's talking about their entries, especially when that talk is positive. It's nice to get a little love once in a while! But more importantly, a blogger's readers might want to see what other readers are saying about a particular blog entry, and with trackbacks, they can easily find a list of the sites that reference it. Using our example of the cream cheese architecture tutorial, let's say that Gail commented in her post that she tried Sue's tutorial, and while it was a great one, she would recommend using blocks of cheddar instead. People find this stuff interesting, and it helps to keep things flowing in a serendipitous manner.

# Relax, Refresh, Reward

You have a handle on commenting and pinging! You're almost a pro! Commenting can build friendships you'd never think you'd have, (we're proof!) so why not make it official.

## Organizing blogger meetups

Send out an APB to bloggers in your local area. Meet for coffee, drinks, or a concert. Meeting people from the Internet isn't as dorky as it once was. Gone are the days of geeks playing Dungeons & Dragons. Okay, so those guys are still around, but the bloggers of today are people from every walk of life. Men, women, business people, parents . . . the Internet isn't just for nerds anymore. Choose a centralized public venue for your meetup (safety first, ladies) and bring a camera. Heck, bring a friend! Bloggers are a wild bunch, and we're willing to bet you make some great new friends, or business contacts, as the case may be. You may even get some good blog fodder out of it.

# 10

## Tags and Tagging:

### To Do List

Get the 411 on tags

Choose your weapon. Tags or categories

Check out services that can help
  organize your content

Experience bathtub Zen

# Your Tag Is Showing

**T**agging made its debut in 2005 as a new way of categorizing material on the web. Until tagging took the spotlight as the new method of making information more accessible, people relied mainly on categories and grouping content into similar lumps. Tagging showed up on the scene and put a whole new spin on how we find things in blogs and websites. Roll out the red carpet for tags!

# Understanding Tagging

A *tag* is a simple keyword (or keywords) that's used to associate or describe the content of something, such as a blog entry, a video, or an image. Generally, people use various tags to describe items they've published on the web. Compare tagging to something teenagers do with spray paint. Tagging in blogging and websites is similar. You are, in essence, putting a label on something, be it a blog entry or a photograph. You are identifying the item with relevant keywords to describe it in simple terms.

## Tagging your content, not the freeway

Let's say, for example, Sue (you remember Sue, she wrote a tutorial about building the Empire State Building out of cream cheese) tags her tutorial entry. She would probably tag it with: *tutorial, cream cheese, New York, Empire State Building, sue*. Choosing a handful of keywords helps readers find exactly what they're looking for on your blog.

Regardless of what you are tagging, there is at least one word to describe what it is. If you write a thoughtful entry on cooking a quiche recipe, for example, you might choose tags like *quiche, recipes, brunch, eggs*. Or you might choose to tag it simply *recipe*. Making your content easily searchable is the objective here. If you tag your quiche recipe with just one identifying word, readers can find it with only that one possible search. The more detailed your list of tags, the more ways your quiche recipe is accessible.

The bottom line is, be descriptive and choose thoughtfully. If you tag your quiche recipe with *motorcycle,* that doesn't really help anyone — unless someone searches for *motorcycle quiche,* but that doesn't sound very tasty.

## Finding the interesting stuff with tags

As people continue to tag items on websites, it starts to create something similar to categories only much more specific in manner. Before tags, bloggers and website developers lumped content into categories. Sue might have put all her tutorials in a Tutorial category, and her readers would then be able to sift through that one category to find what they were looking for.

Tags allow much more specific categorization and thus allow people to search more effectively. When a substantial base of tags is created on a site, people can zero in more closely on the content of their choice. For example, instead of digging through Sue's Tutorials category, a website visitor can find exactly what she's looking for by searching for *tutorial* and *cream cheese*. Any tutorials that Sue has tagged with *cream cheese* are presented in the search results. A good tag base saves people time by pinpointing what they're looking for.

Sites using tags often provide a *tag cloud,* or a group of tags that are popular on that site. The tags in the tag cloud are usually varied in font size, as shown in Figure 10-1. The larger, more prominent words are tags that have the most content entries associated with that tag word, within the site.

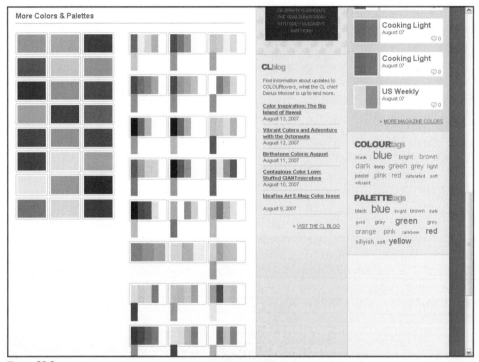

**Figure 10-1**

The nature of tags and the dynamic content they describe means that they're flexible and user oriented — and therefore associated with sites boasting Web 2.0, which is the new generation of Internet, relying more on user-friendly, dynamic methods of presenting information.

For many sites using tags as a method of categorization, such as Amazon.com, the site's users are not limited to one person's point of view regarding a particular subject. Like Amazon.com, some websites allow their visitors to assign their own tags to materials within the site. The more often people tag a particular item, the more diverse the tags become, and discovering that item becomes more likely when someone does a search. Not every website allows users to tag items. In the case of blogs, the tagging is up to the blog owner.

## Using tags on your blog

You want in. We understand the urge to be on the cutting edge! Before you dive in and start tagging, consider the fact that each blog platform or content management system (CMS) has a different protocol. TypePad, for example, allows you to start tagging right away, and you can link it with Technorati from the get-go. (You'll find more on Technorati later in this chapter.) Movable Type and ExpressionEngine require that you add a separate module for tagging. So check the documentation or support forums for your blogging tools for details on how to work with tags.

### Tag— You're It!

Your tags should be relevant to the subject matter – if it's important to you that people be able to find stuff on your site. Tagging is abused on some sites, and people tag things with sentences. These are sometimes funny, so that's okay too. But they're not particularly useful.

# Tagging vs. Categories

You don't necessarily need to choose between tags and categories. Both have their benefits, and many website owners and bloggers utilize both. The pros of using categories are just simple organization of your blog entries, and if people who read your site like a particular post in a certain category, they know just where to look to find others like it. Tags present a better method of finding specific information. You can choose to use one or the other. Or combine them and give your readers the option to use whichever method they prefer.

## Why tags?

Don't see the appeal? Tagging is wildly popular and will continue to become the standard over categories. It may seem like a silly time waster, but tagging can actually make your site much more usable and feature-rich. Tags are more detail oriented than simple categories. Over time, the tags you accumulate on your site will make finding content much easier, allowing readers to search more efficiently and more specifically.

For personal blogs, tagging can be more of a frivolous effort, but if your blog is information specific, such as a blog about real estate or finances, or if your site is a community atmosphere where many people congregate, tagging can become really useful for your readers.

One of our favorite haunts is Colour Lovers (colourlovers. com). Here, members can create a profile, post color palettes that they create (along with their inspiration), and interact with other Colour Lovers by leaving comments and saving other members' palettes as favorites.

Tagging comes in really handy here. The Colour Lovers home page has a tag cloud containing the names of the most recent popular colors people use in palettes (refer to Figure 10-1). You can search for color palettes — to decorate your baby's nursery or to spiff up your home office — by clicking through the tags. You can do a search of the tags, such as *red and white,* and get a list of all the palettes created with those colors.

**Simple Is Smart**

Tags should be one-word or two-word combinations. A big, long, complicated description isn't too helpful, but single words like *red* or *video* can be useful for searching.

## Categories

All this tag talk and no category love. Don't write off categories just yet. Categories are useful too. Whether you're writing a personal journal-style blog or a business blog, keeping things tidy is a good idea. It isn't a law, by any means . . . if you want to have every post you ever do totally uncategorized, by all means do that. But don't forget about the benefits of keeping things in order. For one, your readers can look through your entries according to what interests them.

Most, if not all, blogging software platforms and hosted blogs give you the ability to categorize your blog entries. When you write and publish a blog entry, you can file it into a specified category that you can create. For example, you might want to create four categories for your blog including *Breakfast Recipes, Lunch Recipes, Dinner Recipes,* and *Dessert Recipes.* Then when you post a recipe for Pot Roast, you can assign it to the Dinner

Recipes category. Typically, a list of your categories is displayed in the sidebar of your blog or website. A reader can then select the Dinner Recipe category from either a link list or a drop-down box and see all the entries you filed in that category.

If you have a blog about cosmetics and a visitor wants to know what you have to say on all things lip gloss, all she needs to do is click on your handy Lip Gloss category link, and it takes her to a list of *every post you ever made* about lip gloss and everything lip gloss–related. Handy! But what if you write an entry about lip gloss that comes packaged with body wash? Oh no! The sky is falling! Don't sweat it. You can cross-categorize entries in as many categories as you like.

Categories are typically standard in most blogging tools. A little poking and prodding will produce a spot in your blog's control panel where you can add your categories ahead of time as a timesaver. When you get around to posting an entry, you can quickly assign it to your preset categories.

Adding categories to your blog is a cinch. In this example, we show you how to add and use categories in Movable Type:

1. **Log in to your Movable Type (MT) control panel and click on the blog you wish to categorize.**

2. **From the menu on the left, click the Categories button.**

3. **Click Create a Top Level Category.** A text field appears where you can enter the name of the category you wish to use.

4. **Type in the category name and then click the Create Category button next to it.** Once clicked, a yellow box will appear alerting you that your new category has been created.

5. **When MT prompts you, click the Rebuild My Site button.** A small window will pop up, as shown in Figure 10-2.

Figure 10-2

6. **From the drop-down menu, select Rebuild All Files and then click the Rebuild button underneath.**

7. **Once MT has completed rebuilding, click the Close button from the pop-up window.**

You now have a category in which to file blog entries. To put an entry into a category setup in MT, follow these steps:

1. **Login to your MT control panel and click New Entry.** The Create New Entry page appears, as shown in Figure 10-3.

Figure 10-3

2. From the Primary Category drop-down menu, select the category you would like to save your entry in.

3. After you finish your entry and title it, click the Save button at the bottom of the form.

4. Proceed with the Rebuilding prompts that MT provides as outlined in Steps 5 through 7 in the previous step list!

Your entry is now filed into a category. When users select this category, they will be presented with this entry and any other entries you assign to the same category.

# Popular Services That Use Tags

You've got your tags and categories rocking. Now put them to good use and take advantage of some of the great services and blog communities out there that want to use your content to beef up the Internet. Sites like Technorati use the tags and categories on people's blogs to compile a huge collection of blog information. Other services like Del.icio.us utilize a bookmarking system in conjunction with tags created by its users to produce a massive bookmarking tag-fest.

## Technorati

Technorati (shown in Figure 10-4) is a site that *indexes,* or *crawls,* your site to read and collect all your content. It's much like a newsreader, but a very large public one. By registering your site with the folks at Technorati (or "claiming your blog" as they call it), you're essentially giving them the go-ahead to index your website for relevant links and information.

Claiming your blog with Technorati also lets them confirm that you're the author or co-author of the site. You're then free to use all of Technorati's services to promote or increase the visibility of your blog. People perusing Technorati can click your links or profile and learn more about you and the blogs you author. You can also use Technorati to surf for anything you may be looking for.

### Women with Moxie

"If I'd observed all the rules, I'd never have gotten anywhere."

–Marilyn Monroe

Searching the tag system on Technorati is extensive and impressive. After you claim your blog, you'll end up in their search results, but your posts will also end up in the Technorati tag pages. The nice part is that you don't necessarily *have* to tag your entries to get in there. Contributing requires that you have a blog that supports categories and an RSS/Atom feed, like we talk about in Chapter 11. If they're both operating, it does this automatically.

**Figure 10-4**

Here are the steps to follow to claim your blog with Technorati:

1. **If you haven't already, register for an account with Technorati through the sign up link on the main page** (technorati.com)**.**

2. **Once registered, click the Edit link next to your username to administer your account.**

3. **From My Account, click the Blogs tab.**

4. **To begin the claim process, enter your blog's URL (for example:** http://stellalikescosmos.com**) in the field provided, and then click the Begin Claim button.**

5. **Click the Use Post Claim link.** Next, Technorati presents you with a few steps, as shown in Figure 10-5.

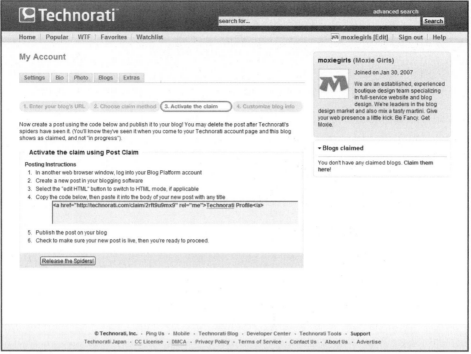

**Figure 10-5**

6. **Copy the code from the window provided by Technorati and paste that code into a new blog entry on your blog. Publish the entry and then continue to the next step.**

7. **Click the Release the Spiders! button.** Technorati will visit your site and look for the link you just published.

After you have successfully claimed your blog with Technorati, your posts will be included in Technorati searches, and people using Technorati can now stumble onto your content. Hooray for bonus blog traffic! If your blog doesn't support categories and RSS/Atom feeds, you can still make it happen. You can manually paste Technorati-specific code in the body of your entry to associate your entry with any tag. Here is Technorati's code example, which you can find on their site in the Site Guide under *Tags*:

```
<a href="http://technorati.com/tag/[tagname]"
    rel="tag">[tagname]</a>
<a href="http://technorati.com/tag/[tagname]+[tagname]"
    rel="tag">[tagname tagname]</a>
```

The tagname can essentially be anything you want, although you'll probably want each one to be relevant and descriptive, such as in the following example for *global warming*:

```
<a href="http://technorati.com/tag/global+warming"
  rel="tag">global warming</a>
```

But hang on, there's one last step. You must ping Technorati to alert them to come and index your blog so they can find the code you just nestled into your entry. As discussed in Chapter 9, you can set your blog to ping other blogs; in this case, you can ping Technorati by setting the ping address in your blog software so that it will ping them automatically, or you can go to Technorati and manually ping the site each time. Check your blog software or hosted solution's documentation to find out where to add Technorati's ping address. You can find more information on pinging Technorati at their site: technorati.com/ping/.

## Del.icio.us

Unlike Technorati, Del.icio.us.com (shown in Figure 10-6) is classified more as a social bookmarking service that is widely used to store, share, and find content on the web using a tag system. Users can tag their bookmarks with various descriptive words to enable people to search and find blogs and other content.

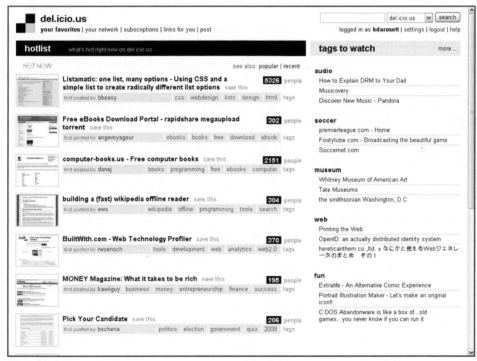

Figure 10-6

With an account, you can add bookmarks and subscriptions by searching the tag system or by subscribing from a site with a Del.icio.us link. Additionally, you can tag your links with relevant items to build a tag cloud of your own, making searching your own collection a snap. You can assign as many tags to a bookmark as you like, and you can edit them if you change your mind. Gone are the days of folders and categorizing. You can also check out the lists and tags other people create.

# Relax, Refresh, Reward

You've got the scoop on tagging, so here's a quick way to decompress and de-stress without pulling a muscle. Chill the bubbly and take a load off. One of our favorite ways to unwind at the end of the day is to take a long, hot bath. Whether bubbles or oil are your thing, add them and take a soak.

## Bathtub Zen

We found these great recipes for fragrant, relaxing bath treatments for you to get your *om* on from iVillage.com, a premier online community for women.

### Green Tea Bath with Jasmine Flowers

Heat a large pot of green tea by combining 4 cups boiling water and 4–5 tablespoons loose green tea leaves. Steep for 10 minutes. Cool a bit, strain, and add to bath water. Sprinkle a handful of fresh or dried flowers like jasmine, gardenia, or camellia.

### Skin-Firming Flower Mask with Orange Flowers

*1½ teaspoons finely chopped orange flowers or scented geranium leaves*

*2 teaspoons orange juice*

*½ teaspoon honey*

*1 teaspoon grated orange rind*

*1 teaspoon clay (green, white, or bentonite)*

Mix ingredients together. Apply to clean face and neck. Leave on for several minutes while breathing deeply. Rinse with tepid water and pat skin dry. Clay draws out impurities in the skin, the orange ingredients cleanse, and honey moisturizes.

## To Do List

Get the dish on RSS and other web feeds

Figure out what all the fuss is about

Subscribe, subscribe, subscribe

Revel in your success without guilt!

# Feed Your Blog Addiction

**Y**ou may wonder how people find the time in their busy schedules to read all these blogs, let alone your brand-new, April-fresh creation. Thanks to something called a *web feed* (or simply a *feed*, if you're hip – and we know you are), reading all the blogs you desire becomes as easy as scanning the newspaper . . . minus the messy thumbprints.

By the end of this chapter, you'll know what feeds do, why they're important to you, and how to really maximize them to your benefit. You'll be reading more blogs more efficiently, all while throwing around the lingo like a pro.

# The Scoop on Feeds

A *feed* is the data format used to deliver frequently updated content, such as your blog entries, your friend's new photos, or CNN.com's latest headline. You may have seen websites with links or references to labels such as RSS, Atom, or XML. These are essentially assorted flavors of the same thing — a way you can get site updates without having to actually visit the site. Here's the skinny on these terms:

- **RSS** stands for a few different things, depending on whom you ask. Recent definitions claim that it stands for Really Simple Syndication, and that sits just fine with us. We like simple! RSS is the most commonly used term you'll find for feeds, as its primary job is to deliver regularly updated content such as blogs and podcasts.

- **Atom** is just another type of feed, for all intents and purposes. Atom has some technical goodies that make it slightly different to those who program such things, but for your purposes, it's really just a matter of preference and what the site you're reading chooses to publish.

- **XML** is not, technically, a feed at all, but really the technology used to create the feeds. However, due to some misconceptions, it's most often used to reference a feed, just like RSS and Atom. You may sometimes see icons or links for XML along with RSS or Atom.

## Feeding the masses

The act of publishing those links and feeds is called *syndication*. Anyone who posts on the Internet can syndicate a feed. Gathering all the feeds in one place is called *aggregation* — although most of us not sporting pocket protectors just call it *subscribing*.

Suppose you have a list of 20 blogs you like to read, and visiting each blog daily takes an hour (or more, if you visit more than once a day). It would be fantastic to be able to check those all at once, saving precious time for a bubble bath, wouldn't it?

Fortunately, content distributors, known as *newsreaders* or *feed readers,* have got your back. These handy services syndicate the content, allowing you to subscribe to it. Think of it like you're customizing your own newspaper, gathering all the headlines and snippets of your favorite websites in one central location to read at your leisure.

## Feeds vs. favorites

For years, people have used bookmarks (or *favorites,* for you Internet Explorer fans) to save and organize sites they've discovered online and want to visit again. To bookmark a website, you simply click the Bookmark (or Favorites) button on your chosen browser when you run across something that blows your dress up. It's still a perfectly valid and reasonable way to keep an eye on sites that don't provide frequently updated content — or that don't offer feeds, such as many shopping and business sites. However, like you, more and more sites are getting on board the RSS party bus.

Then what is the point of feeds, you may ask, if people still use bookmarks? Feeds make it easier to read and manage *dynamic content*, which is content that is regularly and frequently updated, like blogs and news. Whenever your girlfriend Gina posts a new blog entry, you're notified via your feed reader if you have subscribed to Gina's feed. The next time you visit your feed reader, Gina's site is highlighted in some way (perhaps bold or italicized or a different color, depending on the reader you use), usually with some indicator of how many new entries are available for reading. Clicking her name in your list makes her entry (or entries) display in your reader — and there you have it! You're reading feeds.

What if you want to go from your feed reader back to the original website? Let's say Gina's blog entry is all about how her boyfriend is a total jerk, and you want to tell her to kick him to the curb! What to do? Simply click the link in your feed reader, and you're directed away from your reader and sent to her actual blog entry on her site, where you may diss him to your heart's content.

Can bookmarks do all that? Heck no! Bookmarks have their place, especially when you just want to flag something for later, but if you want to get the skinny on your buddy's love life, see the latest headline from Google, or know the moment your sister's baby shower photos go online, feeds and you will be tighter than Nicole Richie's leggings.

## Subscribing to Feeds

Subscribing to feeds is easier than finding a date at last call. In terms we all can understand, subscribing to a feed is a pickup line, and the website is a sure thing. By subscribing to a feed, you're simply telling that blog or website, "You're hot. I want to know more. What's your sign?" Okay, maybe not that last part. But in essence, you're asking that site to send you its updated content because you're interested. If you get bored and decide you want to break up with that site, you simply *unsubscribe.* It's not them, it's you . . . but maybe you can still be friends.

### Lookie Here

Website and blog owners generally try to make it simple for you to subscribe to their feeds by placing the icon or text links in high-traffic areas such as the top of the blog or a sidebar. Occasionally, you'll find the subscribe link in a footer – or even inline with an entry itself. Just keep your eyes peeled for the icon or the acronym RSS, and you should be just fine.

One of the great things about feeds is that they're so easy to recognize and save on a whim. In late 2005, a unified symbol for feeds was established so that no matter what type of feed a website publishes (RSS or Atom), it's easy to recognize. While you may still see text links labeled RSS, Atom, XML, and even sometimes Subscribe, be on the lookout for the little buttons that look like the ones shown in Figure 11-1. You most commonly see these icons in orange, but they can also appear in various colors that complement the owners' websites.

**Figure 11-1**

## Choosing a feed reader

The best way to organize your feeds is with a *feed reader,* which syndicates website and blog feeds so that you can subscribe to them and read them all in one place. You can choose from three types of feed readers. How you choose a reader depends on the web browser you most commonly use and how much flexibility you desire. Here are some quick guidelines:

- **Browser-based:** If you're kind of a homebody and don't plan on reading your feeds anywhere else, browser-based feed readers might suit you just fine. These are generally built right into your web browser and allow you to subscribe to a feed with one click. This is sometimes referred to as *live book-marking.* Examples of the most popular web browsers that include this feature are Internet Explorer 7, Firefox, and Safari (the latter being exclusively a Mac browser).

- **Web-based:** If you're a girl on the go and want to be able to check your feeds from any web browser or mobile device, such as a PDA or a cellphone with Internet access, we recommend the web-based option, as it's the most flexible and most popular of choices. You'll find several web-based feed reader services on the market. The majority of them are free and easy to use. Table 11-1 lists some of our favorites.

- **The Combo:** Most of the newer browsers incorporate (or give you the option to incorporate) a web-based reader, such as Bloglines (which is available in the Firefox browser), with their built-in reader, so you have the best of both worlds. The one-click ease of live bookmarking *with* the go-anywhere convenience of a web-based reader? It really couldn't get better. Our favorite method of reading feeds — using Firefox and Bloglines. You can do *The Combo* with Internet Explorer 7, too; you just need to install an add-on to make it work.

**Table 11-1**          **Our Favorite Feed Readers**

| Feed Reader | Where to Find It |
| --- | --- |
| Bloglines | bloglines.com |
| NewsGator Online | newsgatoronline.com |
| My Yahoo | my.yahoo.com |
| Google Reader | google.com/reader |
| Feedreader 3 | feedreader.com |
| Rojo | rojo.com |

## Creating live bookmarks

Once you've got yourself a feed reader chosen, set up, and ready to roar, you are armed to start subscribing to feeds! With so many different types of computers, operating systems, and browsers out there, you have a cornucopia of options on how you subscribe to feeds. Because we'd need a whole book to go over every one, we're going to cover the basics to get you started.

As we mentioned earlier, newer browsers, such as Internet Explorer 7, Safari, and Firefox, allow you to subscribe to feeds with a built-in feed reader. This is called *live bookmarking.* If a site is publishing, or *syndicating,* a feed, the option to subscribe via live bookmark will be apparent by the orange feed icon appearing somewhere near the top of the browser window. In Firefox, the orange feed icon is located in the address bar. In Internet Explorer 7, it is in the top right-hand side of the browser window.

Using one of our favorite gossip sites, Popsugar.com, in the next exercise, we show you how to subscribe to and read a feed using live bookmarks with each of the top two browsers used today. Just find your preferred browser in the text that follows, fire it up, and get ready to start subscribing to feeds.

### Internet Explorer 7

Follow these steps to subscribe to a feed in Internet Explorer 7. (If you're still using an earlier version of Internet Explorer (IE), don't fret! You can download IE7 at microsoft.com/windows/downloads/ie/getitnow.mspx.)

**I.** **In Internet Explorer 7, type the Web site address in the address box.** For example, type **popsugar.com** to follow along with the example.

When the page fully loads, the orange live bookmark feed icon appears on the top right of the toolbar, as shown in Figure 11-2. (The live bookmark icon appears grayed out on sites not offering a feed, but highlights orange when a feed is present.)

Figure 11-2

**2.** **Click the orange live bookmark icon.** A simply formatted page appears for previewing the feed you're interested in. At the top of the page is a yellow alert box for subscribing, as shown in Figure 11-3.

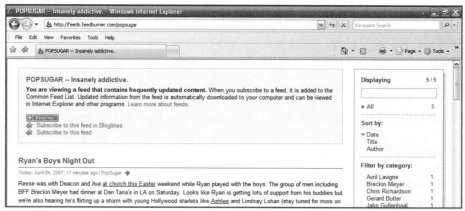

Figure 11-3

3. **Click Subscribe to This Feed.** The Subscribe to This Feed dialog box appears, allowing you to save the feed (see Figure 11-4).

Figure 11-4

4. **Click the Subscribe button.** The dialog box disappears, and the yellow alert message changes, confirming your subscription and inviting you to view your feeds.

5. **Click the View My Feeds link, located in the same yellow alert message box, as shown in Figure 11-5.** A sidebar automatically appears on the left, listing your feeds with the Popsugar.com feed highlighted and the content appearing in the preview area on the right.

**Find Your Feeds in IE**

If the sidebar doesn't appear or you're having trouble finding the feeds you've subscribed to, choose View→Explorer Bar→Feeds from the Internet Explorer toolbar (or press Ctrl+Shift+J) to bring the sidebar on-screen.

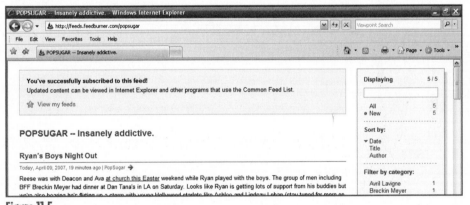

Figure 11-5

Kudos! You just subscribed to the Popsugar.com feed using Internet Explorer 7! If you want to unsubscribe, simply delete the feed from your feeds list by highlighting the feed you wish to delete and pressing the Delete key (or by right-clicking the feed name and choosing Delete from the menu).

## Firefox 2.0 or later

Live bookmarking or subscribing to feeds in the Firefox browser is easier than putting on pantyhose. Here are a couple steps to get yourself started:

1. **In Firefox, type the Web site address in the address box.** For this example, type **popsugar.com**.

   The orange live bookmark feed icon appears at the right side of the address box at the top of the browser, as shown in Figure 11-6.

Figure 11-6

2. **Click the orange live bookmark icon in the address box.**

3. **An Add Live Bookmark dialog box appears, asking you where you want to save this feed (see Figure 11-7).** We recommend creating a folder for your feeds, just to keep things tidy. By default, Firefox saves feeds in the Bookmarks Toolbar Folder located in your Bookmarks list. (There's a Create Folder button right on the dialog box, if you haven't created one already.)

4. **Click OK.**

Figure 11-7

That's it! You're subscribed. Want to unsubscribe? Simply delete the feed from your bookmarks.

To find your list of feeds (if you haven't changed the defaults), you simply look in your Bookmarks list (from the top menu on your Firefox browser); there will be a folder labeled Bookmarks Toolbar Folder containing all your juicy feeds that you have subscribed to, as shown in Figure 11-8.

## What?!
### Where Is the Dialog Box?

If you haven't seen an Add Live Bookmark dialog box when trying to live bookmark a website, it could be that you have changed some of your settings in Firefox. If, for example, you are using a feed reader and set Firefox to subscribe using Bloglines, then live bookmarking will not work as you intend. You'll need to change the setting in your browser. To do so, in your browser, choose Tools→Options→Feeds and set it to subscribe using Live Bookmarks.

Figure 11-8

### The Combo: Firefox and Bloglines

If you're using Firefox as your browser of choice, you may be interested in reaping the benefits of using a web-based feed reader in combination with your browser's live bookmark feature. The basic live bookmark feature of Firefox doesn't offer a whole lot more than the headlines, whereas Bloglines allows you to list your feeds on the left and preview the content on the right, similar to how Internet Explorer 7 displays feeds. This method allows you to ultimately access your feeds from anywhere, read an excerpt or the entire article without ever having to visit the website, and yet still be able to subscribe with a few simple clicks of the mouse directly from your browser.

Following the steps below allows you to set Bloglines as your default feed reader for live bookmarking. This lets you simply click the feed icon or text link, and the Bloglines site loads, with your feed applied to your Bloglines account in one simple step. Pretty slick, huh?

First, you'll need a Bloglines account. Follow these steps to start using your Bloglines account through Firefox:

1. **Visit the site** bloglines.com**.** The Bloglines home page appears, as shown in Figure 11-9.

2. **Click the Sign Up Now It's Free! link in the middle of the page.** Your browser takes you to the Create an Account page.

3. **Enter the email address you wish to associate with this account.** This is your login, so choose a valid email address that you intend to check regularly and that you don't mind being visible to others if you so choose. (*Note:* In your account preferences, after you complete the signup process, you can set your email address to display in your Bloglines profile. It is set to "private" by default.)

4. **Type a password of at least six characters. Re-enter the password for validation.**

5. **Choose the appropriate time zone and language.**

**Figure 11-9**

6. **Be sure that you agree to the terms and conditions before continuing.**

7. **Click the Register button.** You're redirected to a page telling you to respond to a confirmation email to validate your account.

8. **Check the email account you registered with and follow the instructions to validate your account.** You're taken to a welcome page in your web browser urging you to explore Bloglines. After you've finished this step list, you can go nuts.

9. **For now, just click the Feeds tab on the top left of the screen.** Congratulations! You now have Bloglines! The Feeds page, shown in Figure 11-10, is what you see when you visit Bloglines to read your feeds. Now you need to make sure your Firefox browser knows that you have Bloglines.

## The Dog Ate My Email

If you don't see the Bloglines email in your main inbox, check your spam or junk mail filters. Sometimes it slips through the cracks.

**Figure 11-10**

10. **On the Firefox toolbar, choose Tools➜Options and click the Feeds icon.**

11. **Select the Subscribe to the Feeds Using radio button and choose Bloglines from the list.**

12. **Click OK.** Easy as pie!

Mmmm . . . pie. Ah, but that's getting off course. Back to Bloglines! Now when you visit a site that offers a feed or a live bookmark icon with Firefox, clicking the link or icon takes you to Bloglines right in your browser. Just one easy step allows you to preview, organize, and subscribe to feeds on the spot, as shown in Figure 11-11.

## The Combo #2: Firefox and Google Reader

Tons of people use Bloglines, but you aren't cornered into that option if you don't want it. Some, like us, prefer to keep all our information gathered in one central location. Utilizing Google's feed reader, aptly named Google Reader (pictured in Figure 11-12), lets us do just that.

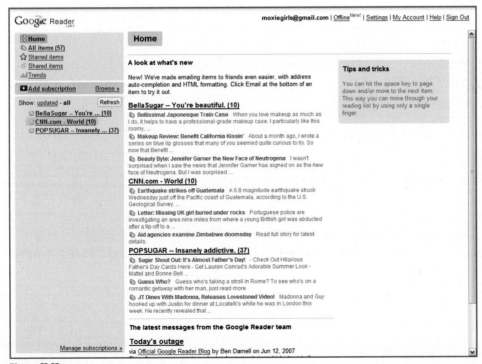

**Figure 11-11**

**Figure 11-12**

Like Bloglines, Google Reader requires you to have an account. Generally, if you are already utilizing Google's other goodies like Gmail.com for your email, chances are you can skip over the signup stuff and start using Google Reader right away. And once you have your Google Reader ready to go, start subscribing. It's addicting, we promise.

# Relax, Refresh, Reward

Look at you! In this chapter, you've investigated the ins and outs of web feeds and feed readers so you can save time reading all those blogs you'll be discovering. Plus, this gives you a more solid understanding of what your readers experience when they subscribe to feeds you may offer on your own blog.

We think you deserve a treat for all that hard work, and because we can't seem to shake the idea of pie, we thought we'd share a quick, easy, and completely no-bake recipe to get your chocolate fix with minimum flab! This pie is a big hit with everyone who tries it, and if you don't tell your boyfriend that it's low-calorie, he'll never know the difference.

## Chocolate cream pie for the baking impaired

*1 tub of fat-free nondairy whipped topping (such as Cool Whip Free)*

*1 large package of sugar-free instant chocolate pudding (Chocolate Sugar-Free Instant Jell-O is perfect.)*

*1 ready-made reduced-fat chocolate pie crust (Keebler's is pretty good, but any will do. If they don't have chocolate, you can use graham crackers.)*

*1¾ cups of nonfat milk (You can use vanilla soy milk, alternatively, if you like.)*

1. **Mix the pudding packet with milk. Let it sit in the fridge for a minimum of 30 minutes.** It won't be like full-on pudding, but it'll be "set" and not liquid goo. It should have the basic consistency of pudding.

2. **Using a spatula, gently fold in the defrosted nonfat whipped topping. Fold — not whip!**

3. **Pour the mixture into the pie crust and stick it in the fridge for at least an hour — but a few hours is best to make it really hold together. Slice into 6 pieces.**

4. **Enjoy!** The beauty of this recipe is even if you totally go CRAZY and eat the whole pie, it's still better than eating one slice of the full-fat version.

If you want to get really fancy, you can top it with a dusting of finely grated chocolate or serve with fresh berries. Get creative and change it up by adding flavored extracts from the baking aisle, such as almond or mint, or change the pudding flavor to vanilla or butterscotch for something different.

## To Do List

- Think of the best way to use photos on your site
- Make friends with Flickr
- Discover photoblogs
- Blog photos on the go!
- Protect your pics
- Power up the paparazzi: Set up moblogging
- Cool off with some caffeine

# Be Part of the Paparazzi

Sharing photos with the blogging community is hugely popular and adds to the voyeuristic quality of blogging. As they say, "A picture is worth a thousand words," and in the case of blogging, a photo can be accompanied by a thousand words. There are blogs that post photos (photoblogs) and a whole barrel of other ways you can incorporate imagery onto your website. You can use photo sharing for personal expression, social fun, or portfolio display, as well as many other purposes.

Of course what you share, how you share it, and if you're sharing too much are all things to consider before you upload your family albums.

# Getting the Picture: Adding Photos to Your Blog Entries

Adding imagery or photos to your posts can have a really positive effect on your entries. People are very visual, and considering that your readers are staring at a computer screen, keeping them entertained can make an impact. Impressions are made quickly with a point of interest to catch the eyes of readers, bringing them in to stay.

Of course, all of this is subjective and depends on the content of your site, your audience, and your goals. If you're blogging for fun, you'll have a totally different set of guidelines than if you're blogging for profit.

Personal bloggers might want to share photos of themselves, their family, friends, or pets to illustrate the point of a post. A blogger looking to build a following might consider posting images or photos to back up a story or show details to drive home a point.

Gossip blogs are the perfect example of blogs with photos. Gossip bloggers spend their days uploading coordinating shots of celebrities to go with the gossip *du jour*. Of course, with publishing anything, particularly photographs, there are copyright issues to consider. If the photos you choose to post are yours from your very own camera, go to town. But posting photos taken by anyone else can pose a problem. The rule is: Get permission.

## On the Line with Lisa Sugar, Sugar Publishing

Lisa Sugar launched PopSugar (popsugar.com) as a gossip blog years ago, and it's since grown to a huge gossip and entertainment hub on the Internet. Her company, Sugar Publishing, is now home to various spin-off sites covering fashion, shopping, home, beauty, and technology. There seems to be no limit to what she plans to accomplish in the coming years. We got a chance to talk to Lisa Sugar, the pioneering voice behind PopSugar, and she had this to say:

**We remember when PopSugar started — we've been reading for a long time! Did you know PopSugar would turn into an actual business, or was it more or less by accident? Or was this the plan all along?**

PopSugar.com started as a personal hobby. I worked in advertising where I had to be aware of the latest entertainment news and trends. I wanted to find a way to combine my knowledge of the media world with my interest in writing.

*(cont'd)*

As I began to write, the audience grew dramatically. That's when I saw an opportunity to start a new career. Being married to an entrepreneur rubbed off on me. When my husband and I saw how successful the site had become, we had a vision for Sugar Publishing, and he helped me turn my hobby into a full-fledged business.

**PopSugar isn't just PopSugar anymore. It's grown into a Sugar Empire! When you realized you had something special, what helped you choose the areas to expand?**

About seven months after starting PopSugar .com, I conducted a survey to see what other topics the audience was interesting in reading about. Based on their responses, my experience from my advertising career, and knowing popular magazine genres and circulations, I determined what topics would generate the largest audiences. If you look at the history of the Sugar Network, you will notice that after starting PopSugar, the celebrity site, we launched FabSugar, the fashion site, and from there we launched sites for a variety of different topics.

**One of the most asked questions from bloggers is, "How do I get people to read my blog?" Other than by posting fabulous content, what did you do in order to get and keep traffic coming to your site?**

Content is the most important differentiator among blogs. We pride ourselves on the voice we created on all of our sites. We also provide our readers with unique content or our opinion on the day-to-day news.

Our site is also interactive — the readers interact with each other through the comments and our social networking site, and the editors interact with the readers through both avenues as well.

Finding the right editors has been critical to our success. We have a very extensive recruitment process. We have hired past bloggers, traditional journalists, and passionate experts for each site.

Finally, word of mouth has been key to growing our traffic. We have established relationships with other bloggers in our fields and have linked to each other. In the blogosphere, competitors are also collaborators, and we have a mutual respect for one another.

**PopSugar posts lots of great photos of celebrities. Do you ever run into copyright problems? How do you handle that, and what advice would you give to someone wanting to post photos on their blog?**

From day one, we have been insistent on sourcing information for every article. We have established relationships with all of the major photo agencies, have contracts in place, and give credit for each photo that is run on each of our sites. This is a must for anyone who wants to be considered legitimate.

**Any tips for beginners who want to turn a blog into a money maker?**

You have to be serious about creating a site that is different from its competitors. You should create your own look, update the site round-the-clock, and show your passion and dedication to the subject matter in how you write. It is also important to learn the ins and outs of blog advertising. There are a variety of advertising networks that are there to help you make money.

# Your Friend Flickr

Flickr (flickr.com) is an extremely popular online photo management and photo sharing website that has transformed into a massive photo community (not to mention, a site we visit daily). If you procrastinate, this is the best way to spend your procrastinating time. Flickr houses the portfolios of thousands of talented photographers ranging from professional to amateur, in addition to a vast collection of photos from people with point-and-shoot cameras. Flickr allows you to upload and share your photos in a gallery format and provides a comment/blog-type of atmosphere. You can have your very own Flickr account to share photos with free of charge, or for $2 a month, you can reap the ProMember benefits Flickr has to offer, such as unlimited photo storage, ad-free browsing, and permanent archiving of high-resolution images. Figure 12-1 shows Flickr's sign-up page.

## Sticky Flickr Fingers

Flickr isn't a free-for-all stock photo joint. Taking people's photos to post on your blog, or for any other purpose, is a no-no. Ask permission – always.

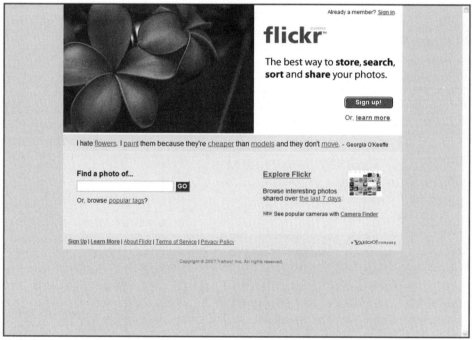

Figure 12-1

## What you get with a Flickr account

Signing up for a Flickr account is pretty easy. Flickr, in its growth, joined forces with Yahoo! (yahoo.com), and you're required to have a Yahoo! account to sign up. If you don't already have one, you can sign up for one in a few minutes. All basic Flickr accounts are free and allow you to post, rotate, tag, and share your photos with the world. You're also granted the ability to sort your photos into sets and collections. Basic free accounts give you three to start off with. You can accept comments, set privacy levels for friends and family-only viewing — and the best part, you can post your photos from Flickr right into your blog. Flickr supports blogging your photos with LiveJournal, Blogger, Movable Type, and TypePad, to name a few. Sweet!

Another charming feature is the note system. You can draw small squares on points of interest in your photos and label them, and you can give your Flickr friends permission to note your photos, too. It's great fun. You can also tag your photos and search all of Flickr using them.

## Getting group therapy

As with any community type of website, people with similar interests congregate. Flickr grants you the ability to create public or private groups for group photo sharing. You can join groups people have created or create your own. You know you want to submit that photo of your dog to the DOGS! DOGS! DOGS! group. The group atmosphere also allows people to post topics of discussion related to the group topic. Photographers post questions, tips, and tutorials to their groups, and dog lovers can share their dog's latest caper with the basket of clean laundry.

### Miss Manners

Flickr is a public forum. Not everyone is there to be a professional photographer. As the saying goes, "If you have nothing nice to say, don't say anything at all." Kindness and courtesy are appreciated on Flickr.

## Browsing for interestingness with Flickr's Explore

Explore is an awesome feature on Flickr that showcases the top 500 most interesting photos on Flickr each day. The folks at Flickr call this *interestingness*. How they select the photos is a bit of a mystery, but getting a photo into the selective group is a perk every member enjoys.

## Managing your contacts

Just as not everyone is a professional photographer, not everyone is on Flickr for innocent photo sharing. Flickr, if you know where to look, can contain quite a bit of adult content. Yes, we mean *adult* as in nude, naked, in the buff, freebird, commando, and otherwise compromised. Shocking, isn't it? Well, it's not that surprising . . . it *is* the Internet after all.

If you receive notifications that users have added you as a contact and you don't recognize their screen names, be sure to check out their profiles to ensure that they're really folks you want to connect with. Check who else they list as contacts in their profiles. You should also check to see if they post any photos and make note of their screen names. Let's say a user's name is XXXILOVE BIGGUNS69, and she has half-naked swingers in her contact list. If that doesn't appeal to you, there's a handy Block This Person link in the upper-right corner of her profile. Clickity click, Bigguns!

# Girls on Film: Photoblogs

Professionals and photography enthusiasts alike enjoy displaying their talents in the form of photoblogs. These photoblogs might stand on their own or work in conjunction with Flickr or other similar photo sharing sites. The increasing popularity and ease of Flickr has made displaying your photos on the Internet simple and easy. Before the wonder of Flickr, personal photoblogs were all the rage. Now, most personal blogs choose to incorporate Flickr. But photoblogs are still fun to have or use, especially if photography is your thing or you're looking to eventually go pro.

## You Say You Want a Resolution

Much like that drawer of last season's lip gloss, posting photos on your site can hog space on your web host. To prevent this, it's wise to reduce your photos in resolution from 300 dpi to 72 dpi to save yourself some space (*dpi* means *dots per inch*). Reference your camera's manual or check out *Digital Photography All-in-One Desk Reference For Dummies* by David D. Busch (Wiley) for more information about image resolution. Or you can beef up your hosting package to accommodate a collection of large image files, but bear in mind that blog visitors who don't have a high-speed Internet connection will sometimes have to wait for your high-res images to display.

## Photoblogs.org

Photoblogs.org (photoblogs.org) is one of a few central hubs where you can look around at the many photoblogs on the web. There is nearly one for every kind of photography style and taste. Many people prefer telling a story through a photograph, in addition to traditional text entries.

There is sometimes a fine line between a professional photoblog and an amateur one. Many times amateur photoblogs are made by those who have such a passion for photography that they often own fancy cameras, lenses, and in-home studios. Their photos can be so fabulous, it's hard to tell the pros from the players. Professional photoblogs typically present larger-format photographs in a portfolio manner and often have them available for purchase.

## Shutterblog.com

Robyn Pollman is an amateur-turned-professional photographer based in Orlando, Florida. Her photoblog, Shutterblog (shutterblog.com), chronicles the growth of her beautiful children, as well as select favorites from her professional shoots (see Figure 12-2).

Some fun goodies that Robin includes in her photoblog, in addition to her gorgeous photos, are resourceful links, camera tips, and helpful methods of protecting your images against theft.

**Figure 12-2**

# Mo' Photos with Moblogging

These days, you gals are always on the go-go-go! You're running off to meetings, catching up with friends for coffee, or picking up your dry cleaning. You're *busy!* Thanks to just about *every* mobile phone and PDA provider, you have constant connectivity in the form of your cute pink Razr phone or your sexy new Blackberry. So you can take and send photos when it's convenient for you.

Now, when you see that hot pair of Kenneth Cole boots on sale, you can snap a camera phone photo and notify your friends — and the entire Internet — that they're on sale for one day only. Originally, *moblogging* (mobile blogging) was used primarily for sending and posting photos to a blog, but you can post full-on text entries on the go too! In the age of *texting,* the act of sending messages from one mobile device to another, you can post photos, blog entries, and video from your cell phone or mobile device right to your blog.

## Call Me Sometime

Before you order a cell phone plan that lets you email photos or send text messages, make sure the phone you have is capable of using the services you're paying for.

# Phones and PDAs: You have the technology

Almost everyone's cell phone comes with Internet access these days. So why not put it to use while you're out taking over the world? Many phones come equipped with a little built-in camera that lets you snap away and then save or send your image to an email address or another cell phone. Or you can send your photo — complete with caption — right to your blog or Flickr. You can do all that right from your PDA or Blackberry while on the bus heading to work. But before you start sending pictures of your latest pedicure color into the great wide Internet, you need a place for your photo or text to land.

## Phone it in

Flickr — and even some blog software — comes equipped with moblogging capabilities ready to go. ExpressionEngine is one of the few blogging software platforms that includes a moblog module built right in. Other blogging software platforms, such as Movable Type and WordPress, require plugins or widgets to enable moblogging.

If you aren't running your own blog software, you can still take advantage of moblogging. Some hosted blogging services, such as Blogger, do provide users with moblog capabilities, but not *every* hosted blogging service allows moblogging. WordPress.com for example, doesn't yet allow it, although this may change as these types of services develop. TypePad and Vox do offer moblogging services, and they've both made it super easy to set up.

## Moblogging with TypePad

Here's how you can set up Moblogging with TypePad:

1. **From your TypePad account online, click Control Panel.**

2. **Click the Profile tab.**

3. **Click the Mobile Settings link.** The Mobile Settings page opens, as shown in Figure 12-3.

4. **From the When I Send Text Messages by Email, Post Them to This Weblog drop-down menu, select which blog to post text messages to.**

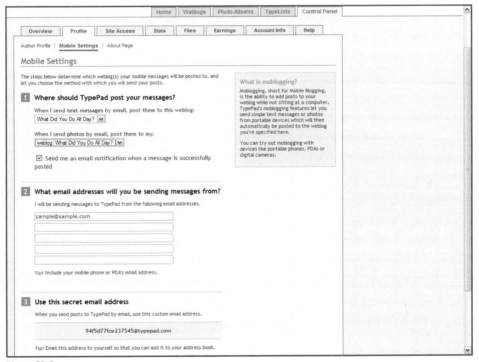

**Figure 12-3**

5. **From the When I Send Photos by Email, Post Them to My drop-down menu, select which blog to post photos to.**

6. **Fill in any email addresses you'll be sending your content from.** For example, if you use a free email account when traveling, a work email, and a mobile or PDA email address, provide those to TypePad in the five available fields.

7. **Copy and save the secret email address provided by TypePad.** This is the email address where you will send your text and/or photos from your phone or PDA. Program it into your phone's address book feature for easy access. Anything you send to this secret address will automatically get published to the blog you specified in Steps 4 and 5.

8. **Click Save.**

### Moblogging with Vox

Here are the steps to get yourself moblogging with Vox:

1. **From your Vox account online, click Account.**

2. **Click the Mobile Settings link from the left navigation link list.** Vox displays your mobile posting options along with a mobile email address to send your text and photos to (see Figure 12-4).

3. **Select your privacy options from the Share With drop-down list and then click Save below the drop-down list to save the setting.** You can choose to have Vox automatically set a default privacy level. Share your moblogging posts with anyone, your Vox neighborhood, or friends and family.

4. **(Optional) Set default moblog tags for your entries from the Tag With drop-down menu.** You can tag your entries with identifying keywords.

5. **Choose when to post from the Create Post drop-down menu and then click Save below the drop-down menu.** Choose Yes to create a new post in the blog with your moblogged photo or text, or No so you can handle it later when you have time.

6. **(Optional) If you've created multiple contact groups, choose to which group these photos should be visible.** Click the link next to Post to Group, and in the small window that appears, select the applicable contact groups. Click Save.

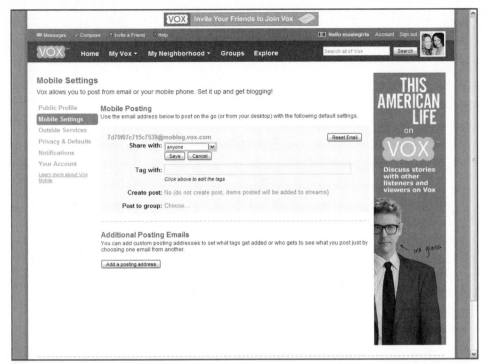

Figure 12-4

## Moblogging with Flickr

Moblogging with Flickr is just a few clicks away. Here's how to set it up:

1. **Log in to your trusty Flickr account at** flickr.com.

2. **Click your screen name, located in the upper-right corner.** This takes you to your account settings.

3. **On the Email tab, shown in Figure 12-5, click the Create an Upload-to-Flickr Email Address link.** Flickr assigns you a special email address that you can use to send photos and text with your mobile phone or PDA.

4. **From your cell phone or PDA, enter this special email address and send your photos.** They are automatically posted to your Flickr account!

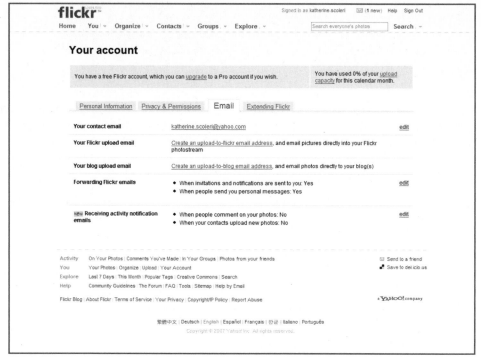

**Figure 12-5**

5. **Click the Your Account link on the top left to get back to the Email tab.**

Now you are ready to post photos from anywhere! Who says you need an office?

# Don't Be a Copy Cat!

Just like any written material, photos are bound to copyright by the owner of the image (unless the photographer says otherwise). If you want to use photos taken by someone else on your blog, ask for permission first.

# Protecting your copyrights

If you post photos you've taken, you need not worry about infringing on someone else's rights. However, you do need to keep in the back of your mind that you have rights to protect, too. Copyright laws are there to protect you, but they don't always cover the seat of your designer jeans. Be sure to place a visible copyright notice on your blog or website and, if necessary, *watermark* your image. Watermarking, or placing an opaque mark over your photo, can deter photo swiping, but also lessens the overall impact of your image, so keep that in mind.

To create a watermark on a photo, you'll need some type of photo editing software, such as Adobe Photoshop. Or plug **watermarking** into a Google search to find out about watermarking software and tutorials. See Figure 12-6 for an example of a watermarked photo.

**Figure 12-6**

*Photo taken by Robyn Pollman*

## Purchasing stock photography

Sometimes you might find yourself needing a photo or image of something that you just can't get yourself. If you run a blog about cooking and you need a photo of a pile of champagne-flavored sorbet, stock photography might be the answer. *Stock photographs* are photos taken by professionals or photography enthusiasts that can be licensed for a fee.

The licensing fees can vary in price depending on what you purchase. Here is a short list of some popular stock imagery websites:

- **Getty Images:** creative.getty.images.com
- **Corbis:** pro.corbis.com
- **iStockphoto:** istockphoto.com

By the way, the champagne-flavored sorbet really exists! Check it out on Chef Melissa's blog, Cooking Diva at cookingdiva.net.

### Stop! Thief!

If you're in doubt about whether a photo is protected, ask permission! The worst the photographer can do is say no.

# Relax, Refresh, Reward

In this chapter, you wrap your brain around the concept of using photos to enhance your website, or otherwise build a blog that will keep people entertained and informed. That's a lot to do in one morning. So get out your blender and start brewing the coffee because we have a wickedly yummy frappucino recipe that will keep you perky in the morning or help you burn the midnight oil.

## Perk up and cool off with a photo-finish frappe

The key to a killer frappe is double-strength coffee. Try doubling the grounds in your coffee maker when you brew it, pour it into a pitcher to cool, and chill in the fridge for a few hours (or even overnight) to have it ready for the morning.

In a blender, blend these ingredients on high until smooth:

*1 cup chilled double-strength coffee*

*3 tablespoons granulated sugar (or Splenda works, too)*

*1 cup low-fat or skim milk*

*2 cups ice*

*Tiny splash of vanilla extract*

*Sprinkle of cinnamon*

Pour into your favorite glass — and top with whipped cream and chocolate shavings if you want to dress to impress. Enjoy!

## To Do List

*Get the scoop on podcasts*

*Become a recording artist*

*Establish an audience*

*Get hip to videocasting*

*Treat your face to a soothing masque*

# the Radio Star!

**W**elcome to the world of podcasting! If your face is twisted up and you're thinking that perhaps you picked up a book about learning a foreign language, don't you fret. Podcasting is a relatively new trend that took form during 2004. It's a fast-growing medium and something you definitely want to know more about.

In this chapter, we give you the lowdown on what podcasting is, why you might want to explore it, and how it can really be a fun way to vamp up your website while enticing visitors to delve deeper and keeping them wanting more. So, climb into your favorite chair and read on!

# What's a Podcast?

A *podcast,* in simplest terms, is a media file that is broadcast over the Internet by the use of syndication feeds. A what? Yeah, that's what we said, too. Podcasters record something, whether it's music or talking, into an audio file, usually in the MP3 format. (Or in some cases, they record video and call it a *videocast.*) The podcaster posts a link to this media file on a blog. The blogging software, in turn, compiles a list of the entries with the linked media files into a list file called an *RSS feed,* as defined in Chapter 11. Subscribers can use these feeds to download those media files and listen to (or view them) at their leisure via a mobile device or web browser.

## Get Hip to the Lingo

Podcasting entails a lot of information and buzzwords that can be tricky to digest, but you can find all of these terms in the handy glossary.

## How a podcast differs from a blog

Most would agree that blogging typically entails a written entry. Podcasts, while they can also include written commentary, include audio and/or video on a regular basis. Posting your favorite song on your blog doesn't necessarily make it a podcast. Podcasts are recognized as regular broadcasts that usually cover a certain topic or range of topics. What you choose to broadcast is up to you, but frequency or regularity is a key component in calling yourself a podcaster. Think of how radio shows air on a regular schedule, and listeners know to tune in at the allotted time. Podcasts don't necessarily need to adhere to a strict schedule, but having some regularity will keep your listeners coming back.

What can be confusing is how the two (podcast and blog) are separate — and in reality, they aren't entirely different in how they're published. It's more about what is published, and how often, that clearly defines podcasting and blogging. The nice part is that while there is a method to the madness, there is also great flexibility. If you have the creativity, you can probably figure out how to combine blogging, podcasting, and video blogging *(vlogging)* all in one neat little package that is packed with juicy tidbits.

## What people are podcasting about

You're intrigued; we can tell! The opportunity to reach millions with the swift click of the Publish button is thrilling. Hang on, though; there's a lot more you must consider. Podcasting has opened people up to endless possibilities for exploring creativity. New podcasts pop up every day, and we're willing to bet there's one for almost every topic you can wrap your freshly highlighted head around.

Podcasting began mostly out of people's desire to broadcast their own radio shows. This is what a lot of people use it for. But as people always do, they pushed the boundaries, and now, podcasting is a useful tool in communicating with the masses. People use podcasting for broadcasting educational classes, updating long-distance family members on what little Suzie is up to, or recording step-by-step instructions and tutorials. No matter what you choose to podcast about, no doubt the Internet has a place for it. Take a look at some unconventional uses of podcasting:

- Group podcasts — get your friends to join in and start a virtual brunch with your long-distance buddies. You can make group podcasts private if you don't want everyone knowing your secrets, or make them public to share your conversation with others.

- Are you a teacher? Podcast extra credit projects and have your students join in on the fun. (Moderated fun, of course. Dang teenagers.)

- Crafty types can videocast a demonstration of knitting in the round or spinning yarn. All the celebs are knitting these days. Who knows, Cameron Diaz might tune in for your latest knit purl podcast.

Just as there are politicians, musicians, artists, mothers, fathers, economists, and footwear fetishists (we know you're familiar with THAT territory), there is a podcast or many podcasts to match. The sky is basically the limit. Want to publish a one-hour show about where to find the best bargains on vintage jewelry or where to find the latest and greatest stock market tips? Go for it!

## The key ingredients to a successful podcast

Keep these few points in mind before you pull out the microphone:

- **Know your topic.** We know that you're the master of making the perfect cupcake in a pinch — or have some other area of expertise that you can speak about. When you start thinking about your podcast, make sure you know enough about the subject you choose to make the podcast meaningful and informative so that people will want to listen again and again.

- **Prepare enough content.** Just like your blog, your podcasts need to have fresh content. It's okay to want to have a podcast about the mating rituals of the grey squirrel. But be prepared with enough material to make more than one show. Think in broader terms. Perhaps covering the mating rituals of animals is a better approach.

- **Express enthusiasm.** Passion is the key to success in anything. If you're excited about your topics, it'll shine through, and your listeners or viewers will appreciate it and become loyal fans.

# Become a Recording Artist

We had a feeling you were going to get hooked on the idea. Podcasting sounds complicated, but in essence, it's no worse than finding a bathing suit that fits right. No no, that's not right. It's much easier than that.

As you may have already guessed, a blog is an easy way to get your podcast out to the masses. If you don't already have a blog, see Chapter 5 for information on how to get a simple one started.

## Tools of the trade

If you decide to podcast, you're going to need a few tools to help you get the show on the road. Here's a handy list:

- **Microphone:** Some computers and laptops have built-in mics. These mics will work for your purposes, but if you're going to put gusto into your podcast, you might consider investing in a good microphone that creates clear audio. Or consider a portable MP3 player with a built-in microphone, which is ideal for on-location podcasting.

- **Recording application:** You need some type of program that records your audio and saves and exports your audio files in MP3 format. Most software gives you the option to edit your audio, which could really come in handy when your cat knocks over your latte in the middle of recording and you let slip something less-than-ladylike. Oops! Ones to try: PodProducer (podproducer.net) and Audacity (audacity.sourceforge.net) are free sound editors. And for the serious podcaster, give ePodcast Producer a shot. It runs you about $250 but can do just about everything. (It's available here: industrialaudiosoftware. com/products/epodcastproducer.html)

### Size Does Matter

If you have a long show, you might consider divvying it up into hourly chunks so your users don't get stuck downloading an enormous file. In this case, bigger isn't better. Not everyone has high-speed these days (why?!), so you still have to keep that in mind.

Doing an Internet search for **podcast recording application** turns up a handful of options. Make sure the software you choose can create MP3 files and not just edit audio. Audacity requires that you download an add-on to convert your shiny new audio file to MP3 format. Don't worry though; it's also totally free.

- **Headphones:** Though they aren't necessary, you can actually increase the quality of your podcast by having headphones. The ear buds you got with your pink iPod do the trick, but having some more serious headphones can aid in creating better audio. Available now are headphones with built-in microphones equipped with noise reduction, so your podcast comes in nice and clear.

- **Extra file space and bandwidth:** You will inevitably upload these audio files. Having a fast Internet connection aids in the transfer time of these large files. Additionally, you'll want to save a backup of your podcasts, which can get large and add up quickly. Having some additional file storage is in the "not necessary, but nice to have" category. Space is cheap these days, so it's not a hassle to find and afford.

## Laying down the audio

Creating an actual MP3 file is not so tricky once you have all the tools you need. If you're still getting your feet wet in regards to creating your first show, don't sweat it. Once you have done it, it will start to come naturally to you.

### Podcast in Your PJs

You don't need a professional recording studio to record a podcast. That's the beauty of podcasting. Find a quiet place and time to record your podcast. Having your three-year old blasting *Blue's Clues* in the background can be distracting, unless it's part of the humor. Limiting background distractions enhances the quality of your show and helps keep you focused on the task at hand.

For these steps, we use the free tool Audacity (audacity.sourceforge.net). It's fast, easy, and works great for beginners. Load up Audacity on your desktop, plug in your headset and microphone, and get started:

1. **Click the Record button (shown in Figure 13-1) and start speaking into the microphone.** Audacity has a nice little toolbar up top with buttons similar to any radio or DVD player with coordinating buttons for record, stop, fast forward, and rewind. Press the red circle Record button and start chatting.

2. **When you've completed your show, go ahead and click the orange Stop button.**

3. **Edit the audio file as desired.** Say you fumbled in the beginning or your dog barked sometime during your heated discussion about politics. Never fear! You can navigate through your podcast and cut out any bits you aren't pleased with. Audacity also allows a few effects to polish your show. Add a fade in or out, put in some silence where your dog barked, or add background music.

## Naming Conventions

If you plan on doing a regular show, or a lot of shows, naming your MP3s something relevant is a smart idea. If you ever need to go back to find a particular show, finding the MP3 will be a cinch if it's labeled properly.

4. **To save your project, choose File→Save Project, name your file, and click Save.** Save your Audacity recording as .aup file in case you need to go back and do additional editing. When you convert your file to MP3, you can't edit it.

5. **When you're pleased with your recording and have edited the car alarm from your introduction, choose File→Export as MP3. Name your show and click Save.** The Edit the ID3 Tags for the MP3 File dialog box pops up, as shown in Figure 13-1, and prompts you to edit the *ID3 tags* for your sound file. These tags, in essence, embed information such as title, artist (in this case, you!), and genre in the MP3 file.

6. **Enter the information you want to include in the ID3 tag and then click OK.**

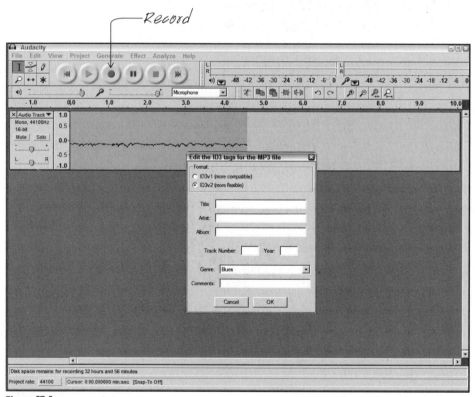

Figure 13-1

# Syndicating a Feed for Your Podcast

Whether you have a hosted blog or are running one on your own, you need to know a few things before you jump in. When you have your amazing podcast ready to go — it's recorded, edited, and converted to MP3 — you're almost there! Remember, your feed syndicates your show. (See Chapter 11 for more on feeds.) People arrive at your site and look for your feed, or they find you in iTunes and start downloading. That all rides on your building an RSS feed that provides a means to distribute your show.

An *RSS enclosure* is a way for an RSS feed to attach some kind of media like a sound file, a photo, or a video. It's most commonly used for incorporating MP3s into an RSS feed for podcasting. You should make sure that by posting your MP3 file, your RSS feed is picking it up. If not, aggregators or other feed readers won't know it's there. This can also affect your listing in iTunes, so it's worth investigating completely.

## Hosted blogs and podcast feeds

Many times, you won't have to worry too much about the details involving things like enclosures and tags if you are using a hosted service. Some hosted services provide RSS creation and feed enclosures for you, and you don't have to do anything but publish a link to your MP3 file in a blog post. However, if your hosted service is of the free variety, such as WordPress.com or Blogger.com, it's best to check the service's site for details on whether it's a supported service. You might have to upgrade to a paid account to gain the ability to upload and store MP3s.

Blogger.com or WordPress.com may not be the best choices in terms of free tools to use in podcasting, but they can be a good place to start as a beginner. You can technically create a podcast feed with any blog. The issue lies mainly in whether you can store the file with your hosted service or whether you need to find web space to store your files. If you have access to a site online where you can store and link to files, podcasting with a free blog tool such as Blogger.com or WordPress.com can work.

One drawback of podcasting with Blogger is that Blogger creates an Atom feed by default. It isn't considered the standard of feeds for podcasting right now, but you can use it. You can use the free service at a site such as FeedBurner.com to translate your Atom feed to an RSS 2.0 feed in a matter of minutes. (You can read more about FeedBurner later in this chapter.)

If you're using a hosted blog service such as TypePad, you needn't worry about enclosures or such technicalities because TypePad handles all of that for you. As long as you publish a link to your MP3 in the body of your blog post, TypePad takes it from there.

## Test Your Feed

When you have your feed running properly, plug it into FeedValidator.org to ensure that there are no errors. An error-free RSS feed is a happy RSS feed.

# Private hosted blogs and podcast feeds

If you've decided to run your own blog on a platform such as Movable Type, WordPress, or ExpressionEngine, you need to fine-tune your RSS files to accept enclosures so that when you publish your precious show on "How to Dress Your Dog in Canine Couture" or "Lisa's Stock Trading Tips," the masses can actually pick it up with their aggregators. Every blog platform has its own protocol for feed enclosures, but generally the steps you need to take are fairly simple:

- **Movable Type** requires you to install a plugin called Feed Manager, which you can download from Movable Type's site. Feed Manager aids you and Movable Type in generating content and enclosures in your feeds so that people can download your podcasts from your site or from podcast directories.

- **WordPress** eliminates the step of having to add plugins. The latest release of WordPress has enclosure support built in, so publishing your podcast is quite simple. You create and upload your MP3 and publish a link to it in your blog post, and WordPress handles the rest. Your RSS feed automatically adds the required enclosure tag to your RSS/Atom feed.

- **ExpressionEngine**, like Movable Type, requires a plugin for your feeds to accept enclosures. A quick search of ExpressionEngine's site turns up its Feed Enclosures plugin and some short instructions. Install the plugin, and when we say "install," it's more like just upload it to a specified folder on your site. Make a couple of minor adjustments to your feed file, and you're in the podcasting business.

## On the Line with the chicks of ChickChat Radio

ChickChat Radio is a show hosted by two of our favorite chicks Heidi Hanzel and Lara Dyan. Heidi and Lara met while working at a telecommunications company and broke free of those 12-hour days, unexpected travel, and unrealistic expectations to realize their own dream of hosting their very own talk radio show.

Heidi and Lara, the beauty and brains behind the talk show ChickChat Radio, define their daily broadcast as a radio show. After all, they *are* hitting the airwaves on XM Satellite Radio these days! However, they distribute and record the show much in the same ways that a lot of podcasters do. As the girls say, "Have a seat on the cheetah couch and pour yourself a drink...."

*(cont'd)*

**Although you define your show as a radio show, how much has the inclusion of syndicating as a podcast played a role in your growing success?**

*Lara says:* "We have embraced podcasting as a way to reach people who don't live in one of the cities we're on the radio.

Radio is an intimate media, and you're supposed to imagine talking to one person when you're on the air. I think podcasting is very similar, but even more intimate — you're whispering right into someone's ear! I imagine that I'm sitting at a bar talking with Heidi and maybe one other person when we're broadcasting. With our show, that other person may be listening to a live stream, the radio, or over an iPod. But they can also time-shift when they listen to our podcast, and take us with them wherever they're going. They're on a treadmill at the gym, on the subway, running errands, or even sitting around at home."

*Heidi adds:* "As we work to play a role in changing the radio industry to include women in the Talk Radio realm, it is a slow process. Reaching people through podcasting is invaluable in areas that have not yet embraced talk radio shows that are not sports or politics."

**What kind of equipment do you girls use to record your show?**

*Lara says:* "I dial in using an ISDN circuit to call in to the studio. The equipment on my end looks like I could land the space shuttle. It's called a Road runner and a mic processor." While the girls do produce the show out of a studio, software and hardware included in creating the audio for their show includes "Cool Edit Pro 2.1 (Adobe Audition), ElectroVoice Microphones, iTunes, and FTP Pro."

**Be honest — you record in your pajamas and fuzzy slippers right? What are some of the pros and cons of doing your job at home?**

*Heidi says:* "I work from our studio 'The Cheetah Lounge,' and it is in an office building. AND, in order to feel the part, I have to dress the part — I have to *dress fun* to *be fun* — which means heels and style as much as possible."

*Lara says:* "I usually do the show in comfortable clothes, often my green cheetah-patterned pajamas! I love working from home because I wasn't a fan of commuting, I like not having to put on 'real' clothes, and I've saved money on not having to buy lunch every day."

**What helps keep you both inspired to come up with new content every day?**

*Lara says:* "I found a $100 bill on the street last year. Rather than trying to figure out what to do with it (spend it, turn it in), my first instinct was to think, 'I can't wait to get on the air and tell Heidi I found a $100 bill!' When I hear a story or something happens and I think to myself, 'I have to tell someone about this,' I know it can make interesting show material."

*Heidi adds:* "Because things on the radio must change . . . there are so few programs by and for women, its just an honor to be among the few around!! And really? It's hard 'not' to have new stuff every day!"

**Have any tips for new podcasters?**

*Heidi and Lara recommend:* "Have fun with whatever you are doing your podcast about. We would think being consistent in the delivery and the sort of show you do would help also. Give the listener what they want and expect! Hosting a podcast is like hosting a cocktail party! Just relax and be yourself! If you're having a good time, your listeners will have a good time."

# Videocasting

*Videocasting,* also known as *video podcasting* or *vlogging* (and sometimes as a *vodcast*), is a podcast done with (or in some cases, in addition to) video rather than MP3 audio. Just as podcasting gained popularity with the increasing trend of portable audio devices, videocasting is yet another phenomenon that's on the rise. Portable devices are now supporting video, and more websites are popping up that can handle and store video, making publishing video a normal occurrence.

As the Internet evolves, the possibilities of what you can do with all these resources become ridiculously abundant. Videocasting can open an entirely new arena of ideas. For example, say our friend Sue, who has those great tutorials on her blog about building architecture with cheese products, wants to expand her blog. She could do a weekly videocast demonstrating different techniques. Move over, Martha Stewart!

## Making the video

You've decided to do a videocast! You don't need a big studio, camera operators, sound technicians, and producers to create your own show. All you need is a camera. A quality webcam or even a video camera will do, and with a little help from some software, you're in

business. Granted, it won't be professional, studio-quality video, but you can get by with a few staples and produce an entertaining video suitable for publishing.

If you're serious, buying a program such as Adobe's Vlog It! software might be a worthy investment. At only $29, you can record and create meaningful videos via your camera, dropping in photos and adding music. You can also create personal newscasts and read from the Vlog It! built-in teleprompter to make it seem as if you're talking right to the camera.

Don't go booking your flight to Cannes just yet; you need to really commit to your project for it to be successful. Be patient, be realistic, and have fun with it.

## Video file formats

You can distribute video a couple of different ways. For some, letting users download video files in advance of watching them allows them to watch at their leisure, offline or on a portable device. *Streaming* allows the viewer to skip around the video without downloading the whole videocast, although viewers can run into speed issues and choppy video streams. Related to streaming, video can be uploaded by the videocaster to third-party sites for viewing, where bandwidth can be less of an issue for the viewer.

MP4 is the file format for storing digital audio and video and is one of the most common formats used for videocasting. You handle publishing MP4 files for aggregation in feeds much the same way that you handle publishing MP3 files for podcasting. Publishing a link to your video in your feed-enclosure-enabled blog should do the trick.

## Where to host your videos

Saving video for streaming can be a strain on bandwidth, causing video to skip or hang. Some people find a solution in a third-party website such as YouTube, shown in Figure 13-2, or Google Video (video.google. com), shown in Figure 13-3. On both sites, users can upload and link to their videos without using their own hosts' resources.

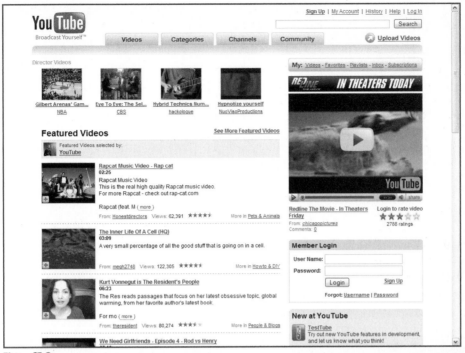

Figure 13-2

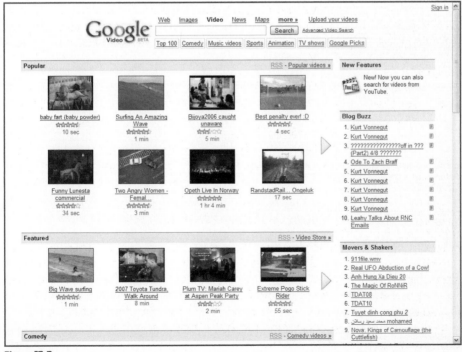

Figure 13-3

## Copyrights and Video

If you do choose to upload video to YouTube or Google, be sure that the videos are your creation or that you've been given proper permission. You don't want the copyright police coming after you for posting protected materials.

Posting video that is hosted on YouTube or Google is pretty easy to do. Sign up for an account on YouTube and follow the easy instructions to upload your video. After you upload it, the site provides you with a code snippet to copy and paste into your blog entry, as shown in Figure 13-4.

Figure 13-4

# Blast It to iTunes

People need to know about your podcast in order for them to download and listen to it. You have it on the Internet, but how is anyone going to find it if you don't publicize?

The first order of business is to march your butt over to iTunes and submit your podcast for inclusion in its podcast directory. To do this, follow these steps:

1. **Download and install the latest version of iTunes on your computer** (apple.com/itunes/download). iTunes must be running when you submit your podcast.

2. **Click the Submit a Podcast button in the iTunes Music Store under the Podcast section (see Figure 13-5).**

Figure 13-5

3. **Submit your RSS feed using the site's simple form, shown in Figure 13-6.**

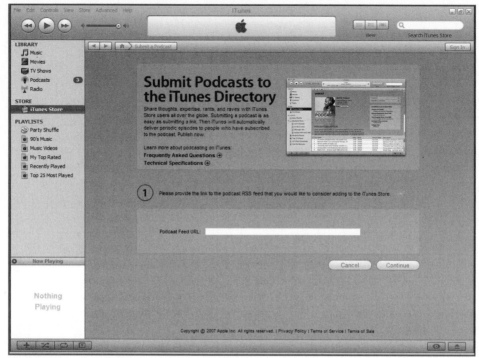

**Figure 13-6**

Working with iTunes definitely gets your show on the road to discovery and makes it accessible to its vast number of users who download media on a regular basis. The numbers vary, but Apple, the company behind iTunes, reports an average of about 10 million active users (and the number is climbing). That's a big opportunity to reach a decent chunk of people.

## Did You Know?

Most say the name *podcast* was derived from Apple Computer's iPod technology, although the term *podcasting* was one of a few names suggested by developers to describe portable audio braodcasting in 2004.

When people find your podcast and start downloading your shows to their iPods, you need to get them hooked and coming back for more.

The beauty of podcasting, especially in tandem with blogging, is that your audience can come from anywhere, as long as each person has access to an Internet connection. Of course, fans won't be piling up at the door for your next podcast unless you build a base of frequent listeners. Your listing in iTunes leaves the door open for any stray subscribers looking for advice on how to sew clothes for their Bichons.

## Stay active!

Staying active in the blogging and podcasting community always helps you obtain valuable listeners and continued subscribers. You have to give only a little to get a lot. Granted, some podcasters have an automatic fan base and simply put up their feed and watch the traffic and downloads go up. But most of us need to get out there and participate.

A tactic you might want to consider is to team with other podcasters to do a side project, or ask podcasters or bloggers you admire to participate in your ventures. Go interview that woman who knits the amazing felt socks, or hit up the chick who has a radio show on Sirius. You won't always get what you're after, but you never know unless you give it a shot.

# Podcasting Services You Need to Know About

When you're ready to rock and roll with your new podcast, promote it in as many places as possible to stir up new subscribers. You're on your way to stardom — just hold your horses and take notice of a few more services you'll benefit from knowing about.

## iPodder

**iPodder** (ipodder.org) has one of the largest podcast directories online, so you may want to look into adding your podcast to the mix. (iPodder was one of the original sites that produced a now-defunct *aggregator* program — similar to the popular iTunes — called Lemon. Lemon allowed people to subscribe and listen to podcast MP3s.) Table 13-1 lists several popular podcast directories.

## FeedBurner

**FeedBurner** (feedburner.com) helps you get your podcast to the masses. Sign up for an account with FeedBurrner, submit your RSS feed, and FeedBurner optimizes your feed automatically. With an account, you can keep track of how many subscribers you have, what they use as a primary subscription service, and be alerted when your RSS feed has any errors. The site is chock-full of tutorials and even provides statistics so you can monitor your growing following.

## Table 13-1      Popular Podcasting Directories

| Directory | URL |
| --- | --- |
| iPodder | ipodder.org |
| iTunes | apple.com/itunes (requires iTunes software) |
| Podcast Alley | podcastalley.com |
| Podcast Pickle | podcastpickle.com |
| Yahoo! Podcasts | podcasts.yahoo.com |

# Relax, Refresh, Reward

In this chapter, you should have gotten a vice grip on what podcasting really is and how to publish one. But before you go running out to the nearest electronics store for recording equipment, we think you should take a break and absorb all that information.

While you're absorbing, why not absorb the cleansing moisturizers in your favorite face masque? All this reading can be tiring to the eyes and skin.

## Podcast pampering sessions

Cucumber is a fabulous and easy treat for tired skin. It's a remedy for many ailments — it can soothe itchiness, tighten your pores, and reduce puffiness. Pamper your face with the recipes that follow, or just toss a couple of thin slices of fresh cucumber soaked in witch hazel over your closed eyes for a few minutes to reduce circles and puffiness.

### Cleansing cucumber masque

For troublesome skin, use this easy recipe to help clear and freshen your face. In a blender, combine the following until smooth:

½ chilled cucumber, peeled

1 tablespoon nonfat dry milk

1 teaspoon plain yogurt

Brush the mixture on your face with a small marinating brush (or paintbrush if that's what you've got) and let it sit for 10–15 minutes. Rinse well with lukewarm water. Ahhh!

### Make me glow masque

This simple mix will brighten and refresh you after a long day, and it helps beat the oilies!

1 teaspoon chilled cucumber, finely grated

Small splash of rose water

Mix well and apply the masque evenly over skin and neck. Allow it to rest for 10 minutes and rinse thoroughly.

# III Love IT

"A girl should be two things: classy and fabulous."

—Coco Chanel

# 14

## To Do List

- Decide if a private blog or a public blog is best for you

- Learn how to protect yourself and why

- Get the goods on Google

- Use your head about what's appropriate to share

- Try out a secret tasty trick!

# Be Mysterious!

**W**hile most bloggers see their blogs as a way to express themselves publicly, it's not always wise to be a completely open book. Sure, you can delete something you've posted, but in the age of RSS feeds, web archiving, and the overall savvy of web users, chances are, if you've put it out there once, it's there for good . . . somewhere. Keep this in mind as you read this chapter about how and when to protect your privacy and whether or not to post that photo of you and your best bud doing body shots at Mardi Gras.

# Covering Your Assets

Blogging, in a way, is a form of exhibitionism, a way for Everyday Jane to shout her opinions from the virtual rooftops while staying somewhat safe and anonymous, tucked behind her laptop. But, not all people want their innermost thoughts immortalized in HTML for the entire world to read. Then why bother blogging, you may ask?

## Private blogs: Behind closed doors

Some people want to blog for themselves as a catharsis, and a blog platform enables them to do so easily, while archiving their writing and providing a simple printable display. While you could do something similar with a word processing program or a good old-fashioned journal, some people are techie types and prefer to use a blog platform to their advantage.

Blog platforms also allow you to categorize your entries, order them easily by date, and clearly chronicle whatever it is you're keeping track of, be it your daily life, food intake, or workout regimen. A blog is usually accessible anywhere that has an Internet connection. The same can't be said for that diary crammed under your mattress.

Some hosted blogging services, like Blogger, offer easy ways to make your blog private by just clicking a few settings. (See more on hosted blogs in Chapter 5.) Your blog is viewable to the public, or open, by default.

With just a few steps in Blogger, you can set your blog to be completely private, visible to you and you alone:

1. **Log in to your Blogger account at** blogger.com. If you don't have a Blogger account but wish to set one up, please review Chapter 5 for help.

2. **From the dashboard, click the Settings link.**

3. **On the submenu across the top, click Permissions.** The Blogger Permissions page appears, as shown in Figure 14-1.

4. **Under Blog Readers, select Only Blog Authors as your privacy permission.** The alert in Figure 14-2 appears, confirming that you wish to allow only authors to view your blog.

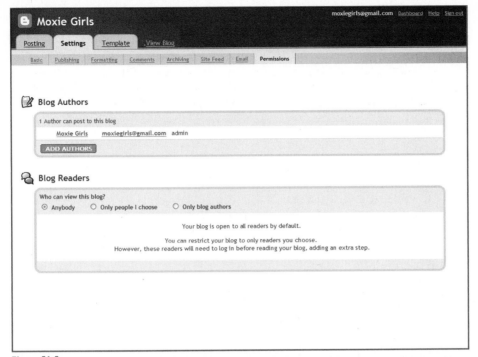

Figure 14-1

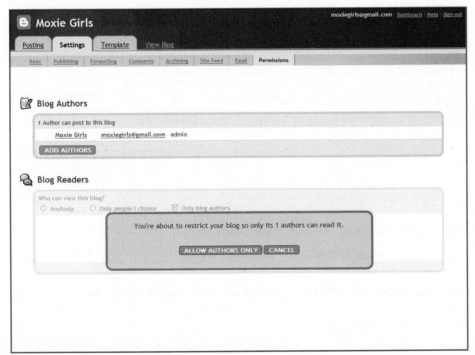

Figure 14-2

5. **Click the Allow Authors Only button in the alert box.** The page changes to display that your blog is now restricted and visible only to you. When people visit your URL, they'll be greeted with a message that your blog is private, just like in Figure 14-3.

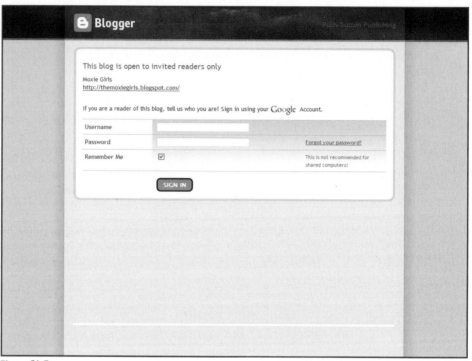

Figure 14-3

## Semiprivate blogs: Peeping through the keyhole

Catharsis is great and all, but sometimes you need to bend an ear. You need someone to listen and perhaps offer some advice. Keeping your blog secret doesn't allow for that. If you're blogging about your new baby, it makes perfect sense to keep the blog private, but what if you want to share with family or close friends? This is where the semiprivate blog comes in.

A *semiprivate blog* is one that allows you to set varying permissions based on membership groups. You can accomplish this with a blog platform such as ExpressionEngine or Movable Type, but the quick 'n' easy way is an out-of-the-box solution. A handful of hosted blogging services allow this, including Blogger, but our favorite for this sort of blog is Vox by Six Apart.

We minced no words in Chapter 5, where we sang the praises of Vox, and this is no exception. The folks at Six Apart have made it extremely easy for you to have a public blog, private blog, and semiprivate blog all rolled into one just by using Vox. As a Vox member, you can set up various member groups in your Vox Neighborhood. From there, you have several options for who can view and comment on each individual entry or the blog as a whole.

With Vox, you have the choice to set your entries to be viewable by:

- Anyone, meaning everyone . . . including your aunt Mabel and your boss
- You only
- Your Vox Neighborhood, which is essentially all of your member groups, but not the public
- Friends only
- Family only
- Friends *and* family

You can see how this would provide the opportunity for you to share only what you want to share and give you some control over with whom you share it. While you still have the freedom to set the permissions by individual entry, in the following steps, we demonstrate how to set all of your blog entries to semiprivate by default. When finished, your entries will be viewable only by Vox members you have marked as friends and family, unless you indicate otherwise.

Follow these steps to quickly change the default privacy setting in Vox:

1. **Log in to your Vox account at** vox.com. If you don't have a Vox account but wish to set one up, go to Chapter 5.

2. **From the home page, click Account in the upper-right corner.** You're taken to Your Public Profile page.

3. **Click Posting Defaults in the sidebar navigation.** The Default Settings for New Posts page appears, as shown in Figure 14-4.

4. **From the Viewable By drop-down menu, choose Friends and Family.**

5. **From the Allow Comments From drop-down menu, choose Friends and Family.**

6. **From the Allow Tags From drop-down menu, choose Friends and Family.**

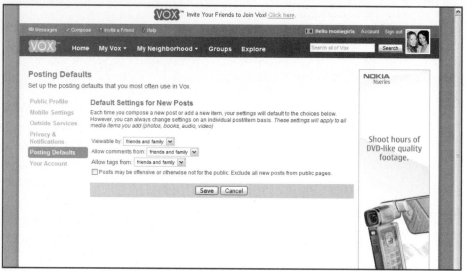

**Figure 14-4**

7. **Determine if your posts could, overall, be offensive and choose whether to mark the blog as such.**

8. **Click Save.** You're finished!

You may change these settings at any time and in any combination. As mentioned, you can also set different permissions on individual entries. If you know that your blog will be primarily private or semiprivate, setting the default permissions is usually a timesaver.

## Public blogs: Open door policy

It's fairly obvious that most blogs are public. If it's out there and anyone and everyone who stumbles across it can read it, it's a public blog. Public blogs consist of a variety of topics, from personal to genre-specific, but the sole fact that anyone can look at them is what makes them public blogs.

Public blog does *not* mean that it belongs to the public at large, nor do the masses have any entitlement over one's blog simply because it's publicly viewable. Some bloggers feel pressure from their readers to *provide*. You don't have to provide anything other than what you've promised. If you have a business blog or a blog that advertises some specific service to its readers, yes, it's important to provide what you've touted. However, if you have a personal blog that you manage and update at your leisure, your only responsibility is to yourself, not the public.

A public blog may or may not have comments open. Again, a public blog doesn't belong to the public; it's simply visible to it. The choice of whether to allow readers to engage with your blog by opening comments or trackbacks is entirely up to you. (See more on comments and trackbacks in Chapter 9.)

# Google: Friend and Foe

Just in case you've been trapped under a pile of shoulder pads for the last decade, Google (google.com) is the world's leading search engine. Google is seemingly all-knowing and just about everyone's go-to when looking for . . . well, anything!

## Public Perk

Public blogs are the most popular sort of blog for a reason. Having a publicly visible blog, especially one with open comments, allows readers to interact with the blog owner, which creates a connection and a reason for someone to become a regular reader. If your blog is relevant to your business, you almost definitely will want to keep a public blog. Just because it's public doesn't mean you can't still take measures to protect yourself and your identity.

## Privacy patrol

To some, the Internet seems relatively anonymous and safe. It's huge! There is a *world* of websites out there! How could anyone possibly discover little ol' *you* in the sea of blogs, commercial sites, and ubiquitous porn? One word, kiddo: Google.

To others, the Internet is a terrifying prospect filled with ne'er-do-wells, trolls, hackers, and child predators. While all of these things may be true on some levels, there is a happy medium. The Internet can be a wonderful tool and resource, letting you forge friendships and create a sense of community. However, if it's not detrimental to your business, consider keeping some things to yourself. Everyone loves a woman with mystery! Here are some ways to guard your privacy:

- Protect yourself by not divulging overly personal information in a public blog.
- Protect your personal life by using appropriate screen names and discretion when discussing your workplace and area of residence.
- Use caution when sharing photos of your family.
- Protect your email address and choose one that conceals your true identity or place of business.
- Register your domain name using private registration to conceal your personal information from WHOIS lookup.

## Go Google Yourself!

If you haven't already, hit Google.com and type your full name. See what comes up! If you have a domain name, type that to see where it comes up in the Google ranking and if others are mentioning you. A little ego check never hurt, and it lets you know what people are saying about you and what others might find if they go looking for you.

The term *Google,* as a verb, was added to the Oxford English Dictionary in 2006. The act of *Googling* means to look someone or something up on Google.com. An example might be, "I Googled your new boyfriend and found out on his blog that he collects toenails in his spare time." Dump that guy, by the way.

## The Google basics

Google sends out what are often called *spiders, bots* (short for *robots*), or *crawlers* to follow links from page to page throughout the Internet. When it finds a new web page it hasn't indexed, it crawls the code on the page and sends the information gathered back to Google. Bots visit indexed websites again and again so the listing stays fresh, but how often they do this is unclear and may vary.

When Google bots crawl your blog's content and links, they pick up the content and send it back to Google to index in the search engine. Google indexes just about anything you talk about, so if you happened to mention frozen pudding pops in an entry, even if you blogged it in 2004, you may get hits for *years* by people searching Google for frozen pudding pops. (Trust us on this one. People *love* their frozen pudding pops.) Remember this if you decide to blog about your boss's bad toupee or your mother-in-law's crappy meatloaf. Things have a way of coming back to haunt you.

## Benefits to blocking and reasons to rank

It's possible to block Google from indexing your website. Assorted scripts are available that — if not on your own, with the help of a web developer or a tech-savvy friend — you can implement into your own blog to block the spiders from crawling your code and content. Try searching Google or the search engine of your choice for terms like **block Google bots** or **script to block Google spiders.** Some blog services, like Blogger, WordPress.com, and Vox, offer to block them for you if you choose to do so in your settings.

There are plenty of reasons folks would want Google to index their sites and a few major reasons they wouldn't. Chew on some of these and decide if blocking Google and other search engines from crawling your site is the best choice for you.

### Business or pleasure?

Do you have a personal or community blog for recreational fun or a blog to represent your business? A lot of bloggers have *both,* so it's important to consider what you're willing to share on your personal blog and if you mind your professional connections stumbling across it. A good rule is that if it's not your clients' problem, they don't need to hear about it. So having them know that you made out with that bartender last Friday, but he hasn't called since, *might* not be the best way to maintain a professional image.

If you do wish to run a blog for your personal use and have a professional business presence online or off, you may want to make your personal blog private (or semi-private) or take the steps to block Google from indexing your blog, even though it doesn't guarantee privacy. It's simply a small step. You may also choose to use a pseudonym for your personal thoughts. You can read more about blogging and business in Chapter 4.

### Help wanted

You've applied for this fantastic job at this hot fashion magazine. It's a high-profile position under the editor in chief. You get to go to all the best parties, get samples of all the haute clothes, and have finally landed the job of your dreams. At least, that's what you thought after nailing the interview. Only, the magazine's human resources department Googled you and found that blog entry from two years ago where you described sneaking into your current boss's office to take sexy pictures on the desk in barely-there La Perla for your boyfriend — complete with photos.

While not all employers would let that deter them from hiring you (we're willing to bet some would even consider that an asset to the team), it's probably not how you *meant* to portray yourself to your new colleagues. There is a very good chance that you might not only lose that career opportunity, but potentially your current job, too. Consider making entries such as this private (or semi-private) and/or blocking search engines overall. Hey, at least you had the good taste to choose La Perla . . . you minx!

### Shameless self-promotion

Are you your own business? Perhaps you're an actor, singer, author, comedian, musician, columnist, artist; whatever it may be . . . you need to be discovered! If the purpose of your blog is to gain exposure, allowing Google to crawl your site and index your URLs is a great step. Make sure you also include plenty of appropriate keywords to help target user searches even further and allow you to climb in the Google ranks. (See Chapter 16 for more on keywords.) You may still choose to use discretion when discussing your personal life, but given the nature of your career, it makes perfect sense to use your name or stage name.

## Protection and Common Sense

If you choose to have a public blog, it's still possible to maintain privacy and distinction between the Internet and your personal life. The power's in your hands to say as much or as little as you're comfortable with. Discretion, along with a few handy web tools, can deter others from prying too much into your offline life, keeping you and your family safe.

# Use protection

Whether you choose to block Google, you can strengthen the protection of your online presence in other ways, including requiring your blog readers to sign in with passwords, adjusting your blog's privacy settings, using a screen name or pseudonym, establishing an email account for your blog only, and registering your domain privately.

### Password protection

If you're hosting your own blog with a hosting provider, you may choose to require users to read your blog by logging in with a global login and password. Some content management systems and blog platforms offer members features that let them grant access with their own login and password. If you use a hosted blogging service, such as Vox, adjust your privacy settings for the appropriate level, and that should work just fine.

### Privacy settings

If you're using a hosted blogging service, like Blogger, WordPress.com, or Vox, you can choose to remove your site from the search engine indexes, including Google, by setting the preferences on your account. You may want to check your particular blog service's documentation for more information.

If you're using WordPress.com, you can change the privacy setting in a few easy steps:

1. **Log in to your WordPress.com account and select the blog you wish to edit.** WordPress.com brings you to your Dashboard.

2. **From your Dashboard, click the Options link at the top.**

3. **Click Privacy in the submenu that appears.**

4. **Choose your privacy level.** WordPress.com gives you a few options, as shown in Figure 14-5. If you wish to have WordPress.com omit you from Google searches, but leave you visible to regular visitors, choose I Would Like to Block Search Engines, But Allow Normal Visitors.

5. **Click the Update Options button.** Your blog is now blocked from Google indexing!

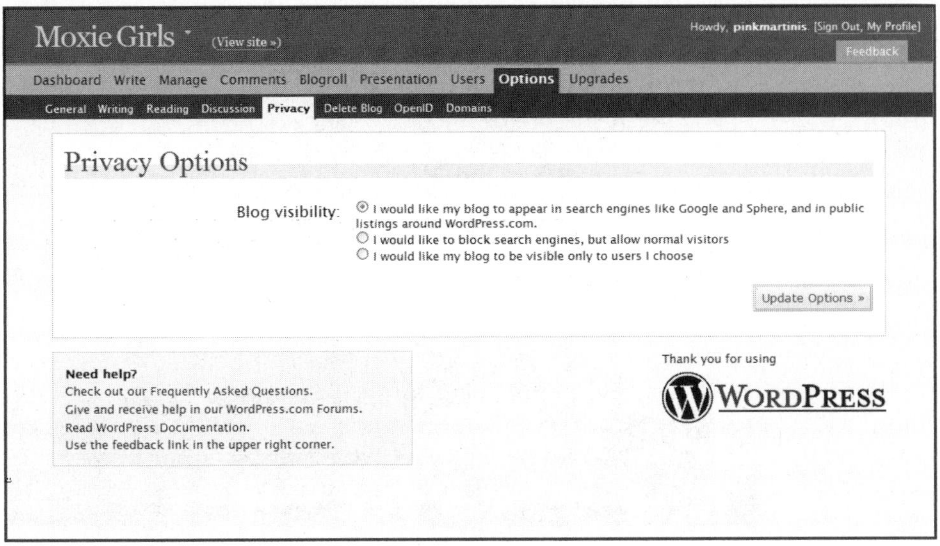

**Figure 14-5**

## Screen names, handles, and pseudonyms

Unless you're a public presence, online or off, it's probably a good idea to avoid using your last name on your blog. If it's not necessary, skipping it can help protect your identity, especially if you have a very unusual name. Jane Smith is fairly common, but if your name is Heaven Tenderfoot and someone hacks your email or uses your name, people will assume it's you. If you'd prefer to avoid using your real name at all, consider choosing an alter-ego! Give her a name and even a different angle of your persona, if that's what you want to put out there. Just because you're Louise the Librarian by day doesn't mean you can't be the Grammar Goddess after the kids are tucked in.

## Anonymous email

Having a blog can generate not only a lot of comments, but also a lot of spam in your inbox, so you'll want to have an email address you don't mind getting picked up by the spam bots when they crawl your site. You also want to avoid using email addresses that include your real name or place of business. Sign up for a Gmail account (gmail.com) or other free email service and choose an email address that you'll use — but that's separate from your personal email accounts. Some bloggers choose to use an email address that is the same or similar to their domain name. If the domain name is StellaLikesCosmos.com, her Gmail address might be cosmostella@gmail.com or the more obvious stellalikescosmos@gmail.com.

## Private domain registration

When registering your domain name (as described in Chapter 6), consider adding private registration to your site. *Private registration* masks your personal information, such as name, contact phone, and registrant mailing address from those who search for your domain in the WHOIS domain lookup.

Private registration carries a small extra fee that varies from registrar to registrar, but GoDaddy.com charges roughly $4.99–$9.99 for this service, depending on the promotion that they're offering. You may think that just entering false information would be the ticket to getting around the fee, but it's against most registrars' policies and prevents you from properly managing your domain and receiving relevant emails and information from the registrar.

## Common sense prevails

When in doubt, use your common sense with regard to what you unleash on the Internet. If you are the type who likes to throw caution to the wind, or you are generally not concerned about your identity being out there, go crazy. But if you're like most, you can find a balance between full-on disclosure and keeping yourself under lock and key. Consider being careful when posting personal identifying details and photos.

### Personal details

Just because you have a blog doesn't mean you need to give us your address, Social Security number, and first-born child. It's wise to protect the identity of not only yourself, but your entire family. Give them nicknames, too! If they're involved in your blog, you can even let them choose their own.

Don't discuss where you live in great detail. Many websites and some blog platforms allow you to use maps to place your exact location at times of posting or where you were when a certain photo was taken. While these features are very cool, think for a moment if you really want the entire world to know that. Do you want to make that information accessible? Do you want *everyone* to know which playground you and your kids frequent? Do you want *everyone* to know exactly which Starbucks you haunt, especially if you've posted photos of yourself?

While you probably won't have throngs of paparazzi camped out waiting for you to emerge — tall, no-whip mocha in hand — and the chances of a stalker are slim, it's generally best to protect yourself as much as possible. Again, discretion is the word of the day.

### Sharing photos

It's important to protect your name, but your face needs protecting, too. While many people choose to share their faces but not their names, you can still be recognized! If you're the head of the PTA but dabble on the dark side, don't be surprised if little Timmy's dad recognizes you as Mistress Leatherlover at the next bake sale. We're just sayin'. . . .

Posting photos of children is more commonplace online these days, but we recommend using caution when choosing where to post them and which photos to post. There are a lot of dodgy creeps out there, so it's best to keep your photos in the family, or at least protected.

## Flickr Family

If you need to feed your urge to display family photos but aren't quite sure how to protect them, try creating an account on Flickr.com. Flickr allows you to create your very own photo gallery (for free!) and you can set image privileges to a few levels of privacy. The privacy levels range from full privacy, to friends, family, or friends and family only. You can find more on Flickr in Chapter 12.

# Relax, Refresh, Reward

After locking down your blog tighter than a sports bra, you might crave a little personal inter-action. Invite a few friends over for a night of *Sex and the City* on DVD, whip up a pitcher of Cosmos, and make these quick-and-easy hors d'oeuvres that seem super fancy — but you can make in 10–15 minutes with stuff you may already have on hand. You don't have to divulge your secret if you don't want to. Let your guests think you slaved for hours over them!

## Herbed Apricot *Amuse-Bouche*

*1 tube of refrigerated crescent rolls (or you can use frozen pastry dough, like Phyllo)*

*1 jar of apricot jam or preserves*

*1 box of Garlic & Herb Laughing Cow cheese (or you can substitute part-skim ricotta cheese combined with herbs like minced parsley, thyme, a bit of lemon zest, and garlic)*

1. Heat the oven according to the crescent roll instructions.

2. Unroll the crescent triangles and lay them out on a cookie sheet, allowing enough space between them to let them puff up without touching. (If you're using Phyllo dough, you can cut the dough into squares to make it easier, if you like.)

3. Take a small spoonful of the cheese and put a little dollop in the center of the widest part of the crescent.

4. Add a tiny dollop of apricot jam to the top of the cheese.

5. Be sure to leave a nice margin so that you can gather up the excess dough and make little pouches, twisting the top and pinching the sides so the good-ies inside don't burst out during cooking.

6. Toss in the oven for about 10–12 minutes, keeping an eye on them to make sure they don't open or that you don't overbrown them. (That's a fancy way to say "Don't burn them!")

7. Let them cool for a bit until they can be handled, put on a tray, and serve!

They taste great with Cosmos, and if you opt to use the reduced-fat or sugar-free varieties of these ingredients, you can keep it figure-friendly. Enjoy!

## To Do List

- Become a joiner
- Share your thoughts
- Link to others
- Get over the newbie blues
- Throw a party for pennies

# Be the Belle of the Blogs

If you ever attended a high school formal, you remember how gut-wrenching (yet exciting!) the whole affair can be. Does your hair look just right? What if you trip when you enter? What will the pictures look like? Do you have the hottest dress? What if you accidentally tuck it into your pantyhose?

Launching your first blog can produce similar preprom anxiety. Take a moment to read through this chapter's great tips for increasing exposure to your blog through forging relationships with other bloggers. A few clever moves on your part, such as appropriate etiquette and overall respect, can take you far and help ensure your blog's debut isn't as bitter as the spinach in your prom date's teeth.

## Make Sure to Mingle

We discussed group blogs and community blogs in Chapter 3, but some sites, such as blog communities and social networks, are much larger than the blogs they contain. Some offer huge resources of link lists and forums, as well as member features that allow you to connect with other people like yourself. Becoming a member of these sites can grant you access to all of their members and sometimes their advertisers, as well as any other tools, contests, or opportunities they might offer.

## Blog communities and networks

Of the many blog communities/networks out there, some are exclusive or topic-specific, and some are more general. Most require registration in order for you to become a member or be listed on their blogrolls. This helps communities keep their sites spam- and troll-free! Here are some of our favorites to get you started.

### Clicking with a Clique

Do a web search for communities that blog about things you're interested in. Visit Google.com (or the search engine of your choice), and type in **blog communities** for a general search. Or, if you want to search for specific communities and networks, include the topic in the search term. Some examples might be *mommyblog communities, mom communities, woman blog network, "blog community" knitting,* and so on. When you find a community or network that strikes your fancy, register and jump in!

### BlogHer.org

BlogHer (shown in Figure 15-1) was created as an opportunity for all kinds of women bloggers to gain greater exposure, education, and community within the blogosphere. In its own words, BlogHer "evangelizes blogging by, for and to *women.*" BlogHer also hosts a conference every year for BlogHer members, and nonmembers interested in joining, to commune and share ideas on panels and through social events. Be sure to check out our interview with one of BlogHer's founders in "On the Line with Elisa Camahort of BlogHer.org," later in this chapter.

### ClubMom.com

The ClubMom community was created with moms in mind! Established in 1999 by Meredith Vieira (of *The View* and now the *Today Show)* and Andrew Shue (social activist, philanthropist, and former regular on *Melrose Place!),* it has more than 40 blogs written by seasoned mommybloggers. (See Figure 15-2.) Plus, you can find on the site an ask-a-mom feature, message boards, sweepstakes, and a library of over 20,000 articles written by moms *for moms.*

**Figure 15-1**

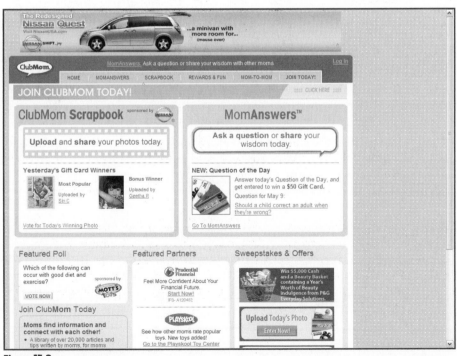

**Figure 15-2**

## ...works:
## ...ace

Social networks aren't always great to *blog* on, but they're fabulous for networking. Much like a game of Six Degrees of Kevin Bacon, these sites allow you to network with other people with similar interests and plenty of other bloggers. You may have someone on your friends list who has a stylist, who has a cousin, who has someone on *her* friends list, who has a Pilates instructor, who knows Kevin Bacon. Who knew? Consider signing up for one or more of these popular sites to help get the word out about your blog and build relationships on the 'net.

The grand poobah of social networks — and by far, the most popular — MySpace (shown in Figure 15-3) is *the* social hub for anyone from 16 to 60. Everyone from artists, authors, and rock bands to teenagers, bloggers, and your receptionist seems to use MySpace.

Some MySpace users are *very* into it and forget there's a whole world of Internet beyond its domain. Many, especially blogging purists and business professionals, have the account as a supplement to their blog or business, not as their primary hangout.

While a lot of negative attention is paid to MySpace, especially when it comes to predators and scam artists, signing up for MySpace can definitely be fun, as long as you maintain the same level of discretion and privacy discussed in Chapter 14. It can be a great boon for your blog and a way to get those who rarely venture away from MySpace to explore life beyond their Top 8.

## Don't make us call Dateline!

We assume you're of the age of legal consent, but if you aren't or you're helping set up a blog or profile for someone who is underage, be sure to use caution when setting up a MySpace account. You can set profiles to private, which is a wise choice if the user is under the age of 18. Private profiles are visible only to those on your friends list.

Make sure you open a dialogue with your kids and teens about what is appropriate to post on their website, blog, or MySpace profile, and remind them that they aren't anonymous. If you're setting up MySpace for your child, make sure you keep the login and password, as well. This is not to spy on your teen; it's merely a way for you to periodically monitor the sorts of people that are contacting her or him.

Do you know everyone who appears on your teen's friends list? If not, ask your teen about them. If these "friends" are adults, let your child know that unless you know them, it's inappropriate. The Internet can be a perfectly fun and safe place to be as long as you protect yourself and your family, especially your kids, from the nut jobs.

Figure 15-3

# Don't Be a Wallflower: Linking and Quoting Etiquette

Linking to other blogs in your entries or in the sidebar of your site is called *blogrolling,* and the list of links itself is called a *blogroll,* as shown in Figure 15-4. It's standard blog practice and usually encouraged. Most of the time, people love to be linked. It drives up their ranking in Google and grants them a tiny slice of advertising to your blog readers. Of course, these perks apply to your blog, too. Most importantly, linking allows bloggers to connect! Quoting other bloggers in your entries is also welcomed. Although, if you do so, don't forget to credit the source and link back.

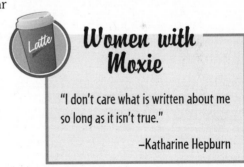

## Women with Moxie

"I don't care what is written about me so long as it isn't true."

–Katharine Hepburn

*Blogroll*

**Figure 15-4**

# Blogrolls and link sharing

The blogosphere is founded on community. If we didn't read each other's blogs, there'd be no point to it all. Part of the fun of blogging is linking to other blogs. It allows you to share your reads with those who read your blog, potentially turning them on to someone new. Perhaps you've been too timid to comment on blogs you like. Linking to them can let the bloggers know that you dig what they're saying. When the blog owners check their referral stats, it leads them to *your* blog. Consider it an extremely subtle calling card.

BlogRolling.com (blogrolling.com) was one of the first services available to bloggers to create link lists. Using a simple script provided by BlogRolling, you can generate a link list, or *blogroll,* as it's most commonly known, to display

## Blogging's Party Favors

Much like the days when you dyed your satin pumps to match your corsage, there was a time when using small rectangular buttons or banners to link back to other blogs was all the rage. Some bloggers do still offer them and display them proudly. Some consider it a bit passé, sort of like banana clips. It's really a matter of personal preference. Our recommendation is to do whatever you want, just do it with style and restraint. Make it work!

on your site. BlogRolling will check whether a blog has updated and display the update on your blogroll with an indicator you customize through BlogRolling.com. Currently, BlogRolling is a free service that lets you create multiple link lists, create private link lists, and add people to your blogroll with one click.

You can also use various RSS feed services (flip back to Chapter 11 if you need to find out what feed services are) to post blogrolls on your site. Bloglines.com offers a small script that produces a blogroll of the public feeds to which you subscribe when you insert it into the HTML on your blog. Some blog services, such as TypePad and WordPress, offer link lists as a feature of the service.

## Being Miss Manners

Whether you're the center of attention or a shrinking violet, it's always important to be courteous. Here are some myths and oversights in linking etiquette that we'd like to clear up for you:

- **Asking permission:** Unless the blog owner specifically requests it on her or his site or it's required by the blog service, it's really not necessary to ask permission if you wish to link to someone. Feel free to link at will. You're welcome to alert the blog owner that you've linked to her or him, but actually requesting a link from a blog author is sometimes met with confusion. "It's nice that they asked, but . . . why?"

- **Linking to images:** Directly linking to people's images on their servers is frowned upon. It is equally frowned upon to right-click and save the image to your desktop and then upload it as your own — unless it's a photo in public domain. If you wish to link to someone's image, use a text link to the entry itself or email the blog author first to ask if it's okay.

- **Tracking it back:** As a new blogger, you'd probably want to know if someone were talking about your entries, wouldn't you? Other bloggers would, too. Trackbacks can help! When you *trackback* to someone's blog entry, that person's blog software creates a link on her or his blog in that particular entry linking back to *your* entry. Thus, anyone visiting that blog entry can click through to your blog to read more. Google and other search bots can also pick up your link on the other person's blog, allowing you a potentially higher rank. (You'll find more on trackbacks in Chapter 9.)

- **Posting direct quotes:** Being quoted can be extremely flattering! However, quoting someone without proper credit is plagiarism, and that's just bad juju. If you wish to quote someone else's blog entry, be sure to include just a snippet of the original entry, not the full entry itself. Also, make sure to link back to that entry and trackback to it as well, if that feature is available. It alerts the blog author that you're discussing her or his entry and allows your users to click through to the full entry on the original author's blog.

# On the Line with
# Elisa Camahort of BlogHer.org

Elisa Camahort is one of three founders of BlogHer, along with Jory Des Jardins and Lisa Stone. As President of Events and Marketing, Elisa generously took a few moments out of her very busy schedule to chat with us.

**BlogHer is such a phenomenon! Why do you feel that a community for women who blog is so important?**

Jory Des Jardins, Lisa Stone, and I decided to hold the first BlogHer Conference in 2005 to answer the nagging question, "Where are the women bloggers?" The conference was designed to answer that question with a resounding "Right here!" After the conference, attendees made clear they wanted to "meet" every day. Hence the BlogHer.org community hub was born.

BlogHer has a pretty simple mission. Our mission is to create opportunities for education, exposure, community, and economic empowerment for women bloggers. That mission and just about everything we do is driven by what the community tells us is most important to them.

**What do you think is the most important feature or portion of your website? Why?**

One of the biggest complaints from women bloggers has been that if you weren't one of the very entrenched uber-geeky bloggers or rabid political bloggers, as measured by the very limited metric of incoming links, then it was hard to be found … and hard to find other bloggers with your interests. There was simply no clearly organized directory of blogs. BlogHer.org functions like the phone book and *TV Guide* at the same time. Our blogrolls list almost 9,000 blogs by women, self-categorized into over 20 different topic tags. Meanwhile, our more than 50 contributing editors cover each topic like a beat reporter, ready to point you to what's hot in the blogosphere every day. So the most important feature is findability, whether by surfing our blogrolls or by following the links our editors write about every day.

**What would a female blogger new to the blogosphere gain and how would she benefit by joining BlogHer? What can BlogHer do for her?**

BlogHer is just about the only place online where a woman can go to follow *all* of her interests, from politics to pets, from food to finance, from entertainment to eco-consciousness. So many sites prefer to silo women into "interest groups," and we think women are much more complex than that! So BlogHer is a great resource for new bloggers to find other blogs and bloggers that interest them … across a great diversity of topics. Further, BlogHer is a community of women bloggers who support and advise each other. Blogging is a wonderful means of expression and a channel to getting great advice and support, but it can sometimes feel solitary. It's hard to feel solitary when you're having an active discussion about anything from the latest technical tools to the best resource for Irish Soda Bread recipes on BlogHer posts or in the Forums. It all does come back to the mission: We want to create opportunities for education, exposure, community, and economic empowerment. Each member can pursue one or all of those goals via BlogHer's conferences, web community, or our advertising network.

*(cont'd)*

# On the Line with (cont'd)

**What are some of the requirements for joining BlogHer, and how do those requirements enrich the community?**

The only requirement to join is that you provide a username and a valid email address. After joining, you do have to abide by the BlogHer Community Guidelines (blogher.org/what-are-your-community-guidelines). To have your blog listed in the blogrolls, it must meet some pretty simple criteria, mostly that it's a real-live blog that hasn't been abandoned. Our pretty simple and consistent guidelines and criteria are about making sure BlogHer is the source to find quality blogs and to find civil discussions . . . even when they're contentious. We're BlogHer, not PornHer, SpamHer, or HateHer. Here are the criteria to have a blog listed: blogher.org/node/1052.

**Tell us about the BlogHer conferences. What are the benefits of attending? Who might we expect to see there?**

BlogHer conferences are really the conferences that the community built. We look to the community for session ideas, speaker ideas, activity ideas. We follow every blog post and comment on or off BlogHer to see what people are thinking would be entertaining, informative, exciting, or challenging. You're going to meet a ton of really fascinating, friendly, talented women at BlogHer . . . and you're going to discover a whole new list of blogs that you simply must follow regularly. And you'll improve your skills . . . technical skills, writing skills, even self-promotion skills! You'll see everyone from very prominent well-known bloggers to people who haven't even started their first blog. But blogging is still such a new endeavor that the difference between the two groups isn't really that wide, in either years or knowledge. Perhaps the biggest benefit of attending for many of us is, for once, not to be one of very few women in the room, but rather to be amongst hundreds of powerful, passionate, creative women.

**Do you have any tips for a new BlogHer on how to make the most of the BlogHer community?**

The answer is pretty similar for BlogHer vs. for any part of the blogosphere: Read and participate. You can become as much of a presence in the community by commenting as you can by posting. It's all about the entire conversation.

**Any final tips or tricks on how to be embraced by the blogosphere at large?**

There isn't really one blogosphere; there are many blogospheres. It'd be pretty tough to be embraced by every blogosphere out there, so find the ones you care about, the ones that intrigue and interest you. And then, just like I said before: Read, write, and participate. And a little respect goes a long way. That means no spamming . . . because it's disrespectful. And attack ideas, not characters . . . because attacking people you don't even know is disrespectful. And if you're going to state "facts" as part of your argument or debate, then cite your sources, because making sweeping statements without supporting data is disrespectful.

# Be the Life of the Party

When meeting people for the first time, it's best to remember the old adage our grandmothers used to say: "You get more flies with honey." You *could* call upon, "If you don't have anything nice to say, don't say anything at all." But there are definitely times when being nice is the *last* thing you want to do. The trick is to be honest, genuine, and respectful when you post comments on another person's blog. You can disagree with dignity.

## Chat them up: Comments count

Comments are the single most important means of interaction in the blog community. Some blogs don't activate comments and still thrive, but they're the exception. They're usually those blogs that have built a following over time or serve as more of a resource rather than a social setting.

Leaving thoughtful commentary can endear you to blog owners — even if you disagree — but fluff comments like "yeah!" or "sure" are often disregarded. Commenting with fluff won't drive people to click your link. In fact, it may even discourage them.

## Social commentary: Everyone is a critic

People sometimes think that because your blog is public, you're entitled to their opinion. And let's face it, not everyone was born with the tact gene. Treating others as you wish to be treated is one of those rules that applies pretty much anywhere, including blog comments. While the occasional jerk is inevitable, how you handle it is what counts. On the flipside, how respectfully you comment on the blogs of others is equally important.

### Put away your claws

You don't have to agree with everything you read. If you're so fired up that you feel the need to leave a heated comment, keep in mind that you (usually) won't be able to edit or delete it after it's posted. When it's out there, it's *out there,* and you really can't take it back — not completely. Okay, so the blog author said that Prada has a lousy collection this season, but did you *have* to call her a "tasteless, dollar store–shopping cow"? No, you really didn't.

You may want to strangle that blogger with her own played-out pashmina, but keep it together! Take a moment to compose yourself before responding. A well-thought-out, intelligent comment or rebuttal can at least be respected, if not agreed with.

## Cool the Trash Talk

Being a bitch is a trend that we'd rather see go the way of bolo ties. Do a quick search for the words *bitch* and *blog,* and you'll find dozens of women wearing the bitch title with pride. While some embrace bitch as being a strong, powerful, opinionated woman, some take it a bit too far by becoming venomous, vindictive, and downright hateful. Come on, you've seen the movie *Mean Girls* (and if you haven't, set this book down right now and go get it. Go on. Go! Shoo!). It *is* possible to be witty, sarcastic, funny, and sharp without being malicious. There are real people on the other side of that blog.

If you're particularly outspoken, be prepared for resistance. Regular readers of a blog tend to rally behind its owner. Kicking in the door and wielding your attitude like you're the Duchess of Know-It-All Kingdom isn't usually the best way to make friends.

This is not to say that you shouldn't speak your mind, but do so with decorum. A witty, well-timed retort and a sweet disposition can leave them wondering. There's nothing quite like delivering a zinger with a smile. It's infuriating to them, satisfying to you. Everybody wins!

### Dealing with toxic comments

Having a blog opens you up to a whole world of wack-a-doos with god complexes, so sometimes you need to chaperone your blog, making sure that everyone plays nice. These wack-a-doos, usually called *trolls*, will leave negative comments on your blog, usually more than once. Most of the time, blog commenters are lovely, fine people such as yourself, but once in a while, you'll get someone who is hell-bent on picking a fight with you, usually over something ridiculous. The troll will usually comment anonymously because mean people are often too cowardly to reveal themselves.

Similar tactics apply, as were mentioned in the preceding section. Take the high road whenever possible. Delete the comments and block the jerk from commenting — or from your site entirely. You can do this by blocking that IP address from the server, or with features that may be available through your blog platform or service. You can track the IP address and use search engines to help you find the offender, but that's usually a dead end. Check with your hosting provider or reference your chosen blog software's documentation for more information about blocking IP addresses.

## Call in Reinforcements

If you're unable to block particular offenders (or trolls) from your blog because they use shady tactics to change their IP addresses – and they continue to pester you to the point of harassment – contact your hosting provider, who may be able to assist you with tracking and blocking the IPs. If the problem persists, contact authorities. You can learn more about what steps to take at HaltAbuse.org (haltabuse.org).

### Relax; it's just the Internet

When someone gives you a hard time on your blog, take it with a grain of salt . . . and maybe a little tequila. It's only the Internet, after all. Unless you feel you're in danger of harassment or stalking, try not to let the occasional negative incident impact your feelings toward the blog community. One or two rude people don't represent the whole of the Internet, and the benefits of blogging and sharing comments definitely outweigh the random troll here and there.

# The Newbie Hustle

When you're new to blogging, it's tempting to go a little nuts. You want to sign up for *every* gadget and display *every* widget! You're going to be the next blogging A-lister! You're instantly going to be best friends with the most popular blogger on the Internet by leaving her one of your magically delicious comments. When you launch, your blog will be flooded with avid readers, and advertisers will be banging down your door. You want to blog and podcast and videocast and photoblog and . . . and . . . and. . . .

Slow down there, hot foot! Success requires endurance and patience. Take a few spins around the dance floor and find your groove. Here are some insider do's and don'ts to keep you from tripping up:

- **DON'T leave comments on other blogs begging people to read *your* blog.** A tell-tale sign of a new blogger is her tendency to leave comments along the lines of, "Great post! Check out my blog at PrincessProtractor.com!" It's bad enough to be so blatant, but not even bothering to leave any thoughtful commentary is even worse. It borders on spam, and it's become a tactic spammers have started using. So unless you want your comment deleted as spam and your IP potentially blacklisted, share a comment, but skip the sales pitch.

- **DO blog often and with quality, easily digestible content.** Consider starting out with snack-sized entries so new readers to your blog can get an idea of what your writing is like. If you're new and your goal is to build an audience, don't write long-winded diatribes about how your sister used the last of your toothpaste. Dooce.com (and other successful blogs like it) might have long entries packed full of hilarity, but unless you're prepared to bring it on a similar level, you'll want to build a readership before unloading *War and Peace* on them.

- **DON'T sign your blog entries or comments.** It's really unnecessary. Most blogs have a Posted By section for both blog entries and comments, so you don't need to close with your name. It takes up space, adding more stuff people have to scroll through and it's just one of those things that make people think, "Hm. She must be new. . . ."

## Women with Moxie

"Delete the negative; accentuate the positive!"

–Donna Karan

# Memes and quizzes

A *meme*, officially pronounced like *dream* (but commonly pronounced *ME-me*), is when something becomes hugely popular, often quite suddenly, through the word-of-mouth and self-publishing made feasible by the Internet. It is sometimes referred to as an *Internet phenomenon* or *Internet meme*. Among bloggers, a *meme* is usually some kind of quiz or survey that makes its way around the blogs, sometimes via an email forward, but usually with the good old-fashioned copy and paste commands. The figure below shows an example.

It's important that you know whether a survey you've found is a meme before you go swiping it from someone's blog to participate. Good indicators are if they've tagged other people to participate in the meme or if they indicate where *they* picked up the meme. Be sure to give the person you lifted it from a shoutout via a trackback (if she or he has that feature enabled) and be sure to credit her or him as your source.

The problem with memes is that newbie bloggers tend to have more quizzes than content. This isn't to say that you shouldn't participate in memes and quizzes. Go for it! But try to limit your memes to once a week . . . twice, tops! Brutal as it may be, it's a rare few that are truly going to care that you're 83 percent Bettie Page or that your Celtic horoscope says you're a chestnut tree.

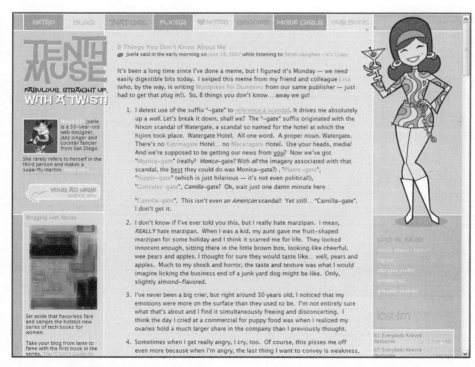

- **DON'T stuff your blog full of surveys.** If surveys and quizzes are your thing, having a MySpace account should do you nicely. The occasional quiz or survey, sometimes called a *meme,* is fine and can be a fun way to engage other bloggers by challenging them — sometimes called *tagging* them — to complete the survey, too. It gets old if surveys make up the bulk of your blog.

- **DO run a spell check.** You never get a second chance to make a first impression, and when the first entry on your blog is titled, "I Want to Loose Three Pounds," you may have blown the only chance you had. Common mistakes are made by people who aren't conscious of the difference between *you're* vs. *your, loose* vs. *lose, it's* vs. *its,* and *their* vs. *they're.* No one says you have to be a scholar, but you'd be surprised how many people judge by grammar alone.

# Relax, Refresh, Reward

Now that you've brushed up on your blog etiquette, why not hone your social skills with a party? Whether it's for someone's birthday or just to celebrate your new haircut, a cocktail party is a great way to gather with friends. Cocktail parties last only a few hours, they're generally given at a reasonable early time (say 6 p.m. to 9 p.m. or 7 p.m. to 10 p.m.), and while it may seem like an expensive undertaking, you truly can host a stylish soiree that won't break the bank.

## Be the hostess with the mostest

With only a few small tweaks, you can take a last-minute gathering from cheap to chic. It's a matter of using your head. Here are a few simple steps that can take your party from lame to fame:

- **Ditch the keg.** It may have been cute when you were 22, but times have changed. While you may be able to squeeze a ton of brew-dogs out of that pony keg for a mere $30, we doubt Colin Cowie would condone the red plastic tumblers.

- **Hit a restaurant supply store.** You'd be surprised how inexpensive simple white plates and generic stemware are. Stock up on the clearance and discontinued items, but make sure to get enough — and make sure that the pieces you've chosen complement each other.

- **Skip the open bar.** Serve champagne cocktails, like the Blogging Betty in Chapter 5, on trays or line them up on a bar. Liquor superstores and warehouse stores like Costco often have great deals on midpriced champagne or sparkling wine by the case.

- **Let them eat . . . petit fours?** Cupcakes have been a big trend in desserts for the last few years, but we're making a prediction that petit fours are the next hot thing. Much like a cupcake, they're portable, small, and you can serve several flavors.

- **Hey there, Miss DJ!** A cocktail party calls for festive but mellow tunes. You want your party guests to be able to chat over the noise without having to yell.

- **Keep it simple; less is more.** You don't need to worry about party streamers and balloons. A simple, elegant display of fresh flowers strategically placed, a smattering of votives, and a few yards of material are all you need to create a beautiful, chic look.

It's time to get this party started. Pop in the tunes, set out the drinks, check your lipstick, and get ready to mingle!

## To Do List

Find out why popularity is important

Make sense of site statistics

Get a free traffic-monitoring tool

Express yourself with art

# Throw a Blogging Block Party

**T**raffic. No, not the bumper-to-bumper you sat in on your way home from work. The traffic we're talking about is the flock of people coming to your blog to read about your latest adventures in knitting a steering wheel cozy while sitting in rush hour. Excluding the folks who would rather not publicize their private blogs, people want a readership and some level of participation. Traffic is what makes blogging such a popular forum. Blogs are a place to converse, trade opinions, collect feedback, share a laugh, or promote a business.

# Traffic Control

Business blogs or revenue-generating blogs rely on traffic to build interest in products or services and to keep people connected to your trade. Traffic can create opportunities to make money, develop ideas for new projects, and make connections with people you would otherwise have never known.

Traffic gives you leverage when it comes to advertising and sponsorship, if that's an important direction for your blog. Some bloggers depend on blog advertisers as their primary income, and some use traffic to turn a hobby into a profession. It all depends greatly on what you want to achieve, of course, but building a following and gaining readers and repeat visits are the bread and butter of the blog world. The question that bloggers ask most frequently is, "How do I drive traffic to my blog?"

## Become a promoter

In order to have a party, you need to invite guests, and you need to be prepared to entertain and keep the party-goers enjoying the event. You don't just put up a party tent and sit back and wait for the guests to flock. You send out invitations, put up decorations, fill the punch bowl, and crank up the dance music. You consider the elements of having a party instead of just expecting it to happen on its own. The blogiverse works the same way. Tossing a blog up and sitting back to wait for the readers to spill through the front door is a surefire way to be sorely disappointed. Put on your party dress, and let's get this venue ready for your guests. Here are a few tips for blog party prep:

- **Tag your entries and register your site with Technorati.** If you haven't already, get your blog into Technorati and start tagging your entries. It sounds like a hassle, but really, helping people find things is a key component to building readers. If your blog is about knitting and you do regular posts about sock patterns, you'll want people who are interested in sock patterns to find those entries. Make them accessible. (Read more about tagging in Chapter 10.)

- **Promote your RSS feeds.** Think of your RSS feed as the party invitation that's going to tell readers where to find your site and keep their curiosity peaked. Hopefully, your RSS feed will prompt readers to visit your site to comment and participate. (Read more about RSS feeds in Chapter 11.)

- **Provide fresh and alluring content.** No one likes to show up to a party that's a total dud. If you don't plan on posting daily, at least make the posts you do put up worthy of the visit. Traffic is about building repeat business. Make sure you keep your readers wanting more.

- **Keep your site free of errors and clutter.** It's important to keep your site running smoothly. That's not to say that the occasional snag will destroy all of your chances at building a readership, but a perpetual code error or a broken feed can deter people from coming back. That's also true about extraneous content. You want people to be able to find your entries; try to keep the extra bling, like distracting scripts and blinkies, to a minimum. Keep it simple, clean, and uncluttered. Deliver your content properly and build from there.

- **Participate in the blogging community.** We can't stress this enough. Interacting with the community from which you hope to aquire readers is essential in getting the word out about yourself. Provide thoughtful commentary on other related blogs, and reply to the people who do visit yours. Just because they visit once doesn't mean they're permanent party guests. You'll need to give them a reason to come to your next soiree. (Read more about participation in Chapter 15.)

- **List yourself in relevant directories and webrings.** Peppered around the web are directories and webrings for every topic you could possibly want to find. Consider listing your blog in a few to get the wayward web traveler to find you. If your blog topic is cooking, you might try visiting Google.com and searching for **cooking rings**, **cooking directories**, and **cooking websites**. See what comes up and visit a few sites to see what strikes your fancy.

- **Link to other blogs.** Consider linking to other blogs that interest you. Not only will you build a list of sites you enjoy reading, but you could also aid in the interconnectivity of blogging. Blogs allow people to discover new sites at nearly every turn. The sites you link could reciprocate and lend their readership the chance to discover you. (Read more about links in Chapter 15.)

## Search party: Search engine optimization

Typically, if you build any type of website, you'll want to keep search engine optimization techniques in mind, and with blogs, it's the same deal. However, your content is constantly changing, so it should be handled differently. Search engine optimization (SEO) is about creating a website with search engines in mind. Search engines *crawl* or index websites in different methods to populate search results. Paying attention to what search engines index, such as certain headings, titles, and content arrangement, can help boost your ranking in search results. Consider picking up *Search Engine Optimization For Dummies* by Peter Kent (Wiley Publishing, Inc.) to find out more about SEO.

Of course, there is always the chance that appearing in search engine results is undesirable for reasons of privacy and spam prevention. There are steps you can take to avoid being indexed by search engines, which we cover in Chapter 14.

A business blog, which we discussed in Chapter 4, naturally has different goals than does a blog for a hobbyist, so you'll need to address specific areas more aggressively, depending on the topics and what kind of ranking you hope to achieve. Paying careful attention to what you title your entries, for example, can influence what and how people find your blog. What you post might not immediately be indexed, so anticipating what could end up in search results may guide searchers to drill into your blog for further information. The bottom line is, search engines get clogged up with blog content so easily that getting in isn't the problem. It's ensuring that what does get in is meaningful or has keywords that invite desired readers to come have a look.

## Quality not quantity

The appeal of tons of traffic can be intoxicating, and sure, lots of adoring fans are a nice idea. But, if you're blogging for the benefit of creating revenue, you'll want a certain type of reader group coming to your site, rather than every bum on the Internet. The Internet is like one big blind date; you never know if you're going to need rescuing or if it's a match made in heaven. Finding your target audience can be tough, but it's not impossible.

Like a trained cockatiel, we keep saying "participate" over and over. And for good reason! Participate on relevant websites that already have the type of readers you desire. Obviously, thousands of hits are great, but if only three of those hits are from people who are interested in your blog, you aren't targeting the right audience with your techniques. You want the bulk of your readers to have a genuine interest in your content, rather than being just "drive-by" readers.

### Traffic Cop

Increased traffic drags in the inevitable troll or spammer, so be armed with the necessary tactics for spam prevention and housekeeping. (Read more about spam control in Chapter 9.)

## Meter Maid

After you build some semblance of regular site traffic, you'll probably want to evaluate it to know where you can make improvements, especially if your blog is for business or you hope for it to turn into a business blog. Various tools are available, some free, some not, that you can take advantage of. Finding out who reads your site and with what browsers, and what kind of activity specific areas of your blog are seeing, can aid you in enhancing your site further and help you make improvements to areas you think deserve more attention.

# Making sense of site statistics

When you start reading about unique site hits and page views, you might want to drop-kick your laptop out the window. But it's not as complicated as it sounds. Stat counters usually summarize your traffic in a graph format, as shown in Figure 16-1. For example, StatCounter (described in the next section) gives you a nice little bar graph to help you monitor general spikes in traffic. But you'll want to drill a little further to see what's really going on. Here's the quick-and-dirty version of what all the traffic-site-stat mumbo jumbo means and the numbers that are worthy of your attention.

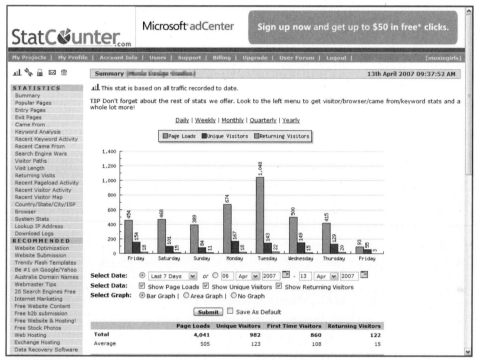

Figure 16-1

## Unique visitors

This is the most important statistic for those who are using blogging for business or revenue-generating sites. This is the total number of people who've come to your website, and you can usually view it by day, week, month, and year. This number includes every person to come to your site, including returning visitors and new visitors. You often need to know this number when selling advertising or obtaining sponsors. Companies buying ad space on a site usually will want to know what you average in unique hits or visitors per week or month.

### Referrers and keywords

In most cases, traffic-monitoring tools tell you where your traffic is coming *from*. Knowing where your readers are coming from or finding a link to your site can be helpful in terms of tracking your promotion progress. It also gives you a clue as to how people are finding your site through search engines. If you run a blog about shoes and 80 percent of your site visitors are finding you through searching for **hairy mole**, you might want to do some tweaking to your content.

### Entry and exit pages

This feature shows you on what page visitors are entering your site and where they exit. Who cares, right? Wrong. You want people to stay and look around, especially if you're marketing a service or selling a product. If you notice that a large number of people are exiting on an entry that links to a lot of outside resources, you might want to change how you present that information. Your goal is to keep people on your site. The longer they stick around, the more they find, and the better your chances they will return.

### Location

You can usually see from where in the world your traffic is being generated, which can come in handy in certain scenarios. If you launch a new local dating site for singles in the metro Atlanta area, you can see how many of your visitors are from Atlanta. If you're getting more traffic from Manhattan, maybe tweaking your site's keywords or rewording your titles can help boost the chances that Atlanta-area folks find your site in a search.

### Browser statistics

The design of a blog or website can really impact how visitors navigate and use your site. It's always important to cater to all current browsers, if possible, but knowing which browser the majority of your site readers use to look at your site can help you weigh options when it comes to design or layout of specific information. If 90 percent of your readers use Internet Explorer 6.0 at an 800-pixel resolution, you better make sure your site is tested and views properly for those people. If you have an even spread of varying browsers and sizes, choosing a layout that is a bit more flexible can be beneficial. The key is to know your audience. These tidbits will help you do that.

Still awake? If you need a moment to digest all of that, grab a latte and get some fresh air. When you're ready, carry on!

## Opting for free site traffic-monitoring tools

There are tons of traffic-monitoring services available. Here are two we found to be popular among the blogging masses.

### SiteMeter.com

Site Meter offers a free stat counter to place on your website or blog that is quick to set up and provides real-time reports on your site's activity. Signing up is a breeze, and as a free service, the service asks that you honor a few simple guidelines.

After a few short questions, Site Meter provides you with a snippet of code you must paste into a visible area of your site, as shown in Figure 16-2. Somewhere near the bottom of the page is usually sufficient enough. The free service puts a small logo icon on your site, but you can opt to pay for the advanced service and be icon free and benefit from the extra perks, such as more advanced visitor information, search engine ranking statistics, and information on up to 4,000 visitors. You can even download all your stats as a .csv or a Microsoft Excel–compatible file for creating reports. For most, the free version is sufficient, but if you plan to use your blog for revenue, you may want to more closely analyze your site traffic.

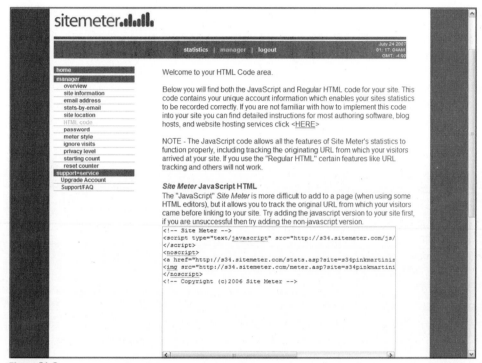

**Figure 16-2**

Installing the tracker code on your site is very simple. If you're confident enough with your site to copy and paste the code yourself, go to town! SiteMeter.com also provides step-by-step instructions (kb.sitemeter.com/entry/46/) for adding the tracker code to almost any blog platform, as shown in Figure 16-3.

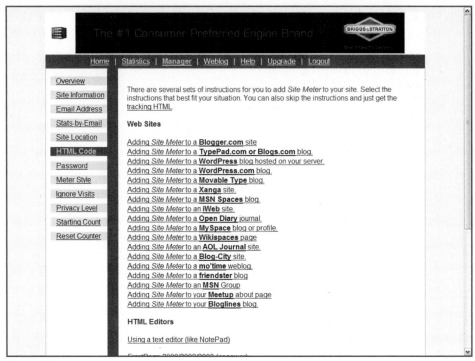

**Figure 16-3**

You aren't limited to Site Meter! A variety of traffic-reporting tools on the web are available for free. You can use the one you like the best or all of them at once.

## StatCounter.com

Another popular traffic tool is StatCounter (statcounter.com). StatCounter's free service provides similar information as Site Meter but has the added bonus of letting you choose an invisible tracker. You still need to install the code snippet, but it will be invisible, so no weird icon button messes up your fancy design. Another added bonus is that the code StatCounter provides can be valid current code, so no funky errors to worry about.

Like Site Meter, StatCounter provides handy, step-by-step instructions for almost any blog or website setup (see Figure 16-4). It holds your hand through the procedure and is there when you wake up. You're a little groggy and disoriented but unscathed overall. Okay, well, it's not *that* big of a deal, but it does have nice, step-by-step instructions. StatCounter provides the neat little code snippet ready to copy and paste, as shown in Figure 16-5. Easy!

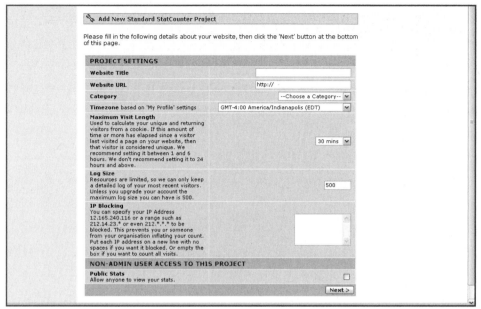

Figure 16-4

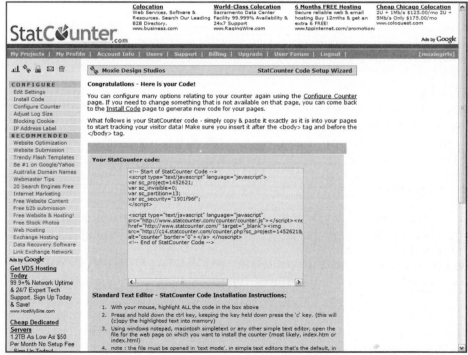

Figure 16-5

## Managing feed subscription traffic

Not only can you ogle your site traffic statistics, but you can also keep track of the RSS subscriptions you have. If you use FeedBurner.com, you get a nifty feed stats dashboard, as shown in Figure 16-6. From here, you can see what types of news readers and browsers people use.

Figure 16-6

# Relax, Refresh, Reward

This chapter should've given you new insight on how to target areas of your site for increasing, managing, and reading the traffic you're already getting to develop a better plan for the future of your blog. Understanding the lingo is half the battle! So now that you know how many unique visitors you get in a week and what browsers they're using. . . .

## Color yourself calm

We all know what stress feels like. It's the twenty-first century — the age of inventions that are supposed to make our lives easier. Wouldn't that be nice? Instead, we all feel the pressures of jobs, family, and responsibilities and get lost in the day-to-day humdrum. Instead of obsessing over your site traffic stats, get away from your monitor and have a little creative fun.

Get out your crayon stash, oil pastels, finger paints, watercolors, or any crafty art supply that looks like fun in the kids aisle at your local superstore or hardware store and get to coloring! Sounds corny, we know, but getting back to your roots as a kid, getting dirty, and having some play time can do wonders for your stress level. Believe us, we're all about reducing stress.

Who knows what you'll come up with. Maybe your creation will end up in the trash, or you'll cut it up and frame it as a fun piece of abstract art for your powder room. Whatever the case, it'll help keep you grounded when you're neck-deep in diaper rash, deadlines, and dinner.

## To Do List

Learn about different types of blog advertising

Consider the potential and drawbacks of ads on your blog

Check out different ad services and networks

Learn tips for increasing your advertiser appeal

Share your extra moolah with others: Donate!

# Support Your Nonfat Vanilla Latte Habit

Everyone could use a little mad money. Or maybe you would like a cushion of cash to supplement your income. If you generate a decent amount of traffic on your blog by providing quality and consistent content, you may be a great candidate for blog advertising. This chapter covers the different ways you can use advertising and some of the services available to you, as well as some tips for making the most of ads on your blog.

Blog advertising comes in two basic forms: text ads and graphic ads. *Graphic ads* tend to appear in sidebars of blogs or along the top of the screen and vary in size from small buttons to large rectangular banners. *Text ads* are just that – simple links containing just a handful of words. These are also usually located in the sidebar of one's blog or sometimes at the foot of the site. Occasionally, bloggers will include some text links in between blog entries. There is one relatively new version of blog advertising that is becoming more popular: paying per post. In these sorts of advertisements, sponsors request that you write an entry dedicated to their product for a flat cost.

# Dollars and Sense: The Pro and Con of Blog Advertising

Back in the day when blogging was in its infancy and the community was much smaller, advertising on your blog was considered quasiconformist. Sure, maybe people wouldn't say anything, but sometimes those who chose to post ads were considered sellouts. Bloggers would sometimes make disclaimers regarding their decision to post ads. Some die-hard blog elitists said if you posted ads, you no longer were in it for the community. You were no longer writing for writing's sake. You were, in essence, The Man. In hindsight, that's one of the most ridiculous things we've ever heard, but in the days of early blogging, ads were just not *en vogue*.

While we occasionally wax nostalgic for the blogosphere's early years, we're very happy to report that advertising on your blog is now quite common and, in some cases, a sign of blogging success! Blog advertising has been liberated! Go tell it on the mountain . . . or at Starbucks — whatever. Here are some things to consider when choosing whether to run ads on your blog.

## The pro: Money, honey!

The real draw to blog advertising, obviously, is the hope of additional funds in your bank account. Advertising on blogs has become more accepted as a way to make legitimate cash. There are bloggers out there who support themselves solely with advertisements. We're not talking about blogs that exist only as a place to host dozens of links or bombard you with so many ads that you're lucky if you can find actual content. We're speaking of blogs such as Dooce.com and other wildly successful sites that run unobtrusive advertisements and use them as a primary source of income.

Now, we're not suggesting that you pick a domain name, quit your day job, and sit back to wait for the advertisers to bang down your door. No, indeed! But, once you've established your blog and can convince potential advertisers, via site statistics and consistent content, that they should throw some bones your way on a regular basis, get ready to slip into your jammies and work from the sofa!

Even if you don't become the next Dooce, you can still make a tidy sum if you place your ads wisely and generate steady traffic. A few bucks here and there add up quickly! Before you know it, you'll have enough for that boob job. Oops. Scratch that . . . we meant, uh . . . trip to Cabo! Right.

## The con: Walking on advertiser eggshells

With great power comes great responsibility. Okay, so it's not all that dramatic, but when you accept ads on your site, you should have a sense of responsibility to your advertisers. Some bloggers have legitimate concerns about making sure their voices aren't compromised by the requirements of certain advertisers. In this day and age of thin-skinned, highly litigious society, advertisers are much more careful about who they align themselves with. So, if you're prone to regularly dropping F-bombs on your blog or are otherwise controversial, don't be surprised if that baby food company passes on advertising with you.

Not to say that all advertisers are that picky, but it's definitely something to keep in mind. If you're hoping to make money with your blog, keep your target audience and target advertisers in mind when you post entries. If you don't wish to compromise your voice or your opinion in any way, make sure your potential advertisers are aware of this. This may allow you to draw in the sorts of advertisers you would be happy to host.

The best way to keep your blog free of influence and truly your own point of view is to call the shots whenever possible. This may or may not be lucrative, depending on the circumstances, but it's your blog and ultimately your choice about what kind of content it holds and what advertisers you choose to partner with.

# Advertising Services and Networks

Various ad services and networks are available for those who are interested in placing ad banners on their blogs. It's become a booming business in the last few years, and until recently, many of the services were by invitation only. Here are a few of the most popular services and networks currently available to bloggers.

## Google AdSense

Google, the oracle of Internet search engines, has a great ad delivery service called AdSense that allows you to run ads based on the content Google indexes from your blog. This method for displaying ads is called

### Okay, no one blogged anything about a donkey!

Google AdSense content is both *dynamic* and *contextual*. This means the content of the ad changes on refresh of the browser window and, as mentioned, is based on your blog's content. If you blog about cocktails, Google may display ads about vodka or martini shakers or maybe even popular martini bars or recipes. Handy! If you blog about chicken wings, you might get ads for Hooters. But, if you blog about weight loss, Google may dish up ads about diet pills or other shady methods you might not endorse along with the usual ads for Weight Watchers or gyms. Keep this in mind when deciding what to blog about and/or whether Google AdSense is right for you. Most other bloggers understand that you're not endorsing the products that appear in Google AdSense, but if it's something that concerns you, you might include a disclaimer in the About portion of your blog.

*contextual advertising.* The ads come in varying sizes, and you can customize them to match your blog design through the Google AdSense web-based interface.

Google AdSense serves both text and graphic ads to your blog in a relatively unobtrusive manner. Google does have to approve your participation in AdSense, so if it deems your site controversial or offensive, it may deny your application. But usually, it's quite simple to be accepted. The best part about Google AdSense is that it's free! Sign up for your Google AdSense by going to google.com/adsense and clicking the Sign Up Now button, shown in Figure 17-1.

Free is great, but you may be wondering how you get paid. Google pays for the ads on either a cost-per-click (CPC) or cost-per-1000-impressions (CPM) basis. What this means is that your potential advertisers pay Google either when your readers click on the ads (CPC) or whenever their ads are displayed on your blog (CPM). You receive a certain portion of this payment via check every month, provided your ads have generated revenue — although a minimum amount of $100 must be earned before Google will issue a check. Google doesn't disclose the exact amount that you receive per click or impression, but we can say from experience that you can make money with Google AdSense if you use it in accordance with Google's guidelines.

**Figure 17-1**

# Text Link Ads

One of the hot new services around today is Text Links Ads (text-link-ads.com). It places very subtle text link ads (hey, just like its name!) on websites and blogs. Unlike Google AdSense, Text Link Ads are not contextual; they're *static* links, meaning they don't change on refresh and aren't served dynamically. The bonus is that you can personally approve or deny the text link ads that are sold before applying them to your blog. Having some say in what gets served up to your readers can give you peace of mind and a feeling of control over the advertising process.

## Equal Opportunity

Some ad services won't allow you to run their ads along with the ads of other services. Google AdSense does have restrictions about how many ads you can run and what other services you can run them with. Text Link Ads allows you to run as many as you like and will even let you run their ads with other services, such as Google AdSense, as it isn't the same type of ad service. Be sure to read the fine print on the services with which you choose to apply.

Text Link Ads proudly touts a 50 percent revenue share on the price of the ads sold to your site. Fifty percent! That's not too shabby. You aren't paid per click or per impression, just for the cost that Text Link Ads charged the advertiser to place the ad. So if an ad on your site costs $20, you get ten bucks — enough for a few lattes! So register for your Text Link Ads account, as shown in Figure 17-2, and start making money!

Figure 17-2

## If You Wanted an Opinion, You'd Ask for It

There are lots of reasons you might choose to include advertising on your blog – and guess what? None of them are anyone's business! Whether you're stashing cash for a handbag or a heart transplant, unless it affects someone's ability to read your blog, you shouldn't feel the need to discuss or justify it. And even then, one always has the option of not reading if one doesn't agree with your advertising selection. If you choose to run ads on your blog, as long as you display the ads tastefully and in line with your content, there's no harm in you putting a few bucks in your pocket.

Another Text Link Ads perk: You're conveniently paid via check or PayPal at the first of every month with a minimum payout of $25. No waiting to break a Benjamin before they show you the money!

## Blogads

Blogads (blogads.com) has been on the scene since 2002 and is a wildly popular choice of advertising among bloggers of all types. Blogads describes itself as "a network of influential bloggers who collaborate to promote and sell blog advertising." In the Blogads structure, the advertisers themselves, with assistance from Blogads, manage, renew, and add campaigns to your blog via a simple web-based interface, as shown in Figure 17-3.

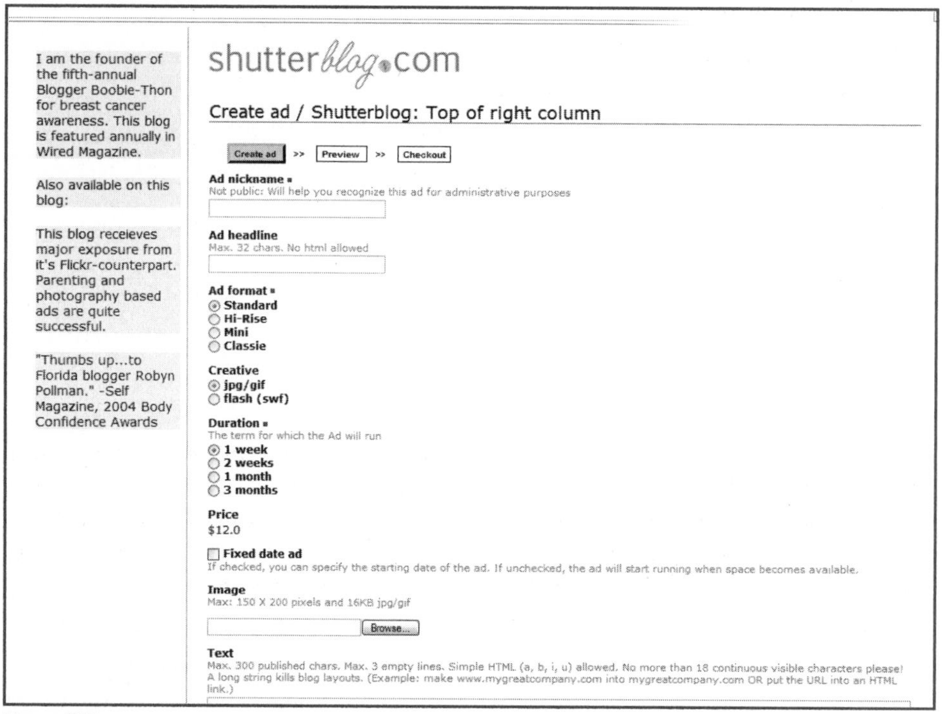

I am the founder of the fifth-annual Blogger Boobie-Thon for breast cancer awareness. This blog is featured annually in Wired Magazine.

Also available on this blog:

This blog receieves major exposure from it's Flickr-counterpart. Parenting and photography based ads are quite successful.

"Thumbs up...to Florida blogger Robyn Pollman." -Self Magazine, 2004 Body Confidence Awards

### shutter*blog*.com

Create ad / Shutterblog: Top of right column

[ Create ad ] >> [ Preview ] >> [ Checkout ]

**Ad nickname** •
Not public: Will help you recognize this ad for administrative purposes

**Ad headline**
Max. 32 chars. No html allowed

**Ad format** •
◉ Standard
◯ Hi-Rise
◯ Mini
◯ Classie

**Creative**
◉ jpg/gif
◯ flash (swf)

**Duration** •
The term for which the Ad will run
◉ 1 week
◯ 2 weeks
◯ 1 month
◯ 3 months

**Price**
$12.0

☐ **Fixed date ad**
If checked, you can specify the starting date of the ad. If unchecked, the ad will start running when space becomes available.

**Image**
Max: 150 X 200 pixels and 16KB jpg/gif

[            ] [ Browse... ]

**Text**
Max. 300 published chars. Max. 3 empty lines. Simple HTML (a, b, i, u) allowed. No more than 18 continuous visible characters please! A long string kills blog layouts. (Example: make www.mygreatcompany.com into mygreatcompany.com OR put the URL into an HTML link.)

**Figure 17-3**

The blogs participating in the service are classified under various categories that Blogads calls *hives*. Hives are groups organized by location and topic — for example, political, health and fitness, parenting, technology, and so on. (Figure 17-4 shows an example of a hive for women bloggers.) Advertisers decide, by visiting your blog or by perusing the list of blogs in their targeted hives, whether to purchase ads based on your blog's advertising cost, audience, traffic, and popularity. They also can purchase ads in targeted group buys based on the quantity, quality, and cost of the other blogs in your hive. For example, if there are four mommy blogs in Boise, but 300 in San Francisco, those mommy blogs in San Francisco may benefit by having more participants in their network, which can ultimately drive up advertising revenue.

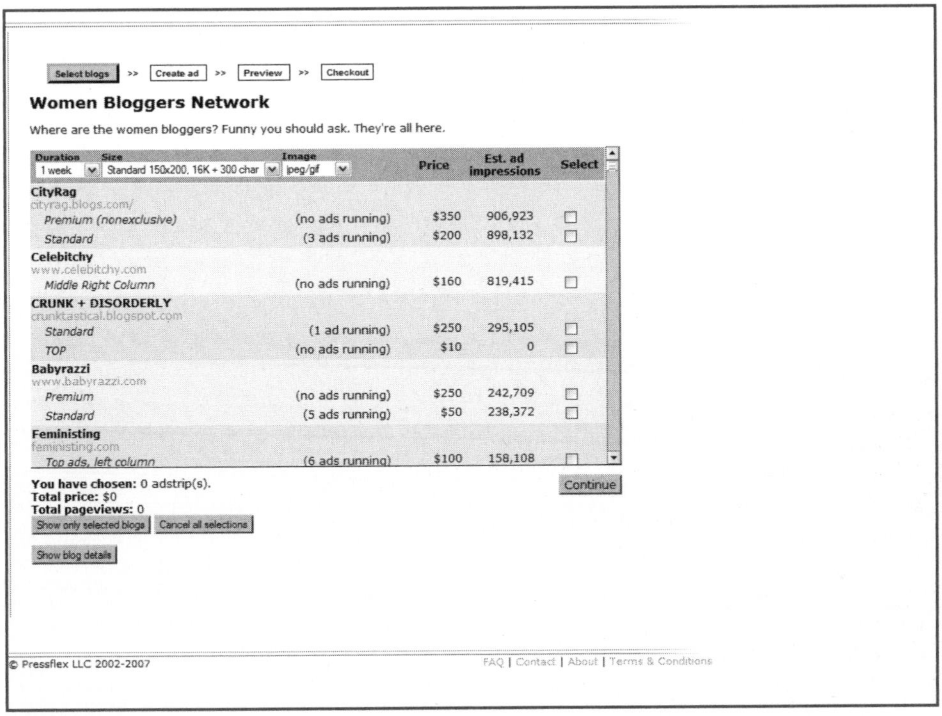

**Figure 17-4**

In addition to having advertising approval, Blogads also allows you to customize the appearance of your ads, set your own prices, and even write the copy to entice potential advertisers. Ultimately, Blogads is one of the most rewarding services. The company takes a mere 30 percent cut from the revenue generated by the ads on your blog. Even relatively small-time bloggers can make, on average, $50 a month.

Some bloggers even generate as much as $5000 in revenue per month! And like Text Link Ads, you can run Blogads along with Google AdSense and other ad services.

At this time, Blogads is by invitation only and requires that you have a sponsor already in the network willing to vouch for you. If you don't have a sponsor, you can send an email to Blogads, and someone will notify you when an available sponsor appears in your potential hive.

## Federated Media

Federated Media, or FM as it's sometimes called, is the Holy Grail of advertising networks (see Figure 17-5). Some of the biggest names in blogging, such as Dooce.com, TheMommy Blog.com, and many others, are members of Federated Media.

FM (federatedmedia.net/authors/index) is currently an exclusive, invite-only advertising network that accepts only blogs with what their staff members consider the utmost in "passion, integrity, authority and strong community support." They choose the bloggers in their network based on how much revenue they think the blogs can generate. FM feels bloggers with the trust of their audience, in addition to high traffic and quality content, are going to lure more potential advertisers.

FM organizes its sites, similar to other services such as Blogads, into groups that they call *federations*. They have federations for parenting, travel, graphic arts, entertainment, and much more, so there's a good chance your blog should fit into at least one federation. FM also allows you to approve or deny all ads that may appear on your site. Federated Media doesn't publicly disclose the amount of revenue you can expect to earn by joining their network, so you need them to accept your blog before they share that info.

While Federated Media is invitation-only, you're welcome to submit your site for consideration. Take a chance! If you feel your blog meets FM's criteria, fill out the submission form on the site (shown in Figure 17-6) and see what happens. You could be listed among some of the best on the 'net!

## Women with Moxie

"I don't judge others. I say if you feel good with what you're doing, let your freak flag fly."

– Sarah Jessica Parker

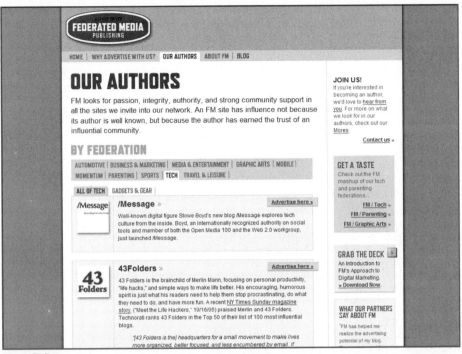

Figure 17-5

Figure 17-6

## Top tips for attracting advertisers

You can't expect your advertisers to beat down your door without a little work on your part. Here are some quick tips to keep in mind for your current and future advertising ventures.

- **Try to keep most ads above the fold.** You shouldn't have to scroll too much to see your most important ads.

- **Offer more than one advertising size.** You have a better chance of accommodating more advertisers this way.

- **Accept both text and graphics ads.** Again, offering more variety allows more advertisers access to your blog.

- **Post consistent, quality entries.** Advertisers want to know that you have solid readership.

- **Keep track of your traffic and site stats.** Advertisers definitely want to know this stuff, especially if you're not using an ad service and it's a private advertising negotiation.

- **Be willing to negotiate.** Don't expect to get $100 per ad right off the bat.

- **Choose ads that are audience specific.** If your blog is about parenting, you may not want ads for hammers on your sidebar. Just a tip!

## PayPerPost

PayPerPost (shown in Figure 17-7) is a relatively new method of advertising for blogs. In essence, you're paid to write an article or post a link in an entry about a particular product or company. Easy enough! Designed to be a self-serve style of ad service, you sign up for an account at payperpost.com and submit your blog for approval. After you're approved (PayPerPost claims a 48–72 hours turnaround time), you can then accept *Opportunities,* which is what PayPerPost calls the postings made by potential advertisers.

An advertiser posts an Opportunity (like a bulletin board message), and when your account is approved, you're free to respond to that advertiser's Opportunity. Most often, the advertiser is looking for someone to blog about her or his product, website, or company in exchange for cold hard cash — although the amount and requirements for each Opportunity varies from advertiser to advertiser.

When you post the blog entries relating to the Opportunities chosen, you submit links to those entries to the folks at PayPerPost. Their staff reviews the links and if all is well, approves the posts. If your post is denied, they do give you an opportunity to revise it once before flat-out rejecting it.

If your post has been approved, you must leave it up on your site for 30 days. It doesn't have to be on the front page of your blog, but it does need to remain live. PayPerPost will spot-check over the course of that time and again at the end of 30 days to make sure it's still visible to the public. If your blog entry is still alive and kicking, you'll get paid. If not, no *dinero* for you, *senorita!*

## PayPal or Bust!

If you aren't familiar with PayPal, it's the leading ecommerce solution for payments and money transfers online. A handy alternative to checks or money orders, it's a popular way to handle money transactions on the Internet, so it's worth investigating, especially if you're interested in PayPerPost. As it says right on the website, the folks at PayPerPost "don't pay in gold, baseball cards, experience points, or food stamps, so please don't ask. If you don't have a PayPal account, please get one or don't sign up." Boy, they're not pulling any punches!

Figure 17-7

Of course, PayPerPost has a moderate list of other requirements that vary depending on the Opportunity selected. You can view these requirements on its website, but it's worth mentioning that you must have a PayPal account in order to receive payment from PayPerPost.

The downside to PayPerPost harkens back to what we discussed earlier in the chapter: the sell-out factor. It's one thing to run an unobtrusive ad in your sidebar; it's quite another to actively push a paid product or service in your blog entries. Whether or not it's the case, some bloggers might feel your blog lacks integrity because PayPerPost makes it so obvious that you're "blogging for dollars." Take your audience into consideration and truly consider the products or services you're willing to endorse before deciding if PayPerPost is right for you.

# Relax, Refresh, Reward

This chapter gives you lots of info for making some extra cash with your blog. Have you considered yet what you'd like to do with your dough? While we definitely wouldn't blame you for wanting to blow it on new highlights or that slinky little skirt you saw at bebe, consider for a moment setting some money aside for a worthy cause.

## Blogging for change

There are a billion charities in the world and so many people in need, but here are some great sites that we feel are worth a buck or two if you have some change to spare.

- boobiethon.com     Since 2002, bloggers have been baring their boobs to save the boobs of others! Now that's humanity, folks. Every October for one week, Boobiethon.com invites bloggers, both women *and* men, to submit photos of their creatively covered nipples in support of the Susan G. Komen Breast Cancer Foundation. To date, they have raised over $27,000. Heads and faces are cropped out and submissions are anonymous. There's even a tasteful, but non-worksafe passworded area for those who donate $50 or more. Hint: It's naked time!

- dressforsuccess.org     Providing professional attire and career development for women in dire financial straits. If you're ever down on your luck and just can't get a break, help these lovely ladies out.

- toasttomom.com     The World's Largest Wine Tasting site visitors offer up virtual toasts to moms on the website. For every e-toast received, Clos DuBois Winery will donate $1 to benefit foundations for women and heart disease.

- aspca.org     American Society for the Prevention of Cruelty to Animals. Say no more! If it's furry (or scaley or feathered!), we love it, and we hope you do, too. Fur looks fab, but would you like it if someone made a purse out of your freshly highlighted locks? We think not.

# Blog Frosting: Make

## To Do List

*Dress up your sidebar*

*Work it with Flickr and Last.fm*

*Check out third-party services*

*Slick it up with plugins and add-ons*

*Keep it simple, less is more*

*Frost yourself!*

# Your Blog Sparkle with a Little Bling

**Y**ou can have just a straight-up blog, with entries and archives. We're not debating your freedom to set up your blog in any manner you see fit. But if you want to make your blog an interesting read for the masses, adding some extras can keep people digging around on your site for more and make it less of a snooze fest for you, too. It's all about having a little fun with your site and checking out the new cool blog toys that so many platforms have to offer.

Of course, every blog is different, right down to its database bones. You don't throw a birthday bash without putting up a few balloons or putting out the "over the hill" joke napkins. So, we'll give you the scoop on what blog toys you can get and where to find the little things that will make your blog party a smash hit.

# Personalize It: Dressing Up Your Sidebar

Your *sidebar* is the section on your blog containing typically a column or two of your About Me information and archive links. Gussying up your sidebar is quick and painless, especially for the folks blogging with tools like Vox. With just a few clicks, your sidebar is ready for the red carpet. If you're using MovableType or WordPress on your own hosted site, it takes a little more work and a little copy and paste, but it's pretty painless nonetheless. Not sure where to begin? Here are a few ideas to get your creativity flowing:

## Speaking Privately

It's up to you how much you share about yourself and your family if you're running a personal blog. Flip back to Chapter 14 to read more about privacy.

- **More about the fabulous you.** If you're not sure what to do with your sidebar, start with the basics. Not only will people who read your blog want to know more about the kind of person you are, but they'll be interested in the things you like, as well. Some bloggers opt to include links to their Amazon.com wish lists, sites they frequent, or places they shop. Bloggers sometimes provide information on how to contact them using various methods, links to their RSS feeds, and maybe short bios about the people they frequently talk about in their blog entries — like a cast list.

- **What floats your boat?** Get a little creative with your interests. If you're an avid book lover or a music junkie, share that with your readers! Display a list of your favorite reads or a list of books you're trying to read by the end of the year. Maybe you can't stay away from your local record store. Compile a list of your most angst-ridden CDs or create a catalog of your CD collection. Whatever your cup of raspberry-infused green tea is, give it a spot in the limelight on your blog. If anything, it'll be useful to you!

- **Miss popular.** There are a bazillion widgets, plugins, and code snippets dedicated to displaying who, what, when, where, and how. Maybe you want to display how many people are on your site at this very moment, show what your rank is in Technorati, or maybe even tell visitors how many people are subscribed to your RSS feed, hanging on your every scintillating word. Perhaps you'll use all three!

- **Paparazzi.** Photos are popular items to include in your sidebar. But now, including them as a more permanent installment of your site is quite the trend. Whether they're part of your overall design or a widget in your sidebar, they can spice up your site with some visual interest — or serve as a useful way to display relevant imagery. If you pride yourself on creating adorable little handmade coffee cozies, pulling in photos from your collection can be a great visual aid to your entries.

# Putting on the Ritz: Flickr and Last.fm

Dazzling your audience with the little nuances that make you unique is just the type of thing that can make or break your little blog. More importantly, you need to keep yourself inspired to blog. Having some fun with your site will keep it fresh and a hoot for you and your readers.

## Pulling Flickr photos into your blog

Pulling photos into your blog from your Flickr account is quite simple. Of course, it requires that you have a Flickr account and, depending on what type of software you use, access to pull that information into your site. For those of you using tools like WordPress.com, it's no more than a simple drag and drop.

Here are the easy steps for adding Flickr to your WordPress.com blog:

1. **Log in to your WordPress.com blog.**

2. **Click My Dashboard.**

3. **Click the Presentation tab.**

4. **Click the Widgets tab.** At the bottom of the screen is a pile of widgets.

5. **Click and drag the Flickr widget into your widget list, as shown in Figure 18-1.**

6. **When the widget's in place, click the icon on the right side of the Flickr widget.** A window appears, allowing you to paste your Flickr account's RSS feed (see Figure 18-2).

7. **Find your account's RSS feed at the bottom of your Flickr page and paste it in the Flickr RSS URL field on your WordPress.com Flickr widget.**

8. **From the drop-down menu, choose the number of photos to display. Then close the widget window.**

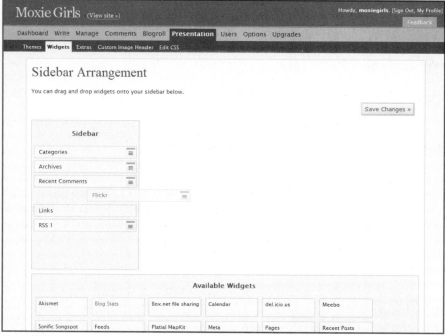

Figure 18-1

9. **Click Save Change to ensure your settings are saved.** Go ahead and preview your site to make sure your Flickr photos appear.

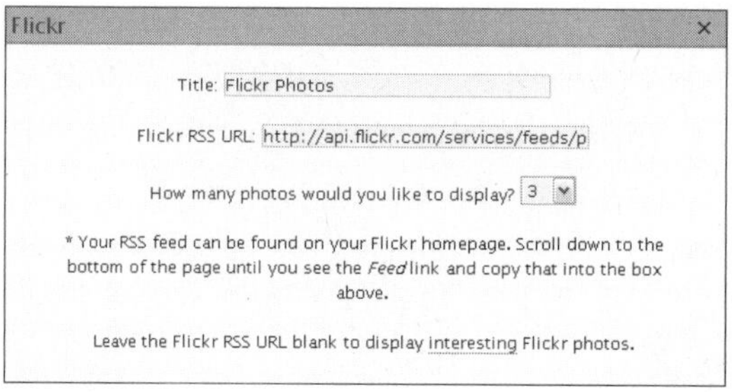

Figure 18-2

If you're running your own show using a blogging tool such as Movable Type or Blogger, you can create a code snippet right on Flickr.com to copy and paste into your sidebar template. Creating and customizing your Flickr code snippet, or Flickr Badge, as they call it, is a simple procedure. You can choose from a couple different looks: a flash badge that has a slow, animated, flip-book style motion or a block of a few thumbnails.

Here are the steps to finding the Badge Wizard and applying it to your blog:

1. **Log in to your Flickr.com account using your Yahoo! ID and password.**

2. **From your Flickr home page, click Upload Photos.**

3. **On the left side, click the Uploading Tools link.** (There's also a link to Tools in the footer of every page of the Flickr site.)

4. **When you're on the Help/Tools page, scroll down the right side until you find the section called Display Flickr Photos on Your Website.**

5. **Click the Build a Badge link.**

6. **From here, Flickr takes you through a number of steps to customize your Flickr Badge. Choose from an HTML badge or a Flash-enhanced badge (see Figure 18-3); choose what photos to display from your account, select your colors to make them match your blog, and then click the Preview & Get Code button.** When you're finished, Flickr provides you with a snippet of code to copy and paste into your own templates.

**Figure 18-3**

# Share your musical tastes with Last.fm

Think you have impeccable taste in music? Consider sharing a list of your favorite artists, or better yet, hook up with Last.fm and display your favorite tunes or currently playing tracks right on your blog. Just think, all your blog friends and readers can see that you have David Hasselhoff's latest track on your playlist. Nothing says instant coolness like David Hasselhoff, we always say. Okay, we never say that.

Last.fm (last.fm.com) is a great community for music buffs. (See more about communities and community blogs in Chapter 3.) With a quick download and installation of the Last.fm software plugin and application, it streams the info from your recently listened tracks from your chosen player, like Windows Media Player or iTunes, to your profile on its website (a method they call *scrobbling*). Last.fm also automatically compiles a customized radio station based on your listening habits, and tallies up your most popular songs so you can see what your own patterns have been. You can link up with friends, find people with similar musical tastes, and find new music through the network. After you build up a bit of information in your profile, you can easily incorporate your playlist or a personalized radio station into your blog or MySpace profile with Last.fm's handy widget code. Last.fm also provides your playlist as an RSS feed.

## Women with Moxie

"Too much is never enough."

–Beverly Feldman

Adding a widget from Last.fm to your blog can be quite simple. Among the features the Widget section has to offer are the following:

- **Charts:** Using Last.fm's widget tool, you can generate a script that displays your playlist of current tracks or top artists based on the music you've played on your computer.

- **Quilts:** A dynamically changing block of images displaying the album covers or photos of artists tracked in your Last.fm profile. You can't sleep under this kind of quilt, but it will spiff up your blog and let people know about your obsession with Kelly Clarkson.

After you've had the chance to sign up and use Last.fm a little bit, you can find the widget code by following these steps:

1. **Login to your Last.fm account using your username and password.**

2. **From the top menu, choose Widgets.**

3. **Click the Quilts tab on the left.** The Share Your Music Anywhere page appears, as shown in Figure 18-4.

4. **Specify the following settings for your quilt as desired:**

   - *Color* of the widget.

   - *Size* (small, medium, large).

   - *Orientation* (horizontal or vertical — this will make a difference depending on the space you have available on your blog).

   - *Type* (images of the artists or the album covers).

5. **Click the Show Me the Code button at the bottom of the page.** Last.fm gives you a snippet of code to copy and paste into your blog templates.

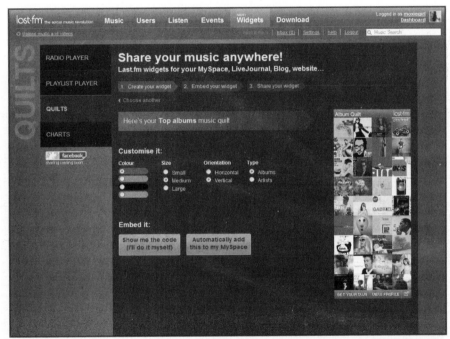

**Figure 18-4**

# Third-Party Services

Flickr and Last.fm are just two services you can use to turn your blah blog into something you'll enjoy more. But that's not all you're limited to! You can add literally hundreds of things to your site to make it sparkle. We can't list them all, but here are a few popular services you can play around with:

- **MyBlogLog.com:** This service allows you to build mini-communities. After you register, you can place a badge on your blog that displays the most recent MyBlogLog members to visit your site. It's a great feature for finding new blogs and for connecting with other bloggers who may be *lurking* (readers who visit but don't comment or participate) on your blog. MyBlogLog is also free, which is always a bonus.

- **Twitter.com:** *What are you doing?* That is the question over at Twitter.com. Have you ever had the desire to tell people what you're doing *every moment* of the day? Twitter is a service that lets you blog in short bursts, from your PC, from your mobile phone, or right from your Instant Messenger. Twitter is completely free and highly addictive. The service provides handy badges to slap on your site . . . a quick copy and paste, and your *every move* is there for public consumption.

- **Amazon.com Associates** (affiliate-program.amazon.com)**:** Amazon has an associates program that allows you to earn a little bit of moolah by promoting items it sells on your site. (Sail back to Chapter 17 for more details about advertising.) You can use it as a money-generating tool, but you can also use it to display what you bought recently or show the items on your wish list. And you make a couple of bucks from it. Bonus!

These are just a smattering of popular items that you can incorporate into your blog. They're popular now, but by the time you read this book, there will be a slew of other cool new toys to play with. It's the Internet — who knows what will pop up tomorrow! Oh, the possibilities! Luckily, nothing is as permanent as that tattoo you got in Daytona Beach during Spring Break '92. If you lose interest with something, you can delete it from your blog and move on. Too bad you can't delete that tattoo. But maybe they'll come out with a cream for that soon.

# Goodies and Gadgets: Plugins and Add-Ons

Depending on the blogging software or service you're using, you can use what is referred to as a *plugin*. Plugins, also known as *add-ons,* are modules of software

## Is Your Refrigerator Running?

Each platform has its own plugins and add-ons to choose from. Many are developed by bloggers just like you who know how to write code. Check the site of your respective platform for complete lists of plugin options, and if you don't see something you think would be cool to add, ask! Forums are generally a great place to find out if others are looking for the same type of functionality. We're sure you aren't the only one who would like a plugin that can make prank calls for you.

that add features or services to the main blogging system. They can help you enhance your blogging experience by adding special functions to the original installation. Plugins can make the reader experience smoother or provide detailed information about varying topics like visitors, comments, and traffic. Checking out the website of your blog software can usually direct you to a master list of goodies that you can download and customize.

Plugins and add-ons can range from practical to downright ridiculous. From a practical standpoint, you can use some plugins to monitor comment statistics and turn URLs into links automatically in your posts and comments, or you may find a plugin that allows you to pull RSS feeds from other blogs you own or participate in into your blog, making it a one-stop shop.

On the fun side, there are plugins that display the birthdays of your readers, list your Netflix rentals, or even convert your posts into Pirate Speak, aye matey? Arg! That's not so practical, but it sure is funny . . . kind of.

## Less Is More: Even RuPaul Keeps It Simple

With all the enticing options out there and the ease with which you can use them, it's tempting to use everything at once. Like excess feathers in a drag queen's headdress, too much can take away from the overall impact. A good rule is, everything in moderation, less is more . . . you know the drill.

Though, now that we think of it, is there such a thing as too many feathers in a drag queen's headdress? Maybe not! The bottom line is this is *your* blog. Do with it what you wish. If you want every single spot on your site filled to the brim with buttons and widgets, feathers and sequins . . . you better work it, girl.

## Do Your Thing

If anyone does their own thing, honey, it's RuPaul! Blogging since 2001 on RuPaul.com, RuPaul has been chronicling his life as an actor, talk show hostess, philanthropist, gay icon, and dance mix diva. One of the most popular blogs by a gay author on the Internet, RuPaul writes with candor and conscience.

We don't mean to sound like a contradiction in this chapter, dangling all these good-ies and then telling you to pare it down. We're merely suggesting that you look at all there is to offer and choose what you like the best, or what you think is fun. Try to make good choices when arranging your content. You need to make sure that all the extra things you have on your blog don't distract from the main event — your entries.

# Hex:
## It's Not a Curse

Every color has a hex value, or hexadecimal color code. You'll often need the codes to color-coordinate widgets and badges to your blog. If you're unsure what the hex values are for the colors on your website, try out a little tool like Color Schemers ColorPix, which is available at colorschemer.com. This free application generates the corresponding hex value for a color that you click anywhere on your screen.

Your blog may be a personal hobby or a method to boost your business. Everyone will have different goals for her or his site, so you'll need to make a judgment call. If you're selling gourmet dog treats and your associated blog is covered in gadgets and hoohas, it could be a distraction from your goal. You want readers to focus on the content that's directing them to your products.

If your blog is a hobby, having all the fun toys is totally your option. If you plan to load up your sidebars with plugins and widgets, take advantage of the option (if available) to customize the colors and fonts to best blend with your blog.

# Relax, Refresh, Reward

Your blog is dazzling, darling! Now that you've beautified your blog's sidebars to coordinate with your entries, why not decorate yourself a little bit. All that hard work copying and pasting surely deserves a reward.

## Frost your blog, then frost yourself

All that glitters is not gold! For truly brilliant treats, check out some of these stellar sites!

- shopfrosting.com    Designer fashion accessories. Need we say more?

- jaquabeauty.com    If you're anything like us, you will jump at the chance to indulge in some buttercream frosting scented body butter. Oh my. . . .

- cakeandfrosting.com    Beauty, fashion, accessories, and spa gifts in a cute little boutique-style website. Shop for great gifts for yourself and read the reviews for the scoop on fashion styles and buying trends.

- sprinklescupcakes.com    These cute little sweet treats are not only pretty to look at, they taste divine. At least that's what Oprah says. Originally based in Beverly Hills California, this company has gained massive clout and acclaim and has expanded to four locations with over a dozen new shops opening in the future. With cupcakes like red velvet, lemon ginger, and chai latte on the menu, these cute little babies will satisfy any sweet tooth. They ship them in gift boxes too. Mmmm. . . .

- sparklelikethestars.com    A blog dedicated to the jewelry and gobs of jewels worn by celebs. While you're enjoying one of those cupcakes, read up on the jewels Cameron Diaz was wearing at the last red-carpet event.

# A

**add-on:** A software module that adds features or services to the main blogging system.

**aggregation:** Combining multiple feeds into one area for easy reading.

**ASCII (American Standard Code for Information Interchange):** Character encoding based on the English alphabet and used to represent text in computers.

**Atom feed:** An XML-based feed used for the syndication of web content, such as blog entries, podcasts, or news headlines.

**avatar:** In blogging, a small photo or graphic, usually square, used as an identifying image or signature icon when commenting on blogs or forums.

# B

**binary file:** A file that typically contains bits of data that are meant to represent something other than textual data.

**blacklist:** A list of known spamming offenders kept in the settings of blog software as an anti-spam measure.

**blog:** Short for the term *web log* (or more frequently, *weblog)*; a journal-like website where the site owner, or blog author, posts data — such as text entries, photos, and other content — most commonly in reverse chronological order. The term *blog* is also used as a verb for the act of writing blog entries.

**blog community:** A collection of bloggers writing about a similar topic or topics, found in one centralized website location.

**blog software:** A program that provides a method for posting chronological text and photos in a journal-like fashion; creates an environment that allows outside users to comment and interact with the weblog. Also called a blog platform.

**blog title:** The name of a specific blog, often represented with text or a graphic treatment.

**blogroll:** A list of links to other blogs that a site owner frequents, often appearing in a sidebar or on a separate page of the blog.

**bot:** A program that follows links from page to page throughout the Internet, and when it finds a new web page it hasn't indexed, it crawls the code on the page and sends the information gathered back to the search engine. Also known as a *spider* or *crawler.*

# C

**Captcha:** A combination of letters, numbers, or both, in a graphic format that users must type into a text box to verify that they are human users, not spam robots or otherwise. It is used primarily in spam prevention and control on blogs and websites. (Captcha stands for Completely Automated Public Turing Test to Tell Computers and Humans Apart.)

**category:** A specific group that a blog entry can be filed in. Typically, bloggers create their own categories and assign entries into them at their own discretion.

**CMS (content management system):** A software package that allows you to edit and manage website content, such as basic site text and images, without fiddling with HTML code.

**column:** A blog nested within a community blog that acts more like a running article in a magazine. The word *column* is also used to refer to a sidebar of a blog.

**comment:** A message that a blog visitor may leave on a blog regarding a particular entry. The blog usually has a small comment form to fill out.

**community blog:** A large-format group blog that typically encompasses multiple authors and encourages visitor participation in forums, message boards, and blog discussions. These blogs sometimes provide memberships and interconnectivity among members.

**content area (body):** The most essential element to any blog; where blog entries live. Traditionally, you find the content area on the left or right side of the web page (if you have only one sidebar) or in the middle (if your sidebars flank to either side).

**contextual advertising:** Ads that are displayed based on the content that search engines or advertising services index from your blog or website.

**control panel:** An interface that allows you to administer a service, usually requiring a login and password. In web hosting, a *control panel* is the web-based interface that the hosting company provides, allowing you to edit and monitor the website. Also sometimes called a dashboard.

**copyright:** The legal protection given to individuals who create written, photographic, or other forms of intellectual property, protecting them from unauthorized copying of their work.

**crawler:** See *bot.*

**CSS (Cascading Style Sheets):** The language used to apply the design elements to a web page.

# D

**database:** A structured group of data that is stored on a computer or server so that a program can access it to find specific information quickly.

**DNS (domain name system):** A service that translates your domain name into an IP address.

**DNS server:** A computer (usually controlled by a web host) that translates the domain name of a website to the IP address of the server on which the web site lives so that the correct website is displayed in the user's web browser.

**domain name:** A simple and unique, but memorable, name used as an address that corresponds to the numeric IP address of a computer on the Internet.

**dpi (dots per inch):** A measure of printing resolution, specifically the number of individual dots of ink a printer can create within a 1-inch area.

# F

**feed:** A data format used to deliver frequently updated content.

**footer:** The area at the very bottom of your blog where you might list design credits, additional navigational links, copyright information, links to privacy policies, or anything else you'd like.

**FTP (File Transfer Protocol):** A method used to move material from one computer to another over the Internet.

# G

**Googling:** The act of looking up information on Google.com.

**graphic ad:** Website advertising that is made up of a banner image. Ads can vary in size and location but always link to the website buying the ad space.

**gravatar (globally recognized avatar):** Unlike avatars, gravatars are the same in many locations. (Avatars can be different from site to site.) See also *avatar.*

**group blog:** A blog that has more than one contributing author and centers around one topic.

# H

**header:** Text or graphic running across the top of the blog, displaying the blog name or an image. Also known as a *banner.*

**hexadecimal:** A 6-digit number or a combination of numbers and letters that represents a color value. Also known as *hex value.*

**HTML (HyperText Markup Language):** The authoring language used to structure web pages.

# I

**IP address:** A number that identifies a particular location of a computer on the Internet.

# L

**live bookmarking:** The act of subscribing to a feed with a built-in feed reader directly from a web browser.

**lurking:** The act of habitually reading a blog but not contributing with a comment.

# M

**masked registration:** See *private registration.*

**meme:** A quiz or survey about yourself that makes its way around blogs or through email. People typically answer questions about themselves, post the answers on their blogs, and link to the source of the quiz.

**moblogging:** The act of posting photos and text to an enabled blog from a mobile phone or PDA device. Also known as *mobile blogging.*

**mockup:** A faux layout created by a designer that demonstrates what your site will look like before it is built; usually provided as a flat graphic image. You can use this design sample to approve the initial work before the designer moves forward with your design project. Also known as a *comp.*

**MySQL:** A mulituser SQL database management system used to organize data in an easy-to-access way. Blog software uses MySQL databases to organize information such as your entries, photos, comments, and archives.

# N

**navigation:** Links (or a series of links) that provide access to other areas of a website.

**news reader:** A service that allows users to subscribe to RSS feeds from various websites so that they can read the content in one central location.

# O

**open source:** Usually refers to software for which the underlying source code is freely available for the public to use and modify. Anyone can work to improve the product or add to its functionality in any way.

# P

**Perl:** A powerful scripting language used for web applications. Perl is commonly used in blogging software.

**personal blog:** A blog written online by one or two people, chronicling their everyday lives.

**photoblog:** A blog that displays photographs as a focal point of the site, either as a portfolio or for recreation.

**PHP:** A programming language typically used for creating dynamic web page content.

**ping:** In blogging, the trackback alert that notifies a blog owner when someone writes an entry concerning the blog owner's original post.

**plugin:** A small script that you can install or add to blog software to enhance it in some way.

**podcast:** A method of publishing audio media to the Internet through a feed.

**private registration:** Masks a user's personal information, such as name, phone number, and mailing address, from those who search for the user's domain in the WHOIS domain lookup.

**public blog:** A blog that is completely open to the Internet; any viewer or reader may view all of the blog's entries and comments.

# R

**registrar:** A company that sells and administers domain names.

**RSS (Really Simple Syndication):** Web feed formats used to publish frequently updated content such as blog entries, podcasts, or news articles.

# S

**semiprivate blog:** A blog that allows the blogger to set varying permission levels based on membership groups.

**SEO (search engine optimization):** A method of tailoring a website and its code to be optimally ready for crawling by search engine bots for inclusion in their directories.

**server:** A computer or application on the Internet that hosts information.

**sidebar:** The area where blog authors display links they enjoy, a short bio, or links to their most recent posts or archives.

**spam:** Unsolicited or unwanted electronic messages that come through email, blog entry comments, and trackbacks.

**spam bot:** A program that crawls the blogosphere and attacks blogs, often leaving comments and trackbacks linking to websites that are irrelevant to the topics of the blogs. Usually, the spam is sales driven, much like the spam you get in your email inbox.

**spider:** See *bot*.

**static content:** Website pages that are not dynamically created, such as with a list of blog entries. A blog typically draws entries from a database, whereas static content never changes.

**stock photograph:** A photograph (or sometimes an illustration) that is made available in exchange for a license fee and restricted usage.

**style sheet:** A document that gives a site's design specifications. CSS is used in conjunction with HTML to build and design websites. See also *CSS*.

**suffix:** The .com, .net, .org, and so on extension of a domain name.

**syndicate:** To make a portion of a website or blog available to other sites via web feeds.

# T

**tag:** A simple keyword that is used to associate or describe a blog entry, a video, or an image.

**tag cloud:** A group of tags or keywords that are popular on a particular site. The tags in the tag cloud are usually varied in font size. The larger, more prominent words are tags that are more popular within the site.

**template:** A blog design that you can download or purchase and install on your blog to give it a certain look and feel.

**text ad:** A link displayed on blogs and websites that describes a product or service and directs a user away from the original site to the advertiser's product.

**texting:** The act of sending short textual messages from one mobile device to another.

**trackback:** An acknowledgement or way for blog authors to be alerted when another blog is discussing and/or linking to a particular entry. See also *ping*.

**trademark:** A mark that distinctly represents the ownership of a product or service and is reserved for the legal owner of the product or service.

**troll:** A blog or community forum visitor who, by a false name or anonymously, comments in a harassing way.

# U

**URL (Uniform Resource Locator):** An address on the Internet.

# V

**videocast:** A method of publishing video media to the Internet through a feed. Also known as a *vlog* or *video blog*.

# W

**watermark:** An opaque symbol or logo that a photographer places on photos to deter photo theft.

**web host:** A company that leases server space to clients for storing all the files associated with their websites.

**widget:** See *plugin.*

**wiki:** An application that lets multiple users post and update information to keep it current.

# X

**XML (eXtensible Markup Language):** A language that helps share info and data over the Internet via a feed.

## See You in the Blogosphere!

That's it, ladies! You've reached the finish line! By now, if you don't have your blog up and running, you should at least feel well-versed in the ins and outs of blogging.

We've covered a lot of ground in this book — everything from basic blog definitions to hosting your own blog to making friends (not enemies) in the blogosphere. Perhaps you've set up your blog on a hosted blog service (see Chapter 5) or hired a professional to help you get started (see Chapter 6). The important thing is that you're trying something new and getting out there to connect with others.

Ultimately, blogging should be a fun endeavor. Whether you're writing for personal reasons or blogging your favorite celebrity gossip with a group of friends, fun is really the heart of it all. We've been blogging since the early days and seen the trends ebb and flow. The blogs with staying power are those with authors that don't let others get under their skin and remember the reasons they started blogging to begin with.

You can meet wonderful, amazing people through blogging and forge what could be life-long friendships. We feel we're a testament to that! Blogging is a great way to bring people together and gives you an opportunity to express yourself in ways you might not be able to do in your everyday life. Believe us, after a month, one of your favorite phrases will be, "I am SO blogging this!"

We hope you've enjoyed reading *The IT Girl's Guide to Blogging with Moxie* as much as we've enjoyed writing it. We laughed, we cried, we laughed until we cried . . . and then we blogged about it. We hope you will, too. See you around the blogosphere, and don't be afraid to say hi!

# O

# P

# X

# Y